Peoples of
AFRICA

Arco Publishing Company Inc.
New York

Peoples of
AFRICA

INTRODUCTION by
JOHN MIDDLETON
Professor of Social Anthropology
University of London

Published 1978 by Arco Publishing Company, Inc.
219 Park Avenue South, New York, N.Y. 10003
Copyright © 1978 by Marshall Cavendish Books Limited
Printed in Great Britain

Library of Congress Cataloging in Publication Data
Main entry under title:
Peoples of Africa.
First published in Family of man.
Includes index.
1. Ethnology-Africa.   I. Singer L. and
GN645.P3   960'.04   Wood Robin L. K.
                                    78-623

ISBN 0-668-04578-7

Contents

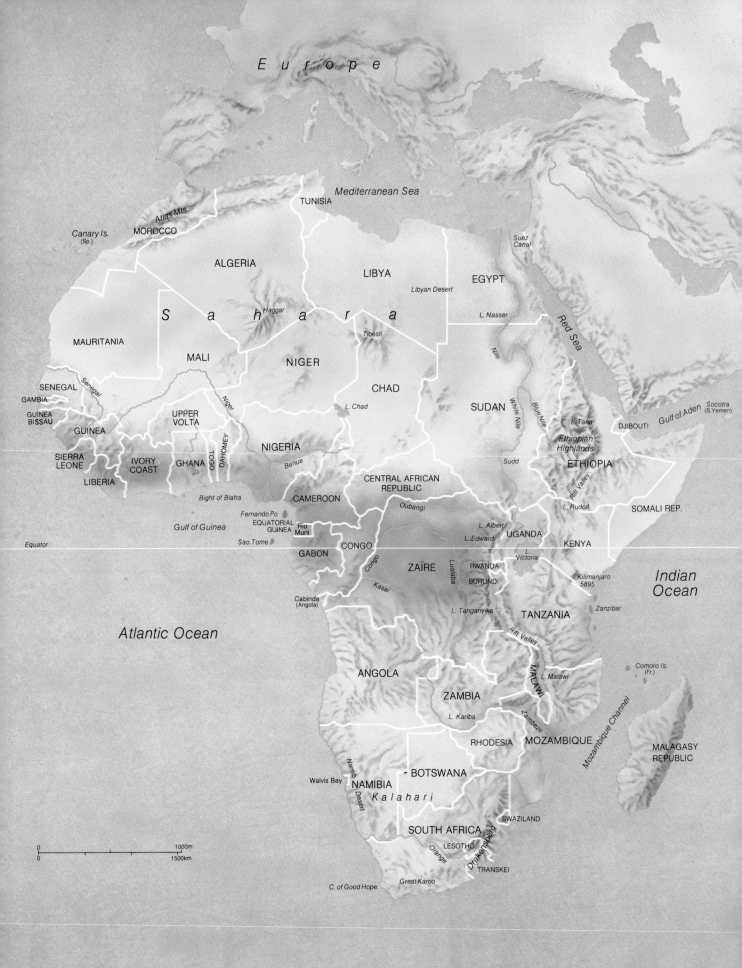

Europe

Mediterranean Sea

TUNISIA

Atlas Mts.

Canary Is.
(Sp.)

MOROCCO

ALGERIA

LIBYA

EGYPT

Libyan Desert

S a h a r a

Haggar

Tibesti

Suez Canal

L. Nasser

Nile

Red Sea

MAURITANIA

MALI

NIGER

CHAD

SUDAN

White Nile

Blue Nile

L. Tana

Ethiopian Highlands

DJIBOUTI

Gulf of Aden

Socotra
(S.Yemen)

SENEGAL

Senegal

L. Chad

GAMBIA

GUINEA
BISSAU

GUINEA

UPPER
VOLTA

Niger

NIGERIA

Benue

ETHIOPIA

Sudd

Rift Valley

SOMALI REP.

SIERRA
LEONE

IVORY
COAST

GHANA

TOGO

DAHOMEY

CENTRAL AFRICAN
REPUBLIC

L. Rudolf

LIBERIA

Bight of Biafra

CAMEROON

Oubangi

L. Albert

UGANDA

KENYA

Fernando Po

EQUATORIAL
GUINEA

Rio
Muni

CONGO

L.Edward

L.
Victoria

Gulf of Guinea

Sao Tome

GABON

Congo

ZAÏRE

Lualaba

RWANDA

Kilimanjaro
5895

Indian
Ocean

Equator

Kasai

BURUNDI

Cabinda
(Angola)

L. Tanganyika

TANZANIA

Zanzibar

Atlantic Ocean

Rift Valley

Comoro Is.
(Fr.)

ANGOLA

ZAMBIA

L. Malawi

MALAWI

L. Kariba

Zambeze

MOZAMBIQUE

Mozambique Channel

MALAGASY
REPUBLIC

RHODESIA

Namib

Walvis Bay

- BOTSWANA

NAMIBIA

K a l a h a r i

Desert

SWAZILAND

SOUTH AFRICA

LESOTHO

Orange

Drakensberg

TRANSKEI

C. of Good Hope

Great Karoo

1000m

1500km

6

Introduction
by J. MIDDLETON

For many centuries Africa was widely regarded by Europeans as the 'Dark Continent', a view that showed the ignorance of Europeans rather than the reality of Africa. That view died long ago, but we may still ask who are the peoples of Africa and what do we know about their societies and cultures. There are immense variations in the cultures of the continent and, of course, African societies are today changing faster than they have done over many centuries. But together with the haste to develop and the tensions and stresses brought about by this haste, we may none the less discern the basic and lasting qualities of African cultures.

There are today some 350 million people in Africa -- 230 million in the tropics, 70 million north of the Sahara Desert, and 50 million in the southern third of Africa. They live in a striking variety of environments. From north to south, the Mediterranean coast gives way to the Sahara Desert, and the semi-arid plains and savannahs of the Sahel belt lie to the immediate south of the Sahara. The thick rainforests of the West African coast and the Zaire-Congo region contrast with the plains and mountains of eastern and southern Africa and the Kalahari Desert in the south-west. There are many islands round the African coast, the largest being Madagascar to the east.

Much of the continent is harsh, with poor soils and little rain. Some societies, such as the Tuareg of the Sahara and the Bushmen of the Kalahari, have always found it difficult to surmount these conditions and still live a precarious existence always near to starvation. But elsewhere the land is fertile, especially in the forested areas of western Africa and the highlands of eastern Africa; and, in these areas, societies such as Ashanti, Yoruba, Kikuyu and many more have flourished, with densely-settled and productive farming communities, and often with towns and long-distance trade routes. Even though each of the several thousand African societies traditionally has its own culture, language and sense of distinctiveness, few of them have ever been isolated from their neighbours. Migrations and trading contacts have led to exchanges of people, ideas, and goods.

It is almost certain that mankind began in Africa, probably in the steppes and mountains of the Rift Valley region of eastern Africa, where remains of early men (of the genus *Homo*) have been found that can be dated to about two million years ago. Archaeology in most parts of Africa is still in its infancy and as yet we are only beginning to learn about the first inhabitants and their cultures. We know a good deal, of course, about the early societies of the Nile Valley, the great civilizations of Egypt that lasted from about 4,000 BC until 1,000 BC when the centre of that civilization moved southwards to Meroe and Kush, in the modern Sudan.

From about the 9th century AD there developed the empires of Ghana, Mali, Kanem, Songhai, Hausa and others in the western Sahel zone. These were trading empires, controlling the trans-Saharan trade in slaves, salt, kola nut and gold (most of the gold used in Europe before Columbus sailed to the 'New World' came across

A Turkana woman of Kenya. The Turkana are nomadic herders, wandering with their animals through the arid rift valley.

the Sahara from these states). Their rulers were mostly Moslem, living in large towns with wealthy and literate populations. Most of those empires are gone or are but shadows of their former selves, but the peoples of the region today are their descendants and many of their traditions are still alive. In eastern Africa, the Swahili-Arab states of the coast had developed by the 13th century, and by the 15th century there had developed the empire of Monomatapa, based on the citadel of Zimbabwe, and many other smaller trading kingdoms across central and southern Africa.

Africa has always exported to the outside world of Europe and Asia. During the European Middle Ages it exported mainly gold and slaves. Except for the Roman colonies in northern Africa, the earliest colonies were those of the Arabs down the East African coast, from where slaves were sent across the Indian Ocean to Arabia, India, and beyond. Later came the European colonization of the continent, beginning with the Portuguese moving down the Atlantic coast in the 15th century and finally reaching eastern Africa on the way to India. This colonization brought about the New World slave trade, with slaves supplied by the kings of new African states along the coast – Kongo, Benin, Yoruba, Fon, Ashanti and others – being shipped by European traders to the plantations of the Americas.

The high period of colonial rule came in the late 19th century, with almost all Africa shared out among a few European powers – Britain, France, Germany, Belgium, Portugal, Italy, and Spain. These countries assumed both economic and political control of the whole continent with the exceptions of the Christian kingdom of Ethiopia and the republic of Liberia settled by ex-slaves returned from the New World. In some areas, mainly in southern Africa and in parts of northern and eastern Africa, the colonizing powers settled non-African immigrant communities – European, Lebanese, Syrian, Indian and Chinese – mostly as farmers, farm workers and traders. Some of these communities. such as the Afrikaners in South Africa, have lived in Africa since the 17th century and cannot be considered newcomers – they have no homeland but Africa. In eastern Africa the Arabs have been settled in the coastal towns for a thousand years. The presence of these 'immigrant' groups has everywhere posed serious political problems as the former colonies have become independent since the 1950s. Many non-African peoples, such as the French in Algeria, Morocco and Tunisia, the British and the Indians in East Africa, and the Portuguese in Angola and Mozambique, have mostly left Africa to return to the metropolitan countries.

There are some three thousand languages and dialects in Africa, only a handful of which were written before the colonial period. There are generally said to be five main language families. The largest is the Niger-Congo family, spread throughout sub-Saharan Africa and including most languages of western Africa and the Bantu languages of central, eastern and southern Africa. Along the southern border of the Sahara and in the upper Nile Valley region are found the Nilo-Saharan languages. In northern and north-eastern Africa the Afro-Asiatic (Hamitic and Semitic) languages are spoken. The Bushmen and Hottentots of southern Africa speak 'Click' or Khoisan languages; and Austronesian languages are spoken in Madagascar, whose peoples originally came from Indonesia. With this bewildering array of distinct languages, the use of non-African languages has become widespread – Arabic from the Middle Ages, and English, French, Dutch (Afrikaans) and other European languages from the colonial period. *Lingua francas* such as Swahili in eastern and Hausa in western Africa are widely used. Both were originally written in Arabic but now generally are used in Roman script.

Africa is famed throughout the world for its art. Perhaps the best-known in non-African eyes is sculpture in wood and ivory and casting in bronze, brass and gold. Pottery, weaving, architecture, ironsmithing and other techniques are all widespread. The most famous art is that of the western African peoples such as the Yoruba, Fon, Ashanti and Dan. Much is the work of court artists and has religious significance, but today traditional religious art is losing its significance and new forms are arising. Music and dance are found in all African cultures, and both have greatly affected non-African music and dance.

The economies of traditional and modern Africa vary immensely. In the inhospitable Kalahari Desert in southern Africa and the forests of the Zaire-Congo basin, for example, the Bushmen and Pygmies survive by gathering wild foods and hunting animals. Remnants of peoples who once occupied most of the continent, these peoples have been driven into these refuge areas where they still cling to their traditional ways of life. In the arid and semi-arid areas, mainly in the Sahel belt, live pastoralists, people who herd cattle, camels or other livestock around which their lives revolve and on which they depend for food. In western Africa are the Fulani and Tuareg; in eastern Africa, the Dinka, Masai, Baggara and Somali. Most African societies, however, are mixed farmers, practising settled agriculture and keeping some livestock. South of the Sahara, apart from the West African forests and the Kalahari, most of the land comprises open plains and savannahs. Here the main crops are grains such as millets and maize, with many other crops such as cassava, groundnuts and plantains. In the forested areas of western Africa, root crops such as yams and cocoyam are more important.

Traditionally, African farmers have been highly skilled, able to produce regular subsistence while avoiding soil erosion by careful shifting cultivation and crop rotation, and in some fertile areas by use of irrigation. But in recent years, with population pressure and the need to grow export crops such as cotton, coffee, cocoa and tea for money, there is often severe land shortage, and soil degradation. An area that cannot grow export crops can only sell the labour of its younger men, who move to the cities. There has been an almost universal drift of poor and landless people to the urban centres. It is here that the social fabric of 'traditional' Africa is breaking down, and another major way of life emerging. This is sometimes based on industrial employment but in most cases relies on small-scale trading and commercial activity, with much unemployment among the unskilled who form the majority of the immigrants.

Karamojong warriors dressing their hair. Adult men wear a headress of coloured clay which hardens and is then painted with delicate designs. Colour schemes vary among the different Karamojong tribes, although the basic style is the same throughout.

Alan Root/Survival Anglia Television

8

Almost everywhere the basic household unit is the conjugal family of a man, wife and children (or a man, wives and children, since in most African societies polygyny is traditionally the ideal). But the ways in which these families are linked together to form local communities vary a great deal and are often very different from those of, say, Europe. Over most of Africa the basic *social* unit is not the small family but a descent group, a clan or a segment of a clan called a lineage. A clan is a group of people who recognize common kinship by descent from an ancestor either through men only (patriliny) or through women only (matriliny). Clans may be small or may have many thousands of members, who may never meet each other but still accept certain mutual obligations, of which the most common is the prohibition of marriage between them (exogamy). Usually lineages act as the cores of large joint or extended families, each composed of many small individual conjugal families. These joint families are large enough to ensure co-operation in economic tasks, to act as a defensive unit in the past when war and raiding were common threats, and to be persistent, since when one husband dies the family does not cease to exist as it does in the case of the conjugal family. It used to be thought by many people, both inside and outside Africa, that these joint families were in some way old-fashioned and inefficient, but in fact they have almost everywhere shown their strength and persistence as a support to give their members a sense of security and continuity.

Marriage in most African societies is not merely the affair of husband and wife alone. but of the lineages to which they belong. In patrilineal societies, such as the Dinka, Zulu, Sotho and Kikuyu, a man marries largely to obtain legitimate heirs, and marriage is marked by the transfer of bridewealth, often reckoned in cattle, from his to his wife's family as a sign that her children will belong to his side. Bridewealth is not important in matrilineal societies, such as the Ashanti, since there the wife bears children for her own line and not for her husband's.

All societies have some form of government. There are and have been many states, from the great mediaeval empires mentioned above to the kingdoms described in this book, such as Ashanti, Fon, Nyoro, Zulu and others. All kings are to some extent regarded as sacred. Often the sacred quality of the kingship is its most important feature and the king has little secular power. But others have traditionally exercised great authority, as did the kings of the Amhara who became the rulers of all Ethiopia. Other African societies lack kingship and manage their internal government by popular discussion and concensus, with disagreements between neighbours often being settled by feud. These politics have sometimes been called 'ordered anarchies', as in the cases of the Dinka and Somali. Others are essentially little more than large families controlled by

For just 45 minutes every February, 5,000 fishermen from all over Nigeria compete in the Argungu Fishing Festival. Along this sacred mile of the Niger's tributary, near Sokoto, men can land Nile perch weighing anything up to 140 pounds. Competitors keep the small fish but present the largest to the emirs who hold the Festival.

the older men, as among the Bushmen and Pygmies. In some societies there were councils of elders, with age-sets (graded social strata based on age groupings) of warriors to act as police, as among the Kikuyu and Masai.

Today most of these traditional policies have lost their autonomy as they have become swallowed up by modern nation-states. Only the Somali of Somalia, the Moors of Mauritania, the Sotho of Lesotho and the Tswana of Botswana, among those peoples described in this book, have been able to base their new states on their traditional policies. Others have become absorbed into wider political groupings based on the colonies found under colonial rule. Naturally there has often been conflict of interest between the traditional small-scale polities (often called 'tribes') and the modern 'inter-tribal' national governments. Some of these conflicts have erupted into wars, such as the attempted Ibo secession from Nigeria with the proclamation of the breakaway state of Biafra.

Religion has always played a central part in political and family life. Everywhere there is a belief in a creator god, who having made the world is believed to have become a High God remote from his creatures and rarely an object of sacrifice or prayer. Sacrifice is made typically to intermediary powers, to ancestors and spirits of many kinds that symbolize the many forces and experiences recognized by ordinary people as having power over their everyday lives. An important feature of these many traditional religions has been that each society has its own religion, its own cosmology and mythology, its own set of spiritual powers to which its members give respect and which are thought to protect only them. Many of these, such as that of the Dogon, are highly complex and sophisticated, even though there is no written dogma. A part of most religions were, and still are, beliefs in the powers of evil people, witches and sorcerers, beliefs used to explain personal misfortune which cannot otherwise be understood and dealt with. In communities where interpersonal face-to-face relations are all-important, individual misfortune tends to be attributed to the evil actions of other people rather than to impersonal forces such as 'fate', and by accusation and threat of punishment the supposed witch may be made to remove the evil.

As the myriad small worlds of traditional African societies were opened up in recent years, these small-scale traditional religions began to lose their force. Instead, the religions of the colonizers – Islam in some parts of Africa, and Christianity in most of it – began to make converts. It must be remembered that both Islam and Christianity are old religions in Africa. Islam spread along the northern and eastern coastlines in the early European Middle Ages. Coptic Christianity flourished in Egypt and Ethiopia from the 4th century onwards, and in tropical Africa the Portuguese brought their faith to people such as the Kongo about the year 1500. Christianity and Islam are world religions, representative of world powers, and naturally people have been attracted to them since their adherents belong to a wider world and seem to be able to influence events more than can ancestors and spirits. Also they are literate faiths, and education has been an important

aspect of their impact on preliterate African societies. Many African Christians are members of Catholic and Protestant churches based in Europe, but others belong to local African sects founded by African prophets who try to include much of the traditional faiths within a Christian framework.

Perhaps the greatest effect of colonial rule has been the growth of cities. There are many pre-colonial cities in Africa – Cairo, Alexandria, Ibadan, Benin, Kano, Kumasi, Tombuctoo and Zanzibar are cities of great antiquity that are still thriving urban centres. But in recent times, often due to the new importance of African mineral resources for the outside world and the need to build administrative and trading centres under colonial rule, there have appeared the new cities such as Johannesburg, Cape Town, the towns of the Zambian Copperbelt, Kinshasa, Nairobi, Lagos, Dakar and many more. These have acted as magnets for rural people unable to make much of a living at home, and unable to make money there for taxes and consumer goods. They see opportunities to do so in the towns. They have come to form an urban proletariat, often unemployed and too often with little future. They live either in impersonal and often heartless towns such as Soweto near Johannesburg, or in the cities of western and eastern Africa in sprawling slums and shantytowns, overcrowded and, although often warm and with a strong sense of community, also dangerous and unhealthy places without proper schools or health facilities. In the towns also live the members of the new elites, educated and powerful in both commerce and government, living in elegant suburbs and enjoying high standards of health and educational facilities, and acting as members of the international business and political world, but often far removed from the majority of their countrymen.

In the following pages of this book are accounts of both 'traditional' and 'modern' African societies, and their cultures. Restrictions of space dictate that only a small sample have been selected, but those included do give a general picture of the peoples of Africa. To distinguish traditional from modern is of course artificial and in many ways misleading. All societies are changing; they adapt the traditional to new and changing circumstances, but do not thereby throw away the past. The scale of societies widens, so that once-autonomous groups become subject to others and find their own traditions threatened. To cling to them is a natural reaction, since without them people become socially and psychologically adrift without a sense of security and continuity of the past and the future.

Comprehension of and sympathy for the traditional are essential for an understanding of the present and the future, to try to see them through African eyes rather than those of an outsider. This of course is never an easy thing to do, but the articles in this book – contributed by a team of international anthropologists and sociologists and superbly illustrated by some of the world's leading photographers – attempt to describe a wide spectrum of African peoples from all parts of the continent and at all levels of change and adaptation to the modern world that has now drawn all Africa into its orbit. Africa and the rest of the world are today interdependent to a degree they have never been in all history, and knowledge of the peoples of Africa is necessary now more than ever before.

In the Sudan, a Dinka man washes children in one of the scarce water sources. For part of the year the Dinka must travel in search of water and pasture.

African Arabs

Victor Englebert/Susan Griggs Agency

Two thirds of all Arabs live in Africa. Some 37 million live in Egypt, 2 million in Libya, 30 million in the three Maghreb countries (Tunisia, Algeria and Morocco) and 10 million in the Sudan – a total of about 80 million people. Greater Cairo, the capital of Egypt, with some 8 million people, alone has more inhabitants than the majority of countries in the Arab East.

The first Arab invaders reached Africa in the 7th century AD and very quickly conquered Egypt and Tripolitania which were thoroughly Arabized. The Berber inhabitants of north-West Africa – known to the Arabs as *jazirat al Maghreb* (the island of the West) – however proved more difficult to subdue and fiercely resisted the Arab conquerors. The struggle for Arab control of the Maghreb and the implantation of the Arab languages and culture was long and hard and after more than a century of conflict the region had not been entirely subdued. Even today about a quarter of the Maghreb population, concentrated predominantly in the mountains of Morocco and eastern Algeria, remain Berber speaking. Most Maghreb Arabs are in fact Arabized Berbers, and the distinction between the Arab majority and the Berbers is essentially linguistic not ethnic.

In the modern-day Sudan, following the overthrow in the 14th century of a once Christian kingdom based on Dongola, Arab immigrants of very varied geographical origins gradually settled in northern and central Sudan so that the Arabic language is now firmly established in these areas and in the major towns and cities of the Sudan. Several non-Arabic languages such as Beju, Nubian and Tigre still survive, but today about two-thirds of all Sudanese are Arabic speakers and acknowledge Islam.

Other Arabs, mainly merchants and seamen from southern Arabia engaged in trade around the Indian Ocean, settled along the East African coast between the 8th and 10th centuries. They remained non-assimilated, but later, especially under European colonial rule in the 19th century, the Islamic religion spread from the Arab trading centres among some of the African peoples of the interior. However, few local people adopted the Arabic language. For several centuries Zanzibar remained the principal Arab trading station on this coast, a great port for the whole of East Africa. The islands of Zanzibar and neighbouring Pemba were ruled by an Arab sultan until 1964, and the Arab minority constituted a big trading element and controlled large clove plantations on the two islands.

Political domination by Arabs however did not long survive Independence from colonial rule and revolution. During the armed rebellion of January 1964 and its aftermath there were violent clashes between the black African majority and the Arabs in which many Arabs were killed; others fled from the islands. Nevertheless Zanzibar and Pemba still retain a significant Arab minority, though one much reduced in size and importance.

Most of the Arabs of North Africa live in the lower Nile Valley and in the Mediterranean and Atlantic coast lands of North-West Africa, while the vast desert lands of the Sahara are largely uninhabitated. Settlement in the dry Sahara is limited to a scatter of oases which form densely populated islands separated by vast empty areas, some of which are visited seasonally by tribes of pastoral nomads. The desert is still an obstacle to communications and

Camels are still among the best forms of desert transport.

separates the relatively well-populated area of North-West Africa from the region of considerable density found in the tropical rain belt. However, the construction of new roads and a great increase in air traffic now permits greater contact between peoples to the north and south of the Sahara.

Throughout the Arab lands of North Africa the impact of modern forces of change has been particularly disastrous for the tribes of pastoral nomads. Many of their previous functions have disappeared. Airplanes and trucks have conquered the desert and replaced the camel caravan. Governments now have the means to prevent raiding by nomadic tribes and can offer protection to the settled communities on the edges of the desert who previously paid tribute to the nomads. Pastoral nomadism has consequently lost much of its prestige and the profit as well as its political power, and most Arab nomads – such as the Baggara Arabs of Sudan, and the Chaariba, Beni Thour and Said Atba of Algeria – are becoming settled, a process which is often spontaneous but also actively encouraged by the central governments of the North African states. As a result, nomads now constitute a small minority of the Arab population in North Africa, although there are significant numbers in Sudan, Libya and Algeria.

The majority of North African Arabs are cultivators and live in villages which are the main nuclei of population distribution. Cultivable land is limited and the rural population is therefore very unevenly distributed. The Nile valley, for example, by far the most heavily populated area, has an estimated 3,000 inhabitants per square mile of cultivated land – among the highest man/land ratios in the world. Most villages are small, compact clusters of dwellings, normally built of mud brick in the plains and along the river valleys and of stone in upland areas. Where population densities are unusually high, the villages become larger, pressure within them increases, and they occur in greater frequency. Some agricultural villages in Egypt contain thousands of Arab cultivators and their families.

Within the village the low dwellings are separated from one another by narrow, winding unpaved streets. The traditional type of dwelling usually consists of a number of dark rooms built around an open courtyard, which the family sometimes share with their animals. Most houses are meagrely furnished one-storey structures. Many have no furniture except mats made of straw or blankets spread on the floor which together with a few cooking untensils comprise most of the villagers' possessions. Few amenities are found in the village beyond the mosque, a bathhouse and a number of shops. A strong sense of group solidarity exists among the villagers who are bound together by the dictates of custom and convention, and by the rhythm of the annual agricultural cycle.

European rural colonization in North-West Africa during the 19th and 20th centuries led to the emergence of two contrasting types of agriculture, one modern commercial and European, and the other traditional, subsistent and indigenous. The Europeans neglected livestock farming, and concentrated on cash crops for export: soft wheat, vines, citrus fruits, market garden products, olives and tobacco. Arab farmers owned most of the livestock and produced food crops such as hard wheat, barley and dates. European farmers employed an Arab workforce, and enjoyed higher yields through better methods of cultivation, better credit facilities, more capital and machinery, and larger properties. Since independence the

European farms have been nationalized, and although some have been sold to local landowners, the majority have been reorganized into state farms and co-operatives or have been placed under the management of workers' committees. These farms continue to produce the major export crops but they employ only a fraction of the rural population.

The distinction between these two types of farming should not be exaggerated for it was not always clear cut, and in recent decades new crops, improved agricultural techniques and new techniques of cultivation have begun to modify the agricultural bases of traditional rural communities. Unfortunately in spite of these advances, many peasants are still forced to eke out a meagre existence on tiny, fragmented plots of land which are unable to provide a livelihood for the farmer and his family. There are simply too many people in the countryside and too little cultivated land to go around. Millions of Arab villagers are landless and have to try and seek work as tenant farmers or as agricultural labourers. The class of landless labourers are among the poorest of the poor in Arab rural society in North Africa.

Unlike the rest of Africa, the Arab lands of the north have a long tradition of urban life, stretching back several thousand years to Phoenician and Roman times. Until the European occupation, however, towns were relatively small and only a tiny proportion of the Arab population were urban dwellers. Colonization in the 19th century ushered in the period of modern urbanism. Soon a growing number of Arab farmers and herdsmen, displaced from the more fertile lands given over to foreign cash crops, were attracted to the growing urban centres.

The march of the peasants towards the towns and particularly to the major towns, continues today in the Arab lands and, together with high rates of natural increase within the cities, is producing rapid urban growth. Over a third of the Arabs are now urban dwellers, a much higher proportion than in sub-Saharan Africa where the inhabitants are much less urbanized. Five Arab cities – Casablanca, Algiers, Tunis, Alexandria and Cairo – contain a million or more inhabitants and Cairo and Alexandria are the largest cities in Africa. The Sudanese Arabs are the least urbanized, but Khartoum which has the major share of the urban population now contains some 800,000 inhabitants.

Virtually all major cities in North Africa are seats of government and administration. Little modern industrialization occurred during colonial rule and most minerals are still unprocessed before export. Manufacturing industries make only a limited contribution to the national income of the North African states and employ a fraction of the urban labour force. For Egypt, the most highly industrialized state in Africa after the Republic of South Africa, manufacturing contributes only 20 per cent of GNP and employs less than 10 per cent of the economically active population – little more than a million people. Thus in spite of substantial advances and although some Arabs are now factory workers, recent industrialization has had little impact on the high levels of unemployment which characterize the overcrowded and fast-growing urban centres throughout North Africa.

It is in the large cities that the contrasts and social tensions in Arab society are seen in sharp relief. In the former European or 'Westernized' quarters, the smart villas and apartment blocks are now occupied by the new privileged classes in Arab society – administrators,

executives, senior army officers, civil servants, directors of state companies, private businessmen, doctors, lawyers and other professional people – and the shops continue to provide a wide range of imported consumer goods, including the latest Western furniture and household equipment and fashionable clothing.

In contrast, in the overcrowded old quarters of the cities (medinas) and in the burgeoning shantytowns (bidouvilles) live migrants from the countryside and the less fortunate urban dwellers who form the vast majority of the urban population. During the daytime the narrow winding streets and alleyways, accessible only to pedestrians and pack animals, possess a tremendous vitality and bustle. Traditional costumes are much in evidence and a majority of the women are veiled. Craftsmen are at work in their shops; the colourful bazaars (souks) are much frequented by the poorer city folk and by visitors from the surrounding countryside; and street traders can be seen everywhere. Throughout these quarters housing conditions in the old courtyard houses are usually poor, and basic amenities such as sewage and piped drainage water are hopelessly inadequate or non-existant. Incomes are low, even for those with jobs, and many have no work

In the midst of profound economic and social changes the family still remains the basic unit of Arab society, and is of central importance in the life of both the community and the individual. But the extended family of the past consisting of a man, his wife, their married sons and their wives and children is fast disappearing, mainly as a result of economic forces. Although it is still common for young couples to begin their marriage living within the extended family, they remain there only for a few years until they

The Arabs spread across North Africa in two great waves in the 7th and 11th centuries, bringing their religion, their language and their culture.

can accumulate enough capital to buy their own house and form their own nuclear family household. Marriage ensures the continuation of the family and the preferred marriage partner in North African societies, as in all the Arab world, is the fathers' brothers' daughter (or son), known as the 'parallel cousin'. Marriage is by contract and is arranged through a series of discussions and negotiations between the women of the two families involved, the negotiations being initiated by the prospective groom's family. While formerly a wife had no say in the choice of her future husband, as a result of the modernization process marriage is becoming much more of an individual matter between the two partners than a family affair.

Although the family provides a bridge between mens' and womens' societies within the Arab community, each society has its own distinctive functions. The men monopolize almost completely the civic and economic activities of the community, whereas the women are generally restricted to the home and family. Women do perform important although normally low level economic activities; some women also work outside the house, generally before but also after marriage. The basis orientation of women however, remains domestic, although many of the traditional values regarding seclusion and restriction of women are breaking down. Since independence efforts have been made, notably in Egypt and Tunisia, to improve the legal status of women in society, to modernize the attitudes of

17

women themselves and of men towards women. The restrictions on movement of women outside the home for instance, have largely disappeared, although women still do not gather in public places and the café remains a male stronghold.

Weddings, circumcision ceremonies and the annual feasts of the *Aid el Kebir* and *Aid es-Seghir* are major events in the lives of all Arab families, rich and poor, urban and rural. Indeed, for most peasant households they represent the only relief in an otherwise hard, un-rewarding and monotonous existence.

On such occasions the immediate and extended family are the most important participants, neighbours and other friends taking second place. Both circumcision and wedding celebrations are now generally held during the summer months when many people are on vacation and relatives return from abroad and from other parts of the country. For both these occasions houses are painted and redecorated and food prepared in advance. In the case of circumcision there are three or four days of actual cele-brations and for weddings about ten days. All male children are circumcised around the age of five and this event marks their passage into the male community,

although not yet adulthood.

Marriage has a similar significance for females. A female does not become a 'woman' until she marries but is referred to as a 'girl' regardless of age or status. Thus particularly for women, but to a lesser extent also for men, marriage signifies entrance into the adult world, and full status in the community. For both the bride and groom, as well as their families, the preparations for marriage involve great expenditures of both time and money. Following traditions the bride price which a man pays to the bride or the bride's parents in her name, is used towards the purchase of her trousseau or dowry which includes many of the possessions she will need for her adult life: clothes, linens, dishes and blankets. Young girls generally collect items for their trousseau over many years and once they are officially engaged they begin to assemble it in earnest, often now together with their fiances. Unmarried young men and women will save almost all of their earnings for five to ten years in order to pay for the trousseau, for the more lavish it is the better because it is displayed for public viewing and comment during several days of the wedding celebrations.

The two major religious festivals are also essentially

family affairs. The *Aid es-Seghir* (literally 'small holiday') occurs at the end of Ramadan and marks the end of the period of fasting. The *Aid el Kebir* (or 'big holiday') is associated with the *Haj* or pilgrimage to Mecca and is more important. Both holidays are occasions for visits among family members and close friends, and for the celebration of the *Aid el Kebir* almost every household sacrifices a sheep – a considerable expense, particularly for poor families. In Tunisia, much of the meat from the sheep is dried to be served with a special *couscus* on *Ras el Am*, the Moslem New Year's Day.

Nearly all North African Arabs are orthodox or *Sunni* Moslems, and religious homogeneity has been a strong characteristic of the whole region since the 11th century AD, in marked contrast to the religious diversity of the Arab East. Furthermore, unlike the rest of Africa, European missionary activity gained few converts to Christianity. Yet there can be little doubt that adherence to Islam as a religious and social code has declined in recent decades. In a modernizing society a strict adherence to Islamic practices has become associated with tradition, to the extent that religion is therefore equated with conservatism in peoples' conception. Most certainly, a notable decline or disappearance of many Islamic institutions has occurred. The once powerful religious brotherhoods, which flourished in the pre-colonial period and represented a major social and political force throughout the region, collapsed under the impact of European centralization and pacification. The Koranic schools attached to the mosques for centuries provided traditional Islamic teaching but they have been eclipsed by the massive expansion of state systems of secular primary and secondary schools since independence. Legislation has been passed unifying the legal systems and making certain changes in that last undefiled sanctuary of Islamic jurisprudence – the field of personal status (marriage, divorce and inheritance). The mosques, though there are more of them, are poorly attended, public prayer is rarely seen and many educated Arabs admit that they have abandoned most of the religious ritual of Islam.

Nevertheless the almost universally strong observance, at least in public, of such religious tenets as fasting during Ramadan attests to the continuing influence of Islam on the daily lives of the Arabs and the existence of a genuine, deep-rooted if somewhat ill-defined religious sentiment. Since independence the North African governments have sought to maintain at least the outer shell of Islam, insisting on a public posture of Moslem conformity and recently attempts have been made to tighten up social and moral legislation. Today, paradoxically, something of a religious revival appears to be taking place and enjoying wide public appeal, especially in Egypt. A large number of young Egyptians interpret the obvious 'backwardness' of their country as essentially a falling away

Many Arab tribes on the southern side of the Sahara use their cattle for transport as well as for food. Though now mixed with the African peoples who inhabited the region before them, they can boast an ancestry dating back hundreds of years to Arabia.

from the true Islam, and see the remedy as a return to a strict, fundamentalist application of all the rules of the *Koran* and the *Sharia*.

Today many of the Arabs of North-West Africa are experiencing an acute crisis of cultural identity. Although dialectical Arabic is the common tongue among the Arabs of Algeria, Morocco and Tunisia, few know classical Arabic, the standard written form of the language. French colonialism, Arab culture and the Arabic language were systematically discouraged and emphasis placed uniquely on the French language and European civilization and its values. Consequently at independence, while the majority of the Arab population remained illiterate, the small educated Arab elite were the products of French-inspired teaching. Thus when the foreign minister of the newly independent Algerian republic visited President Nasser of Egypt, they were unable to speak directly because they had no common language – a bitter legacy for a people who base their identity in large measure on the use of a common tongue.

The dilemma facing the Maghreb Arabs was obvious. On the one hand there was a desire to rediscover their Arab identity and to reaffirm their membership of the Arab family of nations; on the other hand French was recognized as providing the key to the world of modern technology and economic progress. A solution has yet to be found. For although Arabic has been declared the official language of all three Maghreb states and programmes of Arabization have been introduced, major discrepancies remain between official statements and observable reality. In fact the French language continues to be used for business, in many areas of administration, and for most of the instruction in secondary schools and universities; most members of the ruling elites are bilingual; and almost all high level posts are virtually closed to monolingual Arabs. Paradoxically, since independence the French cultural impact has become stronger than ever. The end of colonial rule removed the major psychological barrier to the acceptance of French culture, while the massive expansion of international tourism (over 1,500,000 tourists, mainly French, visited the Maghreb in 1977) and the presence in France of over a million North African migrant workers and their families poses a further threat to Arab/Islamic culture.

This crisis of cultural identity for the Maghreb is a major factor dividing the Arabs of North-West Africa from those of the Nile valley lands who maintain strong political, economic and cultural links with the Arab East. Egypt, containing one third of all Arabs, is one of the front line states in the conflict with Israel; it is dependent for its very survival on financial aid from the rich states of the Arabian Gulf; and its capital Cairo is one of the major cultural centres of the Arab world. Sudan, Egypt's southern neighbour, has staked its future on becoming the granary of the Arab world with the help of massive investment by Saudi Arabia and the Gulf states in major agricultural projects; and both countries receive much needed foreign exchange in the form of remittances from the growing number of Egyptian and Sudanese workers employed in the rich oil states of the Arabian peninsula.

Andrew Baring

19

Afar
ETHIOPIA

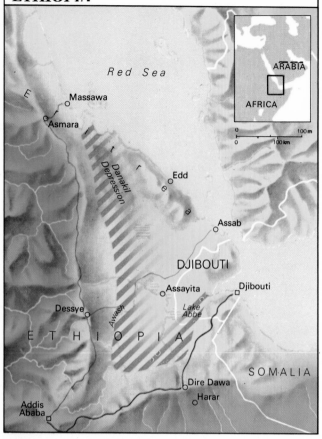

Red Sea

ARABIA

AFRICA

Massawa

Asmara

Danakil Depression

Edd

Assab

DJIBOUTI

Assayita

Djibouti

Dessye

Awash

Lake Abbe

ETHIOPIA

SOMALIA

Dire Dawa

Harar

Addis Ababa

Between the high Ethiopian escarpment and the shore of the Red Sea there lies one of the most inhospitable areas on earth. The rough triangle of the Danakil Desert is for the most part dry rocky land, much of it below sea level, where temperatures can reach 145°F (50°C) in the sun. There is no rain for three-quarters of the year, and what water does flow down from the highlands vanishes into shallow saline lakes. The wind, when it does blow, is too dry and scorching to bring any relief.

Living in this waste of crumbling rock and broken lava-flows are a people as tough and often as hostile as their environment. They are known by the Arabs, who first carried their awesome reputation to Europe, as Danakil. They will usually call themselves by the name of their clan or sub-tribe, but if asked their own name for the people as a whole will say 'Afar'.

In appearance these people are usually lean, often tall, always striking. The visitor is perhaps most impressed by their obvious fitness: weaklings do not survive. The men stand as straight as their spears, but move with a lithe grace and elegance of gesture which are instantly captivating. Their economy of movement is typical of people who live in deserts—they cannot afford to waste energy. When they do move they do so with the most extraordinary speed. When angry they explode violently, their normally smiling expressions become ferocious—and it is instantly obvious why they have been so long feared by their neighbours.

The Afar (pronounced 'arfar') are an independent-minded people, and one who lay great stress on a man's strength and bravery. Prestige comes, as it has always

come, from killing one's enemies. It used to be the case that a man could not marry until he could show his bride the gruesome trophy he had taken from a man he had slain. The dead, the dying and most prisoners would be castrated to provide this proof of an individual's strength. Opportunities for successful trophy-hunting have become fewer, but the tradition remains alive. The custom is recalled with approval over any camp-fire and the visitor is shown with pride, if secretly, the small dried heirlooms which are handed down to a great warrior's sons.

Some Afar in the capital, working perhaps for the Afar service of Ethiopian Radio, wear western clothes, but those in the country wear the traditional *sanafil*, wrapped round the waist and tied in a knot on the right hip. It reaches down to the calves, and is made of natural undyed cotton. Richer individuals wear a top piece, the *harayto*, slung loosely over their shoulders. At the waist men wear the fearsome *jile*—a dagger about 15 inches long, curved and very sharp on both edges and a universal characteristic of the male Afar appearance. Many also carry a rifle or a spear, or both, and a belt around the waist or across the shoulders for keeping the precious ammunition. Bullets are so prized that the cartridges are used again and again and can be used as currency—even mission hospitals will accept payment in bullets.

The women's dress is similar to that of the men but with two exceptions: it is dyed brown (the juice boiled from the bark of a local mimosa tree makes the dye) and is knotted on the left hip. Married women wear a black strip of cloth reminiscent of a veil on the head. All Afar women take a great delight in beads and other forms of jewellery.

Children wear nothing for the first few years. A boy's head is shaved until manhood, when the hair is allowed to grow out into the traditional and distinctive fuzzy style—though it may be plaited. When a man first kills an enemy he can wear a coloured cloth and a comb or feather in his hair. When he has killed twice or more he may advertise the fact with a cut in his ear and by adding brass- or silver-bound leather thongs to his dagger.

Girls undergo infibulation (the sewing together of the vulva) and clitorodectomy (removal of the clitoris). Boys are circumcised, usually in groups. Among the Asaemara (the 'Reds', or dominant political section of the Afar, living around Assayita) this takes place at the age of 15 or so, but among the Adaemara (the 'Whites', who are politically subordinate and live in the more rugged parts of the deserts) at about nine. After being circumcised a boy will try to shout out the names of as many cows or camels as he can in a kind of heroic chant: he is given as many as the number of names he yells. Some are so overcome by the pain that they cannot call out any, which means they receive no animals at all, but most boys manage two or three. Immediately after the operation the boys go out hunting on ponies. They must kill something—even if it is only a bird or a rat—and the girls will make this kill the subject of praise-songs which are sung at the evening's celebration in the young men's honour.

Bravery shown at circumcision and in hunting are essential qualifications for marriage. In the past it was a further essential to have killed a man. A woman would not look at a youth who could not show her a trophy in

Living in the arid wastes of the Danakil Desert, where only the strong survive, Afar nomads reckon a man's prestige by his bravery. Traditionally feared by their neighbours, Afar men always carry a spear or rifle—sometimes both—and advertise the number of men they have killed with leather thongs hung from the sheaths of their vicious 15-inch daggers.

Most of the Afar's land is a desert of volcanic rock weathered down to sand. It forces them to spend much of their life on the move. For most of the year, when water and grazing are scarce, the whole camp must continually move on to another water-hole or new pastures. They transport their matting houses and other equipment on the camels so vital to their existence. Towards the end of the dry season many of the nomads seek the green banks of the Awash River—the only significant water-course of the area.

Easily raised and dismantled, the Afar dwelling solves the problem of frequent moves. Called an ari, it consists of an oval framework of pliable sticks bent over to form hoops and covered with rush mats.

Andrew Baring

proof of his manhood. 'I am a woman and you are a woman,' she would cry, 'so why do you approach me?' Even if he were married, 'affairs' would be impossible without a trophy to show for himself. Insistence is less common now, but the ideal persists. Toughness, bravery and independence are still the standards by which a man is measured.

The ceremonies which the young Afar adolescents go through have a strong ritual and symbolic significance and, though they are performed several years before marriage, are seen as an essential prelude to it. A man, if he can afford it, can have more than one wife (he must then divide his time equally among them) but on the whole Afar men take only one wife.

The union which is considered most beneficial is between a man and a particular cousin, his father's sister's daughter. Men tend to marry girls of the same tribe, but to marry outside it may well gain a family access to water and grazing in different territory.

A man's relationship with his clan is almost as important as the traditional qualities of bravery in determining his social standing. The Afar are organized in clans and sub-sections of clans which trace their descent through the male line from a common ancestor. A man has an inescapable duty to help another member of his clan in certain circumstances, particularly in helping to avenge the killing of a member of the clan. This can lead to protracted feuds unless a death is 'settled' by the payment of blood-money, and if payment is agreed with another clan each man must help to find the necessary number of cattle.

It is by animals that a man's wealth is assessed. The Afar keep cows, sheep and goats for meat and milk, and camels, horses and donkeys for transport. A strict division of labour is observed in caring for the animals. The women look after the sheep, goats and milking cows while the men take care of the cattle, including any cows that are not being milked, and of the camels, horses and donkeys. It is the men's job to build enclosures for the animals and to do any job that entails moving away from the camp.

The camp is chiefly the women's province. They keep it clean, look after the small animals which are kept in it, take care of the children until they are old enough to herd the sheep and goats, and they also build the huts in which the Afar live.

Like other nomads the Afar have found an effective solution to the problem of a movable house. It is called an *ari*, and consists of a framework of pliable sticks with a covering of mats. The sticks (cut by the men) are bent over to make hoops which are arranged to form a rough oval and the mats are placed on top, attached with string at the bottom on each side. The opening left for the entrance is closed by a mat which is neatly rolled up during the day. In a camp occupied for some time a bed is made inside the hut—a framework of forked sticks supporting a number of springy sticks on which another mat or skins are laid. The bed is cool and comfortable and, like the dwelling, it can easily be transported when the time comes to move on.

Because their animals rapidly exhaust the scant grazing which springs up after the rains, the Afar spend much of the year on the move. During the rains, which generally last about three months from November to February, the people go up to higher ground in the hills or to the edge of the escarpment. This move avoids a double hazard in the valleys—the mosquitoes and the floods. As the dry season advances the Afar come down again, and as the water gets more scarce they gather round the few permanent water sources. Many stay close to the Awash, the one significant river in the area, jealously guarding their position on the banks. But some stay away from the river, dependent on permanent water holes fed by underground streams.

The end of the dry season is the most difficult time for both man and beast. Food and grazing are scarce, and competition for the available water often leads to fights. This time also sees increasing concentrations of people flocking to Assayita, the traditional capital of the Sultan of Aussa, who before the 1974 revolution was the most important Afar leader and who wielded political power by providing grain for food. There is only limited land suitable for cultivation in the Afar territory and it offers no real margin of safety in agricultural production. There is certainly no possibility of a surplus, and those few who can grow enough for their own needs are fortunate. In the desert the nomads have to rely almost entirely on their animals for food. Sheep and goats provide most of the meat, but the cattle are more precious and are killed only on special occasions—for an eminent visitor, a circumcision feast or a religious festival.

While milk is the most important part of the Afar diet, it is also important as a social 'offering' and is what is first given to a visitor to establish a proper host-guest relationship. Accepting a drink of fresh, still warm milk from the special water-proof milking basket immediately puts the guest in a protected position, and starts an extensive set of rules of behaviour for both parties. Should a stranger be killed while under the protection of an Afar, for example, he must be avenged as though he were a member of the clan.

The nomads are able occasionally to obtain a little grain from the highland peoples by bartering animals or their produce (chiefly ghee or clarified butter). A handful of millet is a great luxury and is not made into bread

Survival/Lee Lyon

This married woman wears the traditional Afar head-dress. Her dress is made of imported cotton, which is replacing the hand-woven brown dyed skirt of the past. Women do much of the work of the camp: they carry water in goatskin bags, tend the animals, care for the children and look after the dwellings.

In the past an Afar man could not marry unless he had at least one gruesome trophy of a killing to show his future wife—it was customary to castrate a victim. But manhood is also manifested in other ways. Having had their heads shaved until initiation, men then allow their hair to grow into this distinctive style. The special stick is used for cleaning teeth.

Transworld/Victor Englebert

Philip Jones Griffiths—Magnum

Among the Afar the ideals of feminine modesty and masculine bravery and honour are expressed in many ways. On all occasions when the men publicly demonstrate their strength, the women are present.

hand: the left hand is used for sanitary purposes and to use it for food, or for accepting a present, or for shaking hands, is to offer a deadly insult. The symbolism of right and left—already referred to in clothes—is pervasive in Afar social custom. When sleeping with his wife, for example, a man must lie on his right side with his right hand underneath him. If he is to touch his wife's genitals he can do so only with his left hand. She will lie on the left of the bed, on her left side, and is permitted to use her right hand to touch her husband.

While such rules have now been integrated within an overtly Moslem set of religious attitudes, they do in fact pre-date Islam. But although this faith has acquired an overlay of beliefs derived from other sources among the Afar, Islam is of great importance to them. They would not dream of eating pork; they rarely drink alcohol; they pray, if a little irregularly; they go on *haj* (the pilgrimage to Mecca) if they are wealthy enough; some fast for the prescribed holy month of Ramadan; and all make the Moslem declaration of faith, even when they are not as strict in their observance as they should be. Religion is one feature which continues to differentiate the Afar from the Christian highlanders of Ethiopia.

With so many different peoples around them—the Issa Somali and the Ittu and Enia Galla to the south, the Wallo, Yaju, Raya Galla and Tigre to the west, and with the Christian Amhara as the central governing people of Ethiopia, extending their control over them—the Afar have had a turbulent history. A long saga of wars reached a peak of ferocity in the 16th century when the Moslem armies of Ahmed Gran, 'Ahmed the Left-Handed', penetrated far into the territory of the Christian emperor of the highlands. Peace was not established between the Afar and the central government until the second half of the 20th century, and even then sporadic fighting still took place between them and some neighbouring groups, particularly the Somali.

Some of the 250,000 Afar, however, do live in areas where more centralized political authority has developed—particularly the sultanates of the south-eastern part of the desert. It is not difficult to see at least part of the reason why this has happened, for it is in these areas that physical circumstances have permitted a certain degree of permanent settlement. There is one large river flowing down into the Danakil Desert, the Awash. Like the smaller rivers to the north, it fails to reach the sea, petering out inland in a series of lakes. But the volume of water it brings down is sufficient to modify enough of the harsh effects of the desert to allow agriculture and to provide a sure source of water for man and his animals throughout the year.

It was thus in the area of Aussa that the largest Afar sultanate grew up. The former imperial government of Ethiopia saw the Sultan as a means of extending its own control over the Afar as a whole and located a market, school, clinic and other signs of government influence in his capital of Assayita. The Sultan himself acted as main Afar spokesman in the old Ethiopian Senate. In the Republic of Djibouti (formerly Territory of the Afars and Issas) the Afar have tended to increase their power in relation to the Issa Somali in recent years. Modern developments like the establishment of the port at Djibouti and the railway from there up to the Ethiopian capital of Addis Ababa have had a slow but steady influence on a small part of southern Afar territory.

For most of the Afar, however, the day-to-day effect of government activity is slight. Local administrative officers do something by their presence to keep the peace, but life is much as it has been in the past. The proud Afar have never taken very kindly to being governed. □

(many of the desert-dwellers do not, in fact, know how to make it). It is most likely to be roasted and eaten a grain at a time. Where water is a little more plentiful the Afar can find a variety of papyrus root called *burri* which is mixed with milk to make a porridge. Wheat is occasionally obtainable and this is made into a heavy round pancake and eaten with a sauce of ghee and red pepper as one of the Afar's favourite delicacies.

As with most African and all Moslem peoples, food must only be eaten with the right hand. This is the only 'clean'

Victor Englebert/Transworld Feature Syndicate

Afrikaners
SOUTH AFRICA

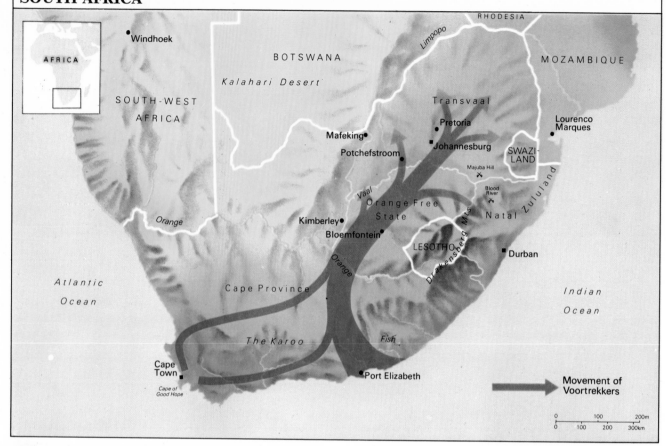

Movement of Voortrekkers

Proud of their own language, loyal to their own church, and practising their own controversial socio-political system, the Afrikaners are a unique people. Today they are the dominant influence in an African country governed by whites and situated at the southern tip of the continent. Yet their separation from the rest of Western culture is much more than a geographical one.

Their language of Afrikaans, evolved over 200 years, is based on the High Dutch spoken by the early settlers in the Cape. It was these people who gradually moved inland to establish themselves as farmers. The Dutch Reformed Church, to which most Afrikaners belong, and which preaches a Calvinist Christianity based on the Old Testament teachings, has long been removed from the majority of the world's Protestant communities. Above all it is their structuring of society by race—apartheid or 'separateness'—which has led to their isolation from most of the Western world.

Apartheid governs much of life in South Africa. It is the system by which each of the major nations of South Africa—the white, the Asian, the coloured and the nine Bantu nations—lives in its own homeland and develops along its own lines. The aim of this is to create a South African common market of independent nations. The precedent for this, however, lies in the policy of the British government in the early years of the 20th century, when the countries now known as Botswana, Lesotho and Swaziland were reserved for the black peoples. The 'homeland' in which Afrikaners, English-speaking South Africans and other whites live takes up 86 per cent of the area of the Republic; the African homelands, eventually to include

one for each of the nations, occupy 14 per cent. There were over 2 million Afrikaners in 1970, about 60 per cent of the white population; there were more than 18 million non-whites. Seen from the outside, it is this imbalance in the area allocated to each group, and the various manifestations of 'petty apartheid', which have resulted in South African whites, and Afrikaners in particular, being condemned by world opinion.

In the face of criticism from both inside and outside the country, the Afrikaners have often used the same arguments to justify their position within the country: it was they who first settled in the southern tip of Africa, it was they who fought for the land and farmed it, it was they who initiated the huge development which has made the country rich. And, if the arguments are old and recurring, that merely lends them weight for many Afrikaners.

The daily lives of most Afrikaners have altered dramatically in the 20th century. They have changed from being essentially farmers, or Boers, into industrialists and townspeople. This transformation has led many of them, and especially the young, to discard the traditions so long connected with the land. Some of these traditions, however, are manifested in other ways.

Sport, and in particular rugby football, plays a major part in their life. On the field the Afrikaner can relive the physical endeavour of the Voortrekkers and, in the international arena, sport becomes a test of the nation's manhood. Many countries of the world, opponents of apartheid, have boycotted South Africa in sport and, of all the international action against her, this has perhaps had the deepest effect on the Afrikaners. It has even led to some cracks in the wall that South Africa presented the black athletes from other countries and contributed to the rift between the *verkrampte* (conservative) and *verligte* (enlightened) factions of the Afrikaner-dominated National Party—a rift which spurred the breakaway of an unsuccessful *verkrampte* splinter-party and produced a wider spectrum of opinion within Afrikanerdom.

Today the Afrikaners, though most survive comfortably on rich farmland and richer mineral resources, are under pressure from many sides, just as they have been in the past. In the 18th century, their struggle was against the Dutch governors of the Cape, who exploited them for the profit of the Dutch India Company, and against the British who then took over; later, pushing north to the veld beyond the Cape area on the Great Trek, it was against the Zulu and the Matabele; and at the turn of the century, in the Boer War, they rebelled against the British.

Nothing symbolizes the hardships, dangers and glories of this past as well as the *laager*, the convoy of ox-wagons formed into a defensive circle to protect the families on the Great Trek. It was from a *laager* that the Voortrekkers defeated the might of the Zulu nation at Blood River in 1838. Monuments to those *laagers* and the trekkers that fought from them stand in prominent positions throughout South Africa.

Afrikaner history dates from 1652, when the Dutch established a garrison at the Cape of Good Hope, halfway along the sea route from Europe to India. Dutch people were encouraged to come out and join the garrison, build the first farms and grow food for the crews of the Dutch East India Company's ships. Though initially they only settled in the area immediately around the Cape, many

Farmers, or Boers as they are sometimes known, still form the backbone of the Afrikaner nation. Despite the Afrikaners' involvement in the growth of South Africa's cities, it is still their attachment to the land they fought for which inspires many of their attitudes.

soon began to move north to escape from the oppressive Dutch administration. Inland, away from its influences, there were vast stretches of land occupied only by Hottentots and Bushmen, who were easily chased off.

Much of the land beyond the mountains of the Cape offered grazing for cattle but was not fertile enough for cultivation. Yet it was here, in the vast loneliness of the Karoo, that the Afrikaner nation was really born. In the meantime, however, the British took over the administration of Cape Colony.

But far more dramatic events were taking place in what is now Natal. This was the violent expansion of the Zulu nation under Shaka. Other African tribes of the grasslands were suddenly confronted by Shaka's warriors, and the result was a chain-reaction of terror and savagery, with broken tribes fleeing to safety in mountainous areas and barren lands where the Zulu *impis* (battalions) would not follow, or retreating into defensive enclaves.

At the Fish River, Afrikaners met this overspill of desperate tribesmen, whose pastoral way of life was severely affected by the pressure of the Zulus to the east, and clashes were inevitable as white and black competed for the grazing lands. But the British government answered Afrikaner requests for increased military protection against this onrush by emphasizing that the African tribes were to be treated as equals. In 1835 many Afrikaner frontiersmen and their families packed up and left, trekking north across the Orange River. There they found the grasslands rich—and miraculously empty. This was the Great Trek, destined to last for two years and to become the central event in Afrikaner history and legend.

The men, women and children who took part in the Great Trek left the borders of Cape Colony for good. The Voortrekkers, as they came to be called, took with them their servants, ox-wagons, sheep, cattle and all their portable possessions. Many sold their farms for a song, others simply abandoned the homes to which they had been attached for years. The Great Trek was much more than a

John Bulmer

Ian Berry—Magnum

South African Tourist Corporation

A river crossing during the Great Trek, the exodus from the Cape which took thousands of Dutch settlers and their families away to the grasslands to the east and north. The hardships they encountered and battles they fought against the African tribes—and later, as farmers, against the British—are proudly remembered and still give Afrikaners a sense of purpose.

A statue of a Voortrekker mother and her children— heroes of Afrikaner history—looks down on today's generation on a hill outside the government's administrative capital of Pretoria in the Transvaal.
Cape Town is South Africa's oldest city, and one of the world's great natural harbours.

movement to escape the British: it meant that the trekkers severed their links with Europe once and for all. They no longer had any home except the soil beneath their feet.

They travelled in the great 12-foot long ox-wagons, whose wheels stood as high as a man's shoulder and which could be easily dismantled for floating across rivers or for navigating slopes. Each day they moved on before the sun was high, and then built a *kraal* or enclosure to protect their animals from wild animals. At night, young and old would join in prayer before settling to sleep.

The Great Trek is remembered with tales of the massacres of the Voortrekkers and their avenging victories. On one occasion 6,000 Matabele warriors attacked a group of about 50 wagons which had been formed into a *laager*. Each of the Afrikaners was allotted a particular section to defend, his powder and bullets laid out next to him. The women helped reload the spare rifles and sewed small buckskin bags to hold the scatter-bullets which were so deadly at close quarters. At first, as thousands of Matabele warriors attacked hurling their spears, the Afrikaners were so outnumbered that many of the tribesmen reached the *laager* and attempted to get inside; it was only the thorn bushes woven between the spokes of the wheels which saved the defenders. When at last the Matabele withdrew they left 300 dead warriors.

There are stories of hardships and dangers triumphantly overcome, and there are the Voortrekker heroes, like Piet Retief and Dirkie Uys. And always, waiting in the wings to snatch away the promised land just as it came within their grasp, was the British government.

In 1843 the British annexed the Voortrekker Republic of Natal; in 1848 the Orange Free State. There were signs that British policy was one of positive expansion when in 1871 they took the newly-discovered Kimberley diamond fields and then, in 1877, the Transvaal. Four years later the Transvalers rebelled. And they won, routing the British troops at Majuba Hill. Under its president, Paul Kruger, the Transvaal—which its people called the South African Republic—faced life with new confidence.

In 1886, there was an event that was to shape the whole future of South Africa: gold was discovered on the Witwatersrand. Thousands of foreigners, mainly British and known as Uitlanders, flooded into the Transvaal, soon outnumbering the Boers. The British sent troops to South Africa to protect the interests of Uitlanders. Kruger, the president of the Transvaal (then called the South African Republic), declared war on Britain, and the Orange Free State followed suit.

After three years of war—a war which was virtually over in a year but was protracted by guerilla tactics, and which left bitter feelings on both sides—the defeated Boers returned to farms that had been reduced to ashes by the British. They were left with little but legends of courage, ingenuity and tenacity to stir the blood of future generations, and the memory gave Afrikaner nationalism an impetus that was to drive it to gain in peace what it had lost in war.

While that impetus came from the Boer War, the unifying mythology and sense of purpose came from the Great Trek and the less spectacular but more populous migrations that followed it. Many Voortrekkers had built a picture of themselves as the Israelites, God's chosen people, fleeing from Pharoah (the British government) to the promised land (the grasslands) which God had ordained as theirs. To ease their physical burden, God provided them with Sons of Ham (the Africans) who were the hewers of wood and drawers of water. Their freedom, as they saw

Terence Spencer—Colorific!

The boys in this group of South African scouts, who are known as Voortrekkers, are reminded by school and family of their unique history, and take pride in their own language and religion.

Two spectators play their own game before the rugby international between South Africa's Springboks and the British Lions at Johannesburg. Boycotts on South Africa's sportsmen by countries who disagree with apartheid have hit Afrikaners harder than most other forms of political action.

it, implied the servitude of the black African population.

It is this freedom that Afrikaners consecrate on their holy day, the 16th of December, the day of their victory over the Zulus at Blood River in 1838—a victory often claimed to be the result of a pact they made directly with God. It is called the Day of the Covenant. And it was this freedom they sought when, in 1908, the Afrikaners from Transvaal and the Orange Free State sat at the conference table with representatives of Natal and the Cape to decide on a constitution for a Union of South Africa.

The Union came into being in 1910, with a flexible constitution, equality with English for the Dutch language, significant voting advantages for the Afrikaners and no vote for black Africans except to a limited extent in the Cape. The English-speakers could afford to be magnanimous. They controlled the towns—and with the towns the administration, communications and much of the economic wealth of the country.

In a matter of two or three decades the discovery of diamonds and gold changed South Africa from a country with a rural, agricultural economy to an industrializing society with the seat of power in the mushrooming cities. The Afrikaners began a new trek, away from the grasslands to the cities, and to power. Low paid, high-security jobs in the government, administration, police and the railways were soon almost monopolized by Afrikaners. Afrikaner business ventures such as Volkskas (People's Bank) were launched to cater especially for Afrikaners. A second, better-educated generation began to enter the professions, particularly teaching.

By 1948 the number of Afrikaners in the cities overtook the number of English-speaking whites. Afrikaners ran the country's administration, communications, and, to a large extent, its education. In 1961 the Union became a Republic and left the British Commonwealth. Since then, internal problems have increased; the allocation of the tribal homeland territories and the unequal distribution of resources between these and the white areas have provoked disputes and resentment. Among urban black Africans, the imposition of the Afrikaans language has produced further troubles. In 1976, in the Bantu township of Soweto, a protest against its use in schools resulted in riots and killings which illustrated the deep tensions existing within the South African community.

Ashanti
GHANA

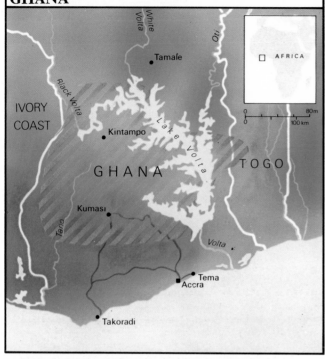

In 1900 the British, under Sir Frederick Hodgson, demanded the submission of the Ashanti Kingdom. He began by asking that their famous Golden Stool should be brought out for him to sit on. He knew it was the symbol of their political authority, and this move would show that he had taken command. He obviously thought of the stool as a throne, the seat of a king. Yet this was no ordinary chiefly stool. It was a symbol, but what it represented was the entire spirit of the Ashanti people. It was their collective soul. Nobody sat on it, not even the Asantehene, the Ashanti King.

The failure of the British to understand this was an expensive one. The Ashanti rebelled and it was a year before they were suppressed. The area was annexed as a crown colony and the independent political power of the Ashanti kingdom was over.

In the past the main items of trade, and those which were the foundation of Ashanti greatness, were gold and slaves. There are no slaves now, of course, though gold is still produced and worked to some extent. Much more important as a source of cash is cocoa. Most of the over one million Ashanti depend directly or indirectly on the success of the cocoa crop, and a fall in world prices can have disastrous effects on their economy. indeed on the whole economy of Ghana.

Within the country other items have some importance

Ashanti is a federal state, and every district or 'nation' has its own chief. These wealthy men and their various retinues have gathered for a special ceremony in Kumasi.

Andrew Rutter

in trade. A certain amount of timber is produced, mainly for internal use, though some is exported. And from Ashanti to the north there is a regular trade in cola-nut—a nut with an astringent flavour chewed for its stimulating effects.

The Ashanti are renowned for their skill at a variety of crafts. In the days when their economy was largely dominated by the gold trade, the associated crafts were vital. Most important of these was the art of casting the small brass weights that were used for weighing out the gold-dust (alluvial gold sifted from the rivers) or small nuggets (dug from the ground). These fall into three classes. The simplest have geometric patterns, which perhaps were once symbolic; then there are a number which represent natural objects like plants or seeds; and the most interesting group is those which represent human or animal form as illustrations of some story or proverb. These are of infinite variety and charm, and have become one of the most sought-after items for collectors.

After the making of weights, the most famous Ashanti craft is weaving. Their earliest cloths were made of

The Ashanti Kingdom founded its power on gold and slaves. Though little gold is worked now, and cocoa provides a livelihood for most Ashanti, it is still a symbol of wealth and prestige.

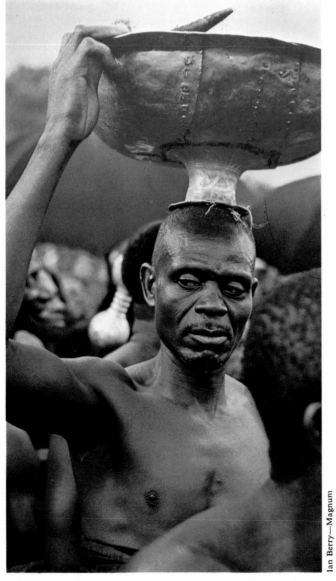

Ian Berry—Magnum

cotton, which suggests that the art was introduced from the north, where cotton is grown more extensively. Silk was brought in later on and the patterns were adapted to take advantage of the greater possibilities, particularly in the range of colours. Weaving is done by men. Spinning is also done by men and now by women, although traditionally women could only do so after they had reached the menopause. The cloth is woven in narrow strips, which are then sewn together to make large cloths. The finest silk ones take many months to make and cost hundreds of pounds.

There is also a flourishing art of carving. Every person may have their own stool, and chiefs will have ones which symbolize their office like a throne. Frames for the flamboyant umbrellas which are an essential part of a chief's regalia are also carved. Drums have carved bodies, and the special drums which are used to 'talk' have a particularly attractive shape. Carving is an art for men, and in the past was associated with a number of ritual observances: women were not allowed to approach a carver working, let alone carve themselves.

Pottery, on the other hand, is a craft at which Ashanti women excel. Men only make pots or pipes if these are to have a human form, and women are forbidden to make these. Pots are still moulded by hand, the wheel having only recently been introduced by European-derived technical education. Decoration is restricted almost entirely to the side effects of the technique of production: a pattern of lines left by the corncob used to smoothe the surface.

The Ashanti believe that a person gets blood from his mother: it is obvious from the menstrual flow that blood is actually produced by women. They understand that conception takes place as a result of intercourse, and consider that the contribution of the man is the child's spirit or *ntoro*—a word sometimes explicitly associated with semen.

The fact that the greater part of a person's physical being comes from the mother finds expression in social terms. The group to which the child belongs, and the group from which social identity is mostly derived, is the clan of the mother, not the father. The members of this *abusua* are united in believing themselves the descendants of a common female ancestor, who is often herself described as being descended from an animal.

The *ntoro* is the male-equivalent. Everyone belongs to his father's patrilineal line as well as to his mother's *abusua*, but the duties and responsibilities to it, and the advantages derived from it, are fewer. Both duties and responsibilities tend to be a religious or spiritual rather than social. There is a special day set aside each week, on which the members of a particular *ntoro* conduct a ceremony of ritual washing and prayer in honour of its name, and there are a number of taboos on eating or killing particular animals with which each *ntoro* is associated. A woman of child-bearing age will also observe the taboos of her husband's *ntoro* since its spirit, if offended, might make difficulties for their children or even cause barrenness.

Members of the same clan are not allowed to marry. This rule is strictly observed for the *abusua*, the mother's clan, no matter how distinct the relationship. In theory the same is true of the *ntoro*, the male line, but in practice marriage may be permitted if it is impossible to trace an actual relationship over five or six generations. It is also more difficult to trace relationships between members of the same *ntoro*, since they tend to be scattered over the whole of the Ashanti territory, while *abusua* members are often localized in one village or quarter of a town.

Local groups and villages are divided into these

Women wear cloth of black, red and brown, the colours of mourning, at the funeral of a king.
Nobody, including the King, is allowed to actually sit on the famous 'Golden Stool', which is thought to embody the soul of the whole Ashanti nation.

'quarters'. Each contains members of the same *abusua*, who can trace their descent back to a common named ancestress over the last six or eight generations. Descent from the ultimate ancestress may be believed but over longer periods of time the actual details tend to be forgotten. The ownership of the land which is used for farming and for the village itself is vested in the *abusua*, and it will be a matter for the head of the clan to decide who shall be allowed to farm it. Use will generally be restricted to members of the clan, but strangers may be allowed to rent land.

The head of the lineage is a man, but the influence of the principal women, especially the 'Queen Mother', is great. She consults the elders when a new head has to be appointed, and she presents the nominations to members of the *abusua* for ratification. She holds a position of great respect and moral authority within the lineage, and her advice has considerable weight with the head, whether he is merely the head of a local lineage, of a district, or of all Ashanti. The principles of selection and political power are the same at all levels.

The head must obviously be a member of the *abusua* himself, and in modern times, with the advantages of education coming to outweigh those of skill and experience in war, there has been an increasing tendency to select a younger man.

Among many practical daily duties, he is also the guardian of the ancestral stools of the lineage. He has to see that the appropriate sacrifices are made to the stools

at regular intervals and on all important occasions. The ancestors must be informed as to what is going on in the world of the living, and their blessing sought on any important undertaking. Their influence is believed to be considerable and nobody would dream of ignoring its possible effects. The ceremonies in connection with the stools are important: the whole unity of the Ashanti nation was largely formed and maintained on the basis of loyalty to the Golden Stool, the symbol of the spirit of the whole nation.

Ownership of the *abusua* land is vested in its head and it is he who will allocate it to its various members for building or farming. He also arbitrates in the many disputes which arise between members, particularly over land, but also over other matters when the heads of the smaller domestic units are unable to settle issues themselves. He must approve all marriage and divorce arrangements for members of the lineage—although approval is now often rather automatic—and more important he will also decide all questions of inheritance.

Because property is inherited through the maternal line, a man's property will not go automatically to his children when he dies, but will go first to his mother's side of the family. His mother will generally waive her rights in favour of her children, the man's brothers. The only exception to the general pattern of inheritance is in the case of certain crafts: the tools of a goldsmith, for example, can pass directly to his son if he also is a goldsmith.

The influence of the *abusua* is also felt at all the important points in the Ashanti life cycle. In the late stages of pregnancy a woman will go to her female relatives and it is they, to the total exclusion of the father or his relatives, who will take care of her during childbirth. The child is immediately named after the day of the week on which it

was born. For the first eight days it is treated rather casually, for it is not yet accepted as a full human being; it may turn out to be a ghost child, coming only for a few days before returning to the spirit world. If it dies during this period the baby will not be formally buried, and the family will rejoice that it has gone rather than mourning as they would do at a proper funeral.

On the eighth day the *Ntetea* rite is held. The father brings gifts for his wife and child, and he or another member of his *ntoro* will name the child, usually after male or female relatives on his side of the family. Twins are treated in a special way: boys become attendants to the king, and girls are his potential wives.

There are few ceremonies connected with puberty. A girl is dressed up in fine clothes and jewellery on her first menstruation, and receives presents and congratulations. Her *abusua* will conduct certain rites including ritual washing, and she will be considered unclean during this period. There are no special rites for boys.

The Ashanti have a number of classes of marriage, depending on the relative status of the two partners, but all involve the exchange of a number of gifts between the groom and his wife's *abusua*. Without these marriage is not legal and, if there is a divorce, some of them will be returned to symbolize the end of the marriage and the termination of the various rights which were created by it.

The basic food crops of Ashanti are yams, cassava and plantains. In the humid forest much of the work is done by the women, although in the more open parts of the north men grow crops on a much larger scale, particularly yams. A variety of vegetables including peppers, tomatoes, greens, egg-plants and marrows add variety to the sauces which accompany the home-grown staple foods or imported grain alternatives. Protein comes from domestic animals (sheep, goats, pigs and some cattle in the northern savannah) and the ubiquitous chickens. ☐

A father and his family. Children are thought to get their blood from their mother and, for most social purposes, belong to her clan or abusua. The father's group, the ntoro, is named after the spirit he gives the child.

A father and son from a village near Kumasi carving wooden stools. Every person may have a personal stool, but certain designs are reserved for the chiefs.

The larger Ashanti houses are often built with verandahs around a court. Many cocoa-farmers now replace the thatch with iron roofing.

Women in the village of Sasa pound cassava in front of a typical Ashanti house. Yams, plantains and cassava are pounded and then boiled to make a thick porridge or cake. The young children stay close to their mothers as they work.

Baggara
SUDAN

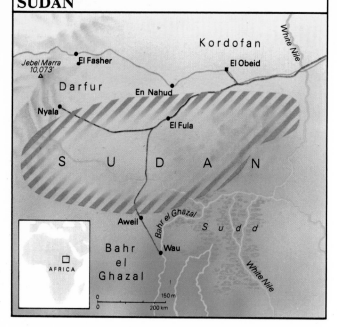

so it is difficult for them to graze and the migration can be completed quickly. By the end of February the hottest and hardest part of the year is on them; water is precious and the cattle are moved to centres with permanent wells. All the water for the vast herds has to be drawn by hand and the animals may have to travel many miles each day to find good grazing.

During April the first rains and the flies arrive, and the slow migration north commences. After the long hard summer the cattle desperately need good grazing and they move forward over a wide area to look for new grass brought up by the rains. June sees the first move north completed and the Baggara's arrival at the most permanent of their camps. If the tribes can be said to settle anywhere it is here, where they have small plots which are weeded, fertilized by the manure of the animals, and then planted with bulrush millet. The rains which drift north bring the flies and mosquitoes, the ground becomes muddy and after only a few weeks it is time for another move.

This time, however, only the herders drive the animals further north, while the wives and children remain behind to cultivate their crops. Once these are established they too move north to join the herds. At the end of September the Baggara start moving south, and by October again reach the millet patches where the cattle are corralled to stop them eating the crops. In November and December harvesting takes place, after which the cattle are allowed to eat the stubble. When the year is completed the migration starts anew.

The various tribes that make up the Baggara are ruled

The Baggara is a collective name applied by the Sudanese to the group of nomadic cattle-owning tribes, living in the dry savannah belt between the Nile and the border with the Chad.

There are several tribes that come under the name of Baggara. They are culturally similar and claim distant kinship with each other but, more important, they are descended from Arabs, speak Arabic and follow the Moslem faith. How they came to live in a land where they are forced to breed cows and not camels has at least two explanations. They may have been part of a circular migration moving west along the coast of North Africa as far as Tunisia, crossing the Sahara and then moving east again; or they could have formed part of the 14th century Arab invasion of the Nile Valley.

The area in which the Baggara move is strictly delineated. To the north of the dry savannah is the semi-desert where the rainfall, although sufficient to allow the breeding of camels, is not enough for cows; to the south is the wet savannah woodland which is not only too wet and muddy to support large herds, but also has the tsetse fly and clouds of mosquitoes which make life unbearable for the animals.

The land through which the Baggara move is the property of the people as a whole. Its frontiers were fixed by the British-Egyptian Condominium government at the beginning of the 20th century, and they were extremely generous considering the Baggara had been the staunchest supporters of the Mahdi and among his most fanatical warriors in his fierce campaigns during the 1880s.

The annual migrations of the Baggara follow a long established pattern. In December, when grazing becomes poor and water sources dry up, the Baggara move southwards to places where there is still surface water and grazing. The animals are bunched together in great herds

Bulls are used for transport from camp to camp and baggage is reduced by the dual purpose of the materials for the tent. The bark is used for padding under the load, ropes for tying it and the straw mats for resting on during halts.

individually by their own leaders, and form neither a political nor an economic force. Each tribe may have one or two leaders called *Nazirs* depending on its size. They hold the reins of power and are the direct link between the tribe and the local administrative officers of the central government from Khartoum.

The individual tribes are split into further sections called *Omodeya* administered by *Omida*, the equivalent of sheikhs. These men collect taxes and arbitrate in disputes. There are further sub-divisions until the smallest unit, the *surra*, a group of people who have a common ancestor five or six generations back.

This is regarded as the ideal social, migratory and herding unit, but due to size the *surra* is usually split into two or three camps which travel in close proximity. These camps are not stable units, and are continually broken up and it is rare for a fixed group to travel together constantly. The camps are arranged in a circle which can be expanded or contracted according to the number of households present.

Even the tents of the Baggara are not permanent, each separate part usually being replaced within two years. They are hemispherical frameworks of sticks (normally cut afresh at each camp site) covered with strips of bark to keep out the wind and then covered again with mats roped into position. Even the rich, owning two or three thousand cows, will live in a ramshackle beehive indistinguishable from its neighbours.

The life of the Baggara is totally dedicated to and controlled by their cattle. Their animals provide milk and

Paul Verity

The Arab features of the Baggara often reflect the influence of intermarriage with Negro slaves, but the Semitic countenance and light skins are still prized. The men shave their heads to deter bugs, then swathe them in lengths of white cloth.

occasionally meat (as for the arrival of an honoured guest), and of course they are the means of transport. Horses are also used by the men during migration, donkeys for carrying water to the camps, a few goats or sheep for meat, and dogs are trained to guard the camp.

A few Baggara own large herds, amounting perhaps to several thousand head of cattle. The larger the herd the greater the wealth, the greater the prestige, and the greater the number of relatives and retainers who will attach themselves to the camp. This in turn leads to political power within the tribal structure. The possession of cattle also attracts women and a man with wealth can take up to four wives.

The amassing of large herds has caused serious problems. Now that the Baggara have access to veterinary techniques and modern husbandry, the herds are no longer being reduced as they were by disease and the land is becoming severely over-grazed.

The Baggara are of Arab blood, although they are far less Semitic in appearance than their camel-owning neighbours to the north. Over the centuries the proportion of Arab blood has lessened with the intermarriage of Baggara and slaves from among the Nuba and Nilotic tribes to the south, and it is now often difficult to tell the physical difference since their skin colour is so similar. This has led to a certain degree of racialism within the tribe—the lighter the skin the better—and though a man will still obey custom and marry his cousin as a first wife, he will search for a girl with light skin for his second wife.

The Semitic features of the Baggara, however, are still in evidence. Their bodies are hard and lean, shaped by the tough life they lead, and their faces are lined and wrinkled by constant exposure to the sun. Their heads, usually

Andrew Baring

The Baggara's tents are made up from detachable parts. Based on a hemispherical frame-work of sticks, usually cut at the temporary camp site, they are covered first in strips of bark and then again with mats roped into position.

shaved to deter the inevitable bugs, are wrapped in a long piece of white cloth under which they wear a small cap. The men wear a long white shirt down to the calves, under which they wear baggy trousers. These loose clothes are ideally suited to the heat of the summer.

Their shoes made from cowhide have soles that extend beyond the uppers all the way round to prevent the wearer from sinking into the soft sand. The men usually wear amulets called *wadjar*, little leather pouches containing written sections of the Koran which provide religious protection from sickness and violent death. When out of camp a man's constant companion is a spear, used both to ward off the predators such as lions and leopards which attack the herds, and as a weapon against raiders.

A Baggara tribesman pays bridewealth to the parents of the girl he wishes to marry, (usually with cattle). She must be a virgin, and this is insured by infibulation (the sewing up of her vagina) at the age of eight or nine. If she is not pure at marriage she will immediately be divorced, but in the past it was not uncommon for her father to kill her

The men, led by the 'best man', whip a bridegroom at a wedding. A Baggara man may take more than one wife if he can afford it—her parents must be paid, usually with cattle—but they must be treated equally in every way.

for the shame she had brought on his household. Although she is worked hard once she is married she is treated with respect and the household possessions and the tent are hers.

If a man has more than one wife he must provide a separate tent for each, and all must be treated equally. If a present is given to one, a present must be given to the other; if the husband spends a night in one wife's tent then he must spend the next night in that of another.

The women are guarded jealously, but with the Baggara way of life it is impossible to hide them away. They play an important part in the running of the camp—erecting and dismantling the tents, milking the cows and doing all the domestic chores. They are not the demure and furtive creatures of the harem. They wear no veils and, in most circumstances, breasts are bare, though when guests are being entertained they cover their breasts. Their hair is braided into many small plaits and periodically rubbed with liquid butter. They wear a dark blue length of material wrapped around the waist to form a skirt with an end falling loosely over the head and shoulders.

Some women wear nose-rings and almost all wear as many silver and gold anklets, bracelets and neck-rings as the husband can afford. This jewellery constitutes most of the tangible wealth of the Baggara and, as women are inviolable under Moslem custom, it is the safest way of transporting their assets. Unlike the camel Bedouin arabs of Arabia, the women are not shut in *utfas* (an enclosed shelter on the camel's back) when moving camp, but sit openly on the bull's back.

In a subtle way women wield tremendous power, for it is through their words, poems and songs that a man's fame is spread and his prestige built up. They tell of his generosity and hospitality; they tell of his prowess in battles in the endless raids and counter-raids which are involved in stealing cattle though this is now dying out.

The Baggara will sell their animals only in extreme need or to pay taxes. The everyday essentials that have to be bought (tea, sugar, pots and so on) are paid for with the money acquired from the sale of liquid butter which is carried out in the villages by the women. Their reluctance to sell or kill their animals is not because of a name association with them as is the case of some Negro cattle-owning tribes, such as the Masai and the Dinka, but because it diminishes the size of their herd and consequently lessens their prestige.

Relations between the Sudanese government and the nomads have never been good, for the Baggara use and graze vast areas of land and contribute little to the national economy. The government levies a tax on each animal, but less than a third of the animals owned are declared, so more money is spent boring water holes than is being collected. Few men know exactly how many head of cattle they possess as it is considered bad luck to count the number of animals. But nobody is prepared to say which came first—the theory about bad luck or the tax.

The friction between nomad and government is increased because the authorities insist that children should be educated in schools, and with the Baggara constantly on the move it means the children must be sent to boarding schools. To the Baggara the education of a child is not the learning to be found in books, but the learning of cattle husbandry, herding, and the locations where good grazing and water may be found. ☐

(Right) The Homr favour cattle of the short-horned 'zebu' type, with dewlap and hump. They walk quickly, which is important in wooded regions, where many days can be wasted searching for stragglers.

Berbers
NORTH AFRICA

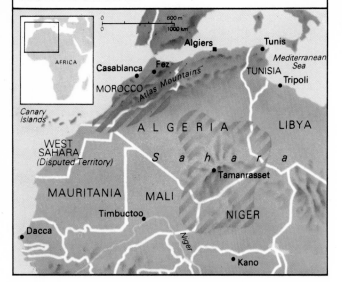

There are about ten million Berbers scattered over the immensity of northern Africa, from the Siwa oasis in Egypt to the Atlantic Ocean in the west and from the Mediterranean in the north to the Niger River on the southern borders of the Sahara. It is thought that the Berbers once inhabited the whole of this vast region, displacing the Negro population who retired southwards through the desert. But where the Berbers came from and how they arrived in North Africa is unknown. They themselves only trace their history back to their conversion to Islam with the coming of the Arabs in the eighth century.

At first the Arabs came peacefully as missionaries, but between the 10th and 15th centuries they came in invading armies, driving the Berbers away from their lands on the fertile plains into the less hospitable mountain ranges of the Atlas, the Rif and the Aures and into the depths of the Sahara. It is in these rugged mountains and desert areas that most of the Berbers are still found today.

About four million live in the Rif and Atlas ranges of Morocco and three million in the mountain ranges of Algeria to the east. The rest are in nomadic groups in the desert or in small pockets around the oases scattered throughout the countries of northern Africa—in Egypt, Libya, Tunisia, Niger, Mali, Mauritania, Senegal, the Upper Volta as well as on the borders of Morocco and in southern Algeria.

Those who remained on the plains readily absorbed the invaders' customs and above all their language; to the Moslem Berbers, Arabic had considerable prestige as the language in which God spoke to their prophet Mohammed. In addition their own language is not only difficult and complex but also unwritten. In Morocco alone there are three regional variations, which although they share a common grammatical structure are mutually incomprehensible. Dialects also vary from tribe to tribe and often from village to village, creating further problems in communication. As a result Berbers from different regions often choose to communicate in Arabic and the majority of them now speak it as a second language.

Few Arabs speak Berber but there are small Jewish and Negro communities in Morocco and Algeria for whom it is their first tongue. Berbers do not just belong to a loose linguistic group but are a distinct section of the Caucasoid race: they are also Sunni Moslems of the Malaki rite.

They have, too, a remarkable uniformity of culture considering their scattered distribution: techniques of agriculture, weaving and pottery show strong similarities throughout the Berber areas, whether on the fringe of the Sahara or in the snow-capped mountains of the Atlas.

But though they share a language, religion and culture and similar racial characteristics, the Berbers do not see themselves in terms of a racial group and have never been united in one kingdom or as a political force. For most, allegiance is to their tribe and they are unaware of any wider bond. It is only in a few places, where they live in small isolated communities, such as in southern Tunisia, that there is a wider awareness of Berberism.

The Berbers are still essentially both a tribal and rural people. The flourishing towns of Morocco and Algeria are basically Arab, and the Berbers who live there are the educated elite or those who have been 'Arabized' over the centuries of contact. Apart from the seven small towns which have grown up around the prosperous Mzab oasis

Traditional Berber dwellings in southern Tunisia. Scattered throughout the vast area of northern Africa, the Berbers are a distinct section of the Caucasoid race with a common language and religion, though their way of life varies widely from region to region.

Elsa Grube

Victor Englebert/Susan Griggs

In the High Atlas mountains of Morocco only the valleys can be cultivated, while the flocks are grazed on the steep hillsides. The Berbers are a rural people, whether they are living in the mountains of Morocco, Algeria or on the fringes of the Sahara desert.

in central Algeria, the Berbers live in scattered hamlets or villages or in small communities of tents.

Wherever they live the majority of Berbers grow crops and keep livestock, although the varieties or breeds and the proportions vary considerably according to the local conditions of climate and soil. The three million Shluh who inhabit the Western and Anti-Atlas ranges of Morocco, like the Berber tribes in the Rif mountains further north, are mainly settled agriculturalists. With the aid of extensive irrigation and terracing high up the mountainsides every possible patch of ground is cultivated. Wheat, barley, vegetables and fruit are grown on the lower slopes while higher up barley and rye are the only crops which will survive the harsh and snowy winters. At these high altitudes sheep are kept for their meat, wool and milk, while in the valleys and on the lower slopes the Berbers rely on herds of goats and cattle.

The houses in the mountain areas are made of stone or mud with flat roofs built around a courtyard. They are often built so closely together up the steep mountainside that the roof of one house forms the courtyard of the one above.

Further east, in the Middle Atlas mountains, where the winters are longer and harder, animals are more important than agriculture. This beautiful mountain range, heavily wooded with pines and cedars, is the homeland of the Imazighen tribes who speak the Tamazight Berber dialect.

The dominant feature of their lives is transhumance, moving up and down the mountains according to the seasons to find the best pasturage for their animals.

Although often on the move, they are not totally nomadic, maintaining a permanent dwelling in a village or hamlet. The winter nomads maintain permanent villages with their distinctive tower-like granaries, high up in the mountains, and migrate with their herds to winter pastures in the valleys before the heavy snows fall. The spring nomads' villages are in the foothills at the base of the mountains and in the surrounding steppes. To escape the scorching heat of the summer sun these Berbers move with their herds up to higher ground in late spring, when the mountain pastures are clear of the winter snow. A few tribes are 'double transhumants', building their villages halfway between the winter and summer pastures. Constantly on the move, they live for most of the year in black goat-hair tents.

However frequently the Berbers move and however long they are away, their villages are never left without a small number to guard the collective granaries and to grow essential cereals such as barley, maize, wheat, rye, millet, vegetables and, in the sheltered lowland river valleys, various fruits.

Where the foothills of the mountains ranges reach the fertile Atlantic plains in the centre of Morocco, Arab and Berber agriculturalists are closely mixed. In the south the foothills of the Atlas merge with the steppelands of the Sahara zone and the soil becomes increasingly arid. Except around a few fertile river valleys, crops are rarely grown and the local tribes are mainly nomadic. They rely on flocks of camels, sheep and goats, and trade their products for cereals and fruits grown around the fertile oases.

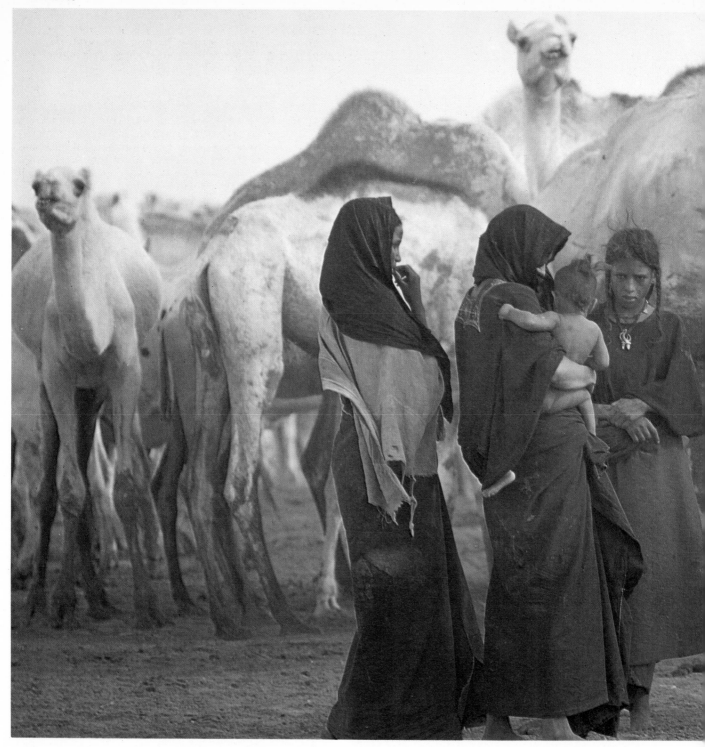

The most famous of the Berber nomadic groups are the Tuareg—the 'Blue Men' of the Sahara. Numbering about 300,000, these aristocratic camel-owning warriors are famed for the distinctive blue veils worn by the men to protect them from the scorching sun and the blown sand.

They traditionally range the barren wilderness of the Sahara, through southern Algeria to northern Nigeria and from western Libya to Timbuctoo in Mali, wandering with their herds of camels, and trading salt from southern Algeria. But with the establishment of firmer political frontiers in the second half of the 20th century, their traditional nomadic life is being severely restricted, particularly by the Algerian and Niger governments. Permission to cross the border must be officially obtained

and only a certain number of camel caravans are allowed to pass through every year.

Algerian independence from France in 1962 also led to the abolition of the Tuareg slave class, the *iklam*, who traditionally looked after the herds and the salt caravans and did the domestic work. As a result of these restrictions many Tuareg moved south into the states of Niger and Mali but their numbers were severely depleted in the early 1970s by disastrous droughts. Of those that remained in Algeria many became semi-nomadic and a few even sedentary, tending their gardens around the oases. These were formally worked by the black *harritine* class who tended the crops in return for one fifth of the harvest. In these oases the principal tree is the date palm, and in its

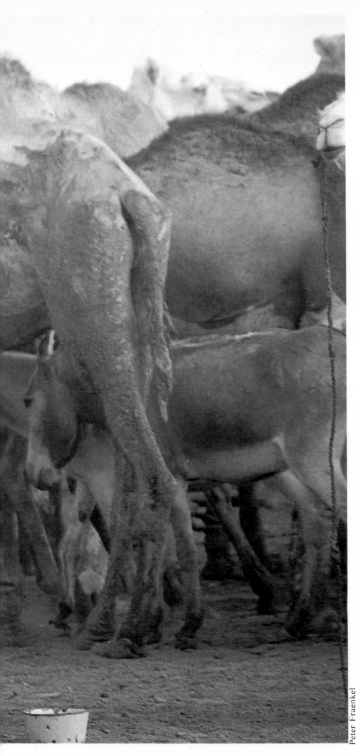

Tuareg nomads halt their wanderings to water their camels. These aristocratic warriors used to roam the length and breadth of the Sahara, but with the establishment of firmer political frontiers their movements have been severely restricted.

Three or four villages may group together in one valley to form a canton of up to 800 extended families. The headmen of the hamlets form a small council, sometimes with an elected president, to decide matters of common interest. The organization of the larger units of tribe and confederation is looser, and these are of little importance except in times of inter-tribal warfare and feuding, which have grown increasingly fewer.

Among the nomadic Berbers, however, the most important grouping is the fraction, which corresponds to the canton of the sedentary peoples. It is usually composed of a number of *duars* or groups of tents in a specific area. The fraction is both a political and a fighting unit for the nomads, particularly the Tuareg. Its council is made up of the heads of the important families and they nominate a war leader—'the leader with the tuft of grass.' At his election a piece of grass or basil is inserted in his headband and his clothes are rubbed with these plants. In the past these fractions often owned communal lands, acquired by con-

These towering castles of mud and straw are found throughout the Atlas mountains of Morocco. They are the homes of the large landowners or of the holy men and their families, who may claim descent from a saint or from Mohammed himself.

Peter Fraenkel

Dr. Werner Wrage

shade grow apricots, peaches, citrus fruits, figs, vegetables and cereals.

The social organization remains local and tribal for most Berbers. Among the sedentary agriculturalists the social groupings are on four levels: the village, the canton, the tribe, and the confederation. The smallest and the lowest is the village, often no more than a collection of hamlets or scattered farmsteads. Each hamlet is inhabited by a group of 10 to 15 extended families—brothers, cousins, and second cousins—who all trace their descent from a common ancestor. Each village has a council composed of all the men of an age to bear arms who meet to supervise the distribution of community expenses and the maintenance of the mosque, footpaths and irrigation ditches.

The weekly 'souk' or market is a potentially explosive situation, the time when Berber men from rival villages, districts and tribes meet to exchange goods. A council is elected to keep the peace or the market may be presided over by a holy man.

quest, to which each of its members would have equal rights. Many fractions also have distinctive female tattoos which are registered at the religious sanctuaries.

Another method of social control which has occurred throughout Berber history is the maraboutic state, or rule by hereditary holy men. These 'saints' still play an important role in many Berber areas, both as arbitrators and conciliators in disputes and in supervizing elections to representative village or canton councils.

It is these holy men who still maintain order in the High Atlas mountains of Morocco. Here the valleys are invaded every spring by the inhabitants of the plains in order to graze their flocks in the fertile pastures. The permanent population of the mountain valleys is not large enough to use up all the pastures; nor is it strong enough to prohibit the southerners who come in vast numbers with their flocks of sheep, goats and camels. Disputes inevitably arise, and it is the holy men who act as the professional neutrals in settling these quarrels and in supervizing the grazing of the pastures. Both sides accept their authority because their ancestry connects them with the founder of Islam, their shared religion, and excludes them from identification with either side.

The one day of real peace in traditional Berber society is the weekly market or *souk*, held by villages, cantons or whole tribal groups. To keep order between rival groups while the essential transactions are taking place these markets are presided over by the village or tribal council, who own the market, or by a holy man. Both the council and holy man can impose fines or other penalties on anyone who dares to break the peace.

Each market meets weekly on a fixed day, and in a fixed place, so that anyone in the district can visit the *souk* and return home by foot within a day. As a result the great majority of *souks* are held on a fairly deserted site, away from a village or any buildings, usually near the boundaries of two or three districts or by an important crossroads.

Vendors are divided according to their wares, and all *souks* place a butcher as far as possible from the other stall holders—his goods are thought to attract evil spirits. Every market has at least two officials who are hired by the organizers to act as market crier and as official weigher and measurer. These men are regarded as the 'shameless ones', and are universally despised.

In all the countries in which the Berbers live they are a minority. But although they differ linguistically and racially from their countrymen, both Arab and Negro, they have never formed a distinct political unit either within a region or on a larger scale. In both Algeria and Morocco, where the largest groups are found, educated Berbers have played important political roles—the first prime minister of Morocco was a Berber—but these men have rarely acted as spokesmen for their racial minority. The Berber minorities seem content to continue their traditional rural lives with their strong loyalties to village, clan or tribe rather than to their country or the Berbers as a people.

But for those nomadic tribesmen whose homeland has been divided between different political states the situation is more difficult. Not only must they attempt to adapt their traditional lives into smaller territories, but in addition the inhabitants of the central Sahara have had to share their territory with oil drills and, in more recent years, with tourists.   □

(Right) The hustle and bustle of a camel market.

Unlike the heavily veiled Arab women, a Berber does not cover her face and her position in her society is generally far higher.

Bushmen
KALAHARI DESERT

The Bushmen of the Kalahari have for centuries attracted the attention of Europeans as exotic remnants of an ancient past, people different in appearance and way of life from both Europeans and Black Africans of southern Africa. The harshness of their environment, the unique 'click' language, and their assumption that as hunters they could freely kill other people's cattle, set them apart from their more powerful neighbours. Indeed, in the early days of colonization they were sometimes regarded as non-human and were cruelly hunted, almost as a form of 'sport', until their numbers were severely reduced. But they have fought back and made a successful adaptation to life in the Kalahari Desert into which they were driven.

It is almost certain that the Bushmen once roamed the whole of southern Africa from the Cape to Zimbabwe, Angola and Mozambique, hunting game in the well-watered grasslands and scrub forests. Where they had first come from, and indeed whether they had actually evolved in southern Africa isolated from all other African peoples, is not known. Although relics of their culture, including rock-paintings and engravings, have been found through-

(Left) A Bushman woman.

Bushmen bands build these small dome-shaped grass scherms wherever they pitch a new camp. All the members are related by kinship ties.

B. Mertens

Members of a Bushmen family warm themselves by a fire in the early morning. Even in the Kalahari there are frosts and icy winds at night, and fire also provides some protection against prowling animals.

The Bushmen are well adapted to living in the heat of the Kalahari desert. Their slitted eyes are protected from glare by fat-laden lids; they have no hair except on their heads; and their skin reflects twice as much sunlight as the darker Negro skin.

out the region, nothing has yet been discovered north of the Zambesi River to indicate a route from the north which they might have followed.

Over the course of several hundred years the Bushmen were gradually driven from these fertile hunting grounds into the arid and empty wastes of the Kalahari Desert. First it was the Bantu-speaking Negroid peoples who pressed upon the Bushmen's territory. They came from further north, between 400 and 500 years ago, in large groups driving their herds of cattle—hitherto unknown to the Bushmen as domesticated animals—before them. Later it was Europeans, pushing up from the Cape, who intruded on the Bushmen's lands.

Although there are about 55,000 Bushmen in southern Africa today—around half of them in Botswana (Bechuanaland), slightly fewer in Namibia (South-West Africa), and a few thousand in Angola—only about a third continue to lead their traditional nomadic lives. The others have abandoned the desert, and the hunting and gathering way of life. In the past, many were kidnapped and made to work in the households and on the farms of Bantu and Europeans who had settled around the Kalahari.

Intermarriage with any other people is rare among the Bushmen. Belonging to a unique racial group, they differ profoundly both from the Negroid peoples of Africa and from the Europeans. Their yellow skins are loose fitting and wrinkle easily; their faces flat and wizened; their figures slender and their stature slight—the average height of the men is between 4 feet 10 inches and 5 feet 2 inches, and women are about an inch shorter.

Although they have not always lived in the Kalahari, the Bushmen are ideally adapted to its harsh climate. Their eyes are protected from the glare by slitted and often fat-laden lids which are so Mongoloid in appearance that the Bushmen were once identified as a lost race of Chinese. Their bodies are free of hair except on the head where the dark, tightly coiled peppercorn hair leaves patches of the scalp exposed to help keep them cool; and their skin reflects 43 per cent of the sunlight—nearly twice as much as that of Negro peoples. To withstand the frosts and icy winds of the winter nights the Bushmen have specially adapted blood vessels to conserve heat—an adaptation which is shared only by the nomadic Lapps and the Aborigines of the Australian outback.

The most noted physical characteristic of the Bushmen is the large accumulation of fat on the buttocks (known as steatopygia), which is particularly noticeable among the women. It is a feature they share not only with their Hottentot neighbours, but also with some of the Negrito peoples of the Andaman Islands in the Bay of Bengal. The large buttocks in fact serve as a store of energy, and in times of drought or famine they shrink in size.

B. Mertens

Although the shells of ostrich eggs are used primarily as water containers, here one is broken up to make beads. The skin cape, or kaross, that this woman is wearing serves both as clothing and as a kind of pouch for carrying her baby.

Bushmen also have other unique characteristics: for example, until they have suckled their first child, the nipples of many adolescent girls are swollen to form small orange balls, and throughout the lives of many male Bushmen the penis remains in a state of constant semi-erection.

Except for a small leather loin cloth the Bushmen go naked and, in spite of the burning sand, thorns and scorpions, they rarely wear sandals. Women have a long, leather cape or *kaross*, belted at the waist and knotted at the shoulder to form a pouch to carry the baby or the ostrich egg water containers. These white shells are also used to make beads which the women thread in their hair or string in bracelets around their arms and knees.

The Bushmen groups, scattered in small nomadic bands over the Kalahari, are usually named after some local characteristic, like the Heikom (the 'People who sleep under Bushes') and the Sekhoin, whose name means 'People of the Plain'. The size of the band varies from group to group and is sensitive to changes in local conditions. Among the !Kung of the north-eastern Kalahari, for example, a band will number 25 to 30 people, while among the Gikwe in the south there may be twice as many. Contact between the various bands is frequent through trade, visiting and marriage. But there is no overall political organization of Bushmen.

On a larger scale, however, communication between the groups is limited, for although they all speak languages belonging to the Khoisan or click group, there are wide variations and many mutually incomprehensible dialects.

There are many Bushmen families who now live on the fringes of the Kalahari. Unable to survive in the desert because of its depleted resources, the Bushmen way of life is vanishing as they turn to work on the farms of other Africans and Europeans.

Gerald Cubitt

B. Mertens

Using a block of wood as a cutting board, a Bushman shapes a strip of tanned leather into a loin cloth. For Bushmen who still follow the traditional ways of their people this is their only item of clothing.

These languages are characterized by short pops and clicks made with the tongue in various parts of the mouth. To outsiders the language is difficult to understand and harder still to speak.

Languages as well as social customs, myths and legends, may vary from tribe to tribe, but the means of survival in the wastelands of the Kalahari differ only according to the terrain. Nowhere in this desert region is there enough water to grow crops or to keep livestock, and the Bushmen rely on digging up roots and tubers, picking berries, fruits and nuts, and hunting game. The few precious water holes that last the whole year are carefully husbanded according to stringent rules.

Antelope such as gemsbok, springbok, wildebeest and eland are the main source of food and clothing. And during the long droughts, they often provide water as well. They are hunted with feeble-looking bows and almost child-sized bone arrows smeared with a deadly mixture of animal and vegetable poisons. Once shot the animal is tracked until it falls and can be killed with a spear. From a whole herd a skilful hunter can pick out the spoor of the wounded animal and is capable of tracking him for hours over the veld, running without food or water in the stifling heat. Once the hunter has killed his prey, the animal is butchered on the spot on a bed of leaves. Nothing is wasted: the flesh is cut up and dried for food, the blood collected for drinking, and the undigested grass in the stomach is squeezed dry for its moisture. The hide will be used to make clothing, the aprons and *kaross* worn by the band, the bones cracked for their marrow and then used to make arrow heads. Only the contents of the gut are discarded as being of no use.

The members of a Bushmen band are related to each other by blood and marriage ties. Everything is shared between them, food and water automatically divided according to seniority, and objects like bows and arrows constantly passed on to avoid jealousy. Only through trust and co-operation can the Bushmen hope to survive the hardships, the famines and the droughts of the desert.

In the search for game, or for the roots and fruits which are such an important part of their diet, the Bushmen cover vast distances on foot. But although nomadic, each band has its own territory whose boundaries are rigidly observed. The territory may be several hundred square miles in area, and the Bushmen must know it intimately if they are not to starve or die of thirst during the long drought.

Always on the move and with no beasts of burden, the Bushmen can have few possessions. They build their small dome-shaped grass *scherms* wherever they pitch a new camp. Their only protection by night against the lions, leopards, and other predators of the Kalahari, is fire. By day they roam the plains armed only with their small bows and arrows. Reflecting their own skills in survival, the heroes of Bushmen legends are always small animals like jackals who trick, lie and narrowly escape while the lions are scalded, singed, cuckolded or killed.

The size of Bushmen families, like that of the bands, is necessarily limited by the resources available to the group. Unable to support a large number of dependants, they nevertheless take care of the aged and infirm. Mothers give birth to their children alone, away from the safety of the camp in the bush where the night is dangerous with prowling lions and the spirits of the dead. Unless it is a woman's first child, or if she has a long and difficult labour, she tells no one and asks for no help. The baby is born onto a bed of grass, the umbilical cord cut with a stick and, together with the afterbirth, is covered by branches and stones. If the mother buries these in the earth, the Bushmen believe she will have no more children. The spot is marked with a tuft of grass to warn men away, because the power of the place is so strong that a man might lose his ability to hunt.

A baby is usually welcomed by the band, but on occasions a child is born that cannot be supported. If the season is exceptionally hard with little food or water, or if the mother is still suckling another child the problem is sometimes solved by infanticide. The Bushmen say, euphemistically, the child is 'thrown away' before the mother returns to camp. Similarly, if a child is born deformed or crippled it too is killed for it would never be able to support itself. It would be a constant drain on the meagre resources of the band.

In times of extreme hardship it is not only the very young who suffer, but also the old. Travelling through the veld in search of food is always hard but in the high summer, after months of drought and with midday temperatures rising to 140 degrees Fahrenheit, only the strongest can survive.

The dead are buried in graves, the body bound with the arms crossed over the chest, the knees raised, the ankles tied together and the head resting on the fists which are drawn up under the chin. Wrapped in an old *kaross*, the body is placed in a sitting position in the grave and supported by a forked stick. Each person present throws a handful of earth onto the body to make sure they will be remembered and that the spirit departs peacefully. The grave is filled up and covered with thorn branches to protect the corpse from hyenas.

For the ancient culture of the Bushmen, the future does not hold out much hope. A way of life so completely dependent on the resources of the desert, cannot sustain itself when those resources are depleted. The Bushmen, so afraid of captivity, are becoming increasingly timid and more easily imposed upon. On the fringes of the Kalahari, many now live almost as serfs, or gather around the villages of their negro neighbours. In the most isolated wastelands of the desert, only the will to survive enables the remaining Bushmen bands to endure. ☐

Copts
EGYPT

David Holden

As the infant Saviour Christ came with his parents to Egypt to avoid Herod's persecution, the family passed the decayed glories of Ptolemaic Heliopolis. The statues of the Ancient Egyptian Gods, recognizing, so it is said, the Truly Divine when they saw Him, fell crashing to the ground. To this day one can see, in the Cairo suburb of Mattariya, a trough in which Mary is said to have washed her son's clothes, and the interested can still visit the crypt of a Church which is said to have been the home of the refugees in 'Babylon-on-the-Nile.'

These traditions have been preserved by the Copts, the Christian minority of Egypt, who now number over three million, and are still distinguished from the Moslem majority of their fellow countrymen by their particular religious beliefs.

The name Copt is itself a corruption of the Greek 'Aigyptos'—which has also given us our word Egypt. The Ancient Egyptians had been conquered by the Greek forces of Alexander in the fourth century BC, and for the next few hundred years the dominant intellectual climate of Alexandria was a mixture of Greek and Egyptian. The Coptic tradition asserts that Christianity was introduced into this mixture by the Evangelist Mark, and this eclectic cultural background was important to the forms which Egyptian Christianity eventually took. The Coptic language in which the Scriptures were written was the final form of Ancient Egyptian. It was written in Greek characters, with seven additional letters to represent Egyptian sounds for which there were no Greek equivalents. One of the best known survivals from Ancient Egyptian hieroglyphic writing found in Christian iconography, is the 'ankh', the looped cross symbolizing life. As the Christian religion developed, a large number of Greek words were included to represent concepts which the Ancient Egyptians did not

have. This remained the liturgical language of the Coptic Church until recently, although it gradually gave way to Arabic as a spoken language after the Arab conquest of Egypt in the 7th century, and had largely disappeared from daily use by the end of the 13th century.

The term Copt has three different meanings: it refers to all the Egyptians during the 'Coptic Period' from the conversion of Egypt to the Arab conquest; it is mainly used to describe the section of the Egyptian people who did not accept Islam but remained Christian, that is a member of the Egyptian Church. By extension, it is loosely used for members of the Ethiopian Church which derived from Egypt.

Although Christianity was originally transmitted to Egypt by the Jewish-Greek-Egyptian intelligensia, it was not initially a religion for the rich and powerful. However, the poor adopted the Christian teachings with enthusiasm. For both the artisan and the peasant Christianity seemed to offer an escape from the harsh realities of life. Perhaps this is why Coptic art has retained its realistic, earthy, humourous quality in spite of the classical influence which appears in the work the Greek-Egyptians commissioned. It is primarily a domestic art, some of its most vivid works being tapestries. Its intimacy comes through its domestic bronzes like lamps and incense burners for the churches and in its bone and ivory carvings and stone sculpture. Coptic art shows little influence from the stylized Pharaonic art which preceded it, either in style or choice of decorative motifs.

Christianity was well established by the end of the 2nd

The Copts are the direct descendants of the Ancient Egyptians. By remaining firmly Christian, they have avoided integration with the Moslem Arabs, who conquered them more than 1,300 years ago.

M. Desjardins/Top

century. The 'Great Church' of Alexandria was mother of 40 bishoprics in the north of Egypt. But Egypt was not a free country; it was a province of the Roman Empire, and a personal possession of the emperor since Augustus had inherited it following the machinations of Caesar, Cleopatra and Antony. Successive Emperors had taken all the corn and tribute they could from Egypt, to feed the hungry masses of Rome and to finance their own spending. The tax burden on the Egyptians was heavy. Many emperors, including Septimus Severus, Decius, Valerian, Diocletian and Galerius persecuted the Copts. Their persecution under Diocletian, in particular, was so severe and bloody that they dated their calendar from it.

For the Copts, the Christian search for a quiet life thus coincided with the desire of an oppressed people to flee from persecution. Many of them sought peace and solitude in the deserts which surround the valley of the Nile, living at first like hermits. Soon, however, groups of people began to gather, notably around St. Antony, and thus, monasteries, collections of cells, came into being. The monastic movement, organized by St. Pachomius at the beginning of the 4th century, had a great and permanent influence on Egyptian Christianity. Famous monasteries like those of St. Paul and St. Antony close to the Gulf of Suez, and St. Catherine in Sinai, still exist today.

The adoption of Christianity by the Roman Emperor, and the establishment of the capital at Constantinople

removed some of the pressure from Christians; they were no longer persecuted for their religious beliefs, at least. But for the mass of the Copts there was still the threat of the tax gatherer, who was usually from the sophisticated Greeks of Alexandria, and this increased the hostility which the 'real' Egyptian majority felt for them. Even when the privileges of the Alexandrian Greeks were withdrawn by enforcement of the same heavy tax demands by Justinian—who even decreed that the Egyptians pay the cost of the transport of their corn to Constantinople—the Greeks were still the official tax collectors.

By the 5th century virtually the whole of Egypt had been Christianized, and when, in 451 AD, the doctrine of Monophysitism, (the single nature of Christ) which the Patriarch of Alexandria supported, was condemned by the Council of Chalcedon, the nation supported him and withdrew from the Orthodox Church. The reasons for the split were thus originally political rather than simply religious. The result has been the adoption of the belief that Christ's nature was single, a mixture of human and the Divine. Their Church has remained Monophysite since that time and the Copts of Egypt and the Christians of Ethiopia still practise this faith. For the Copts their support of Monophysitism was as much a calculated political decision as it was a religious choice. The hostility towards the Greek Empire which it reflected was an important part of their decision to accept the Arabs when the Moslem

Colin Maher

The relative freedom from social restriction enjoyed by Coptic women allows them to undertake many activities, such as selling fruit, which are still denied to some of their Moslem compatriots.

Andrew Baring

(Previous page) One of the oldest Christian monasteries in existence, the monastery of St. Anthony was built by the Copts, who fled to the deserts of northern Egypt to escape their Roman oppressors.

Early Coptic art had the earthy and plebeian character of the artisan class that produced it. It owed little to late Pharaonic or Classical pagan art although some was put to similar ritual use.

John Moss

An Ethiopian priest: Coptic missionaries first reached Ethiopia about 340 AD, and although their message took several centuries to reach the mass of the people, the Ethiopian church is still Coptic.

armies of Amr ibn Al-As arrived in 641. They hoped that they would be more independent and that the burden of taxation would be lighter if they accepted the Arab conquest peacefully.

However, the difference between the two masters was slight: if anything the Copts were even worse off under the Arabs. Their corn was still removed—this time to Arabia—and they still had to pay local money-taxes, a land and village taxation, often in kind, and a personal tax for those who remained Christian. That Moslems did not have to pay the personal tax accounts for a large part of the mass conversion to Islam which the Christian Church suffered over the next few centuries. Thus while the Caliph's receipts from the head-tax went up in the 7th and 8th centuries from 10 to 15 million dinars, by the 10th century they had fallen to little more than 3 million dinars. Even Copts who were converted to Islam had still to pay the land and village taxes, leaving an intolerable financial burden on the remaining Christians. This resulted in many Copt riots during the 8th and 9th centuries.

Under the Moslems the Coptic minority suffered occasional disabilities, but they were not systematically persecuted. The removal of external images from their churches was common to the Islamic world. Haroun al-Rashid, the hero of many of the Thousand and One Stories of the Arabian Nights, ordered them to wear a distinguishing headdress. And in spite of serious persecution by Al-Hakim, the mad Fatimid Caliph, they usually maintained good relations with their Moslem masters. These relations generally depended more on external factors than on internal ones: they were bad when Christian-Moslem relations were bad, particularly during the Crusades.

The Moslems had always employed Coptic artisans to decorate their buildings which accounts for a considerable continuity between the art-forms of the two periods. Many Copts were employed by the Arabs in administrative positions, although the numbers decreased as the Moslems grew more literate towards the end of the Fatimid period. The Fatimids had disagreed with the majority of their subjects, whom they had failed to convert to Shia Islam, and so were obliged to rely on the Greeks and the Copts. The Copts also acted as scribes to the Ayyubids and, after the Ottoman conquest of Egypt in 1517, as tax-gatherers to the Mamelukes, the ruling military class, to enable them both to pay their tribute to Constantinople and to support themselves. Mohammed Ali, the founder of the dynasty under which Egypt achieved independence from the Turks in the 19th century, despised the Copts, but allowed them to serve as officials. This continuous role made them unpopular with many of their countrymen: they were identified with the foreigner and the oppressor—a curiously ironic position for the only direct descendants of the original Egyptians—and were identified with anti-nationalist elements. Sir Eldon Gorst, financial adviser to the Egyptian Government, in his efforts to create a body of moderate opinion to back a co-operative Khedive, drew the Copts away from the rest of the Nationalist movement, and the first Egyptian Prime Minister after 25 years of British rule was Boutros Pasha, a Copt. However, he was regarded as the personification of the collaborator and this further embittered Copt-Moslem relations. The appointment of Mohammed Saad Pasha after the murder of Boutros Pasha was seen as an important nationalist victory.

Many Copts supported the Nationalist movement of Saad Zaghloul in the late 1920s, but there are a few remaining tensions. The socializing policies of the Nasser government meant that some of the wealth that the Copts had acquired as bankers and property-men during British rule was bound to be expropriated, and in 1958 accusations of unfair discrimination against the Copts were made.

Fortunately, these conflicts are very much a thing of the past and there is little to distinguish the Copts either as a class or economically from the rest of the Egyptians. They have a tendency to congregate in the same suburbs of the towns, and there are still country villages which are mainly Copt, but whether businessmen or peasants, they are involved in the same activities as the Moslems, separated only by religious differences. It is easier to distinguish these religious forms in the city than in the countryside, where followers of both religions often share the same festivals, acclaim the same miracles and recognize the same saints. Coptic and Egyptian women are now practically indistinguishable since the veil has declined in popularity. Occasionally the richly decorated hearses which distinguish a Christian from a Moslem funeral can be seen outside Cairo churches and weddings are still an occasion for festivity in their rich, sombre interiors.

Although the Copts had a great influence on the early development of Christianity, and in particular the growth of monasticism, they did not produce great theologians. The reasons for this are reflected in the nature of the Copts themselves, who, because they were primarily drawn from the artisan classes were always practical rather than intellectual. □

Dan
IVORY COAST AND LIBERIA

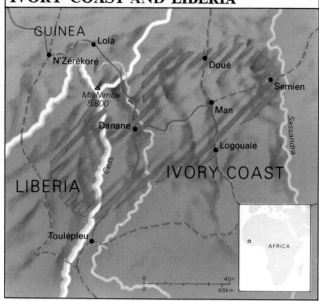

The haunting ceremonial masks of the Dan, found in museums throughout the world, are visible representations of the powerful spirit world which traditionally ruled their lives.

The homeland of the Dan people is a long way from any major population centres, and this isolation helps to explain why their reputation for superstition, cannibalism and magic has persisted for so long.

The Dan now live on the border between Liberia and the Republic of the Ivory Coast in West Africa. Their gently undulating country reaches from the heavy forest zone in the tropical south to the open savannah plains in the north and is notable for the great variety of soils which are found there. These soils are derived from granite, gneiss and many other substances which produce a wide range of ecological conditions. The Dan have developed a complex agricultural system which skilfully exploits these geographic variations.

The rainfall too is extremely variable in this region. There may be over 78 inches of rain one year and only a half or two thirds of that the next, so only an extremely flexible economy can accommodate these conditions. The

A typical village of the Dan people showing the closely grouped houses with their conical thatched roofs. Each of these villages is politically independent having its own headman and council of elders.

Marc and Evelyne Bernheim/Susan Griggs Agency

Marc and Evelyne Bernheim/Susan Griggs Agency

Snakes play an important part in the mythology of the Dan. As in some other parts of Africa, the ability to handle them without injury like this Dan snake dancer, creates fear and awe among bystanders.

rain falls with great force during the wet season of *duei* from late March to early October but during the other half of the year there is very little. At the height of the rainy season in July the paths through the forest become muddy and difficult, and the humidity is intense. In contrast, the dry season, *blay*, from October to March, is uncomfortably hot and dry. In the north it becomes so arid that animals cannot survive.

The Dan now number about 175,000. They are handsome in appearance, and generally tall, unlike most forest peoples. This fact tends to support the idea that their original homeland was the Sudanic region, north of where they now live. According to their historical traditions, they were driven south by Moslem warriors who had superior weapons and horses, and only when they reached the forest zone where the horses of their enemies were destroyed by the tse-tse fly, were they safe.

The Dan men traditionally wore a long robe of locally woven cotton, but today shorts and shirts of imported cloth and European cut are common. The women have needed to adapt less: the long strip of cloth which they used to wrap round the waist, leaving the breasts bare, is now made of brightly coloured imported cotton. It reaches from above the breasts to the ankles and is often used to support a baby on the back.

The Dan spend most of their time involved in agricultural activity. The patterns of social life are dominated by the agricultural needs of the moment. One traditional indication of the beginning of this annual cycle is the appearance of the constellation of the Pleiades, or 'the hen and her chickens' which occurs at the beginning of June. The lighter rains of April have already washed the ashes of the burnt areas of forest into the newly cleared fields, helping to fertilize them. The main crop sown is rice—the Malaysian kind introduced to the Sudan by the Arabs more than 500 years ago.

It was probably this particular grain which enabled the Dan to make such productive use of the forest environment, and they have names for at least 40 distinct varieties. The earliest kind, *zakwale*, is sown in March to take advantage of the early rains. Later varieties are planted in April, (*ge*), May (*mleupou*) and June (*somleu*). May is *alos*, the time to prepare the fields for yams which involves heaping the earth into piles.

In July the really heavy rains fall, when 'the hen and her chickens have fallen in the water'. The previous year's manioc, maize and plantains are eaten during this period, along with a supplement of meat from hunting. Hunting is the favourite occupation of the men, while the women must keep busy weeding until the harvesting can begin. It is also the time when granaries and storehouses have to be repaired and made ready for the new crops of rice which is cut at the end of July. Harvesting the later varieties successively keeps everyone employed until the end of November.

The Dan have a regular system of markets at which agricultural produce is exchanged and sold for cash. This time of year, when the stores are full, is devoted to this commerce and distribution; it is not until December that people can relax a little, and pick up the threads of family and social contact, arrange marriages, hold memorial services for the dead, visit distant relatives or take up paid work. The beginning of January is also relatively relaxed, but as it passes and February begins, the social aspects of life must take second place and the hard work of clearing the forest and preparing fields begins again. New houses must be built or old ones repaired before the rains come again.

The basic vegetable foods of the Dan are rice, manioc, yams, maize and millet, which are generally prepared as a thick porridge and eaten with a highly spiced sauce made of palm oil, peppers, okra, tomatoes and onions. At special celebrations, or to entertain guests, various kinds of meat will be added. The Dan keep a few cows for this purpose, as well as goats, sheep, dogs, chickens, and guinea-fowl which are all eaten on occasions. Some fishing is done and any game brought home by the hunter —small deer, perhaps, or monkeys—will make a welcome addition to the stew.

The Dan have evolved a unique system of rotating the uses of their land, which shows a profound understanding of the natural cycles of the soil. For the first two or three years they will plant rice on a new field. During the third, when rice yields fall off, they add sorghum millet and maize since these plants have longer roots and can use soil at lower levels which is still fertile. These are used alone in the fourth year, and subsequently replaced by manioc for the next three. Manioc and yams, both root crops, finally exhaust the land which must then be left fallow for the next four to ten years before being reused.

The Dan are most renowned for their artistic skills. They are marvellous carvers, making wooden masks with plumes, shells and tin cans for their secret societies, and a variety of ritual figures which have magical significance. They also practise the lost-wax method of casting bronze —a skill which is supposed to have originated in Ancient Egypt and have produced ornaments of great beauty; their

Marc and Evelyne Bernheim/Susan Griggs Agency

Dan carvers produce objects for ritual purposes such as this mask decorated with shells, plumes, and bells. The masks are worn with traditional costumes and used at the ceremonies of secret societies.

Mary Fisher/Colorific!

Improved communications have brought the Dan out of their isolation, and their way of life is changing rapidly. These men, wearing Western shorts and shirts, are threshing rice at the tribal capital of Man.

(Left) A forest village of the Dan.

jewellery is famous. They also produce bracelets and anklets with minute designs cast on the surface, or decorated with bells. Aluminium from Second World War plane crashes was often salvaged for this purpose. They also incise intricate designs on calabashes and carve beautiful wooden domestic implements which resemble spoons. The art of the smith and the jeweller used to be surrounded with great ritual, but this has grown less in recent years since factory-made products have been introduced from outside.

Dan villages consist of up to 300 circular huts, with conical palm thatched roofs and painted walls, clustered closely together. The most important houses belong to the chief, and contain accommodation for guests and a larger house for hearing legal cases and settling disputes. Each village is politically independent, with its own headman and council of elders and there was formerly no large-scale political authority. Each village will contain people related through the male line, and it is through this lineage that inheritance, succession and names pass. Women go to live in their husbands' village when they get married.

The traditionally inferior position of women is changing as an economic necessity. They are now responsible for a great deal of the agricultural work and their economic influence in markets is increasing. A wife is always something of an outsider in her husband's family and she may be criticized if she punishes the children too much. Marriage

involves the payment by the husband of a bride-price to the wife's family, and at one time it was possible for a man to have many wives although this is now less common. The first wife is the senior but each has her own hut. Dan children are weaned at two and the extended family where the mother lives always helps in bringing up a child.

Both boys and girls are initiated at puberty. Boys are circumcised and the girls undergo a clitoridectomy. There are schools in the bush where the children are taught hunting, bush lore and respect for their elders and this leads to admission into a secret society which provides an education and ensures the correct social and ritual conduct on the part of members. The carved masks produced by Dan craftsmen are mainly used in the ceremonies connected with these societies. Each sex has its own society—*Gbasa* for the men and *Togba* for women.

Gbasa members can detect the souls of evil men which they follow home from spirit-meetings by night. When the soul reaches the hut where its body lies sleeping, it gets in through a chink in the roof and falls to the floor with an audible thump. This is the signal for masked *Gbasa* men to burst in and seize the man, who is taken to the chief's court, accused, usually found guilty, and fined. In the old days he might have been executed. Debtors are sometimes embarrassed into paying by *Gbasa* members who pile up all the village's rice mortars in front of his door by night. The next morning, as the stack of mortars cannot be dismantled till his creditors are satisfied, the women are unable to grind the rice for the day's meals. But *Gbasa* can also act as an organized political pressure-group, influencing even the most important community decisions that are still made by Dan chiefs.

The *Togba* society gives protection against spirits with magic powers, black magic and leopards. When a leopard is suspected to be near a village, a *Togba* woman must go out by night armed only with magic medicine and a torch to frighten the animal away.

The influence of both these societies has greatly declined with the introduction of greater governmental control, and the haunting stories brought back by early travellers describe practices which are now forgotten. The Dan are no longer cannibals. But many of the early beliefs survive, modified to suit the modern world, and are evidence of the great adaptability of this fascinating people.

Roland Michaud

Dinka
SUDAN

The lives of the Dinka people of the Sudan are strongly identified with their cattle, whom they imitate in their songs and dances. Most of their words for colours and many of their aesthetic standards are derived from their animals.

Flowing down from the watershed which separates the Congo basin from that of the Nile, and which forms the boundary between Zaire and the Sudan, are a number of rivers which eventually run into the White Nile by way of the Bahr el Arab, and the Bahr el Ghazal. Occupying the middle reaches of these rivers, in a broad arc and stretching across the Nile on the other side there live a large number of people—about a million—who speak a common Nilotic language, Dinka. They are divided into about 25 groups, each giving its name to a particular area. Together these areas make up about 150,000 square miles, which makes the Dinka one of the most extensive peoples in the Sudan.

The configuration of the land means that the Dinka do not rely exclusively on either agriculture or cattle-herding for their subsistence, but on an interesting combination of both. Most of the country is flat savannah and dry, open steppe. As it slopes down to the Nile and the Bahr el Ghazal (the River of the Gazelle) the number of papyrus thickets and swamps increases. The land is intersected by many small rivers and streams which flood during the rainy season, and this restricts the area that can be occupied all the year round.

The only area suitable for the permanent villages is that which is high enough not to be flooded, but not so high as to be without water in the dry season. For this reason, although the women and the older men stay in the permanent settlements throughout the year, looking after the crops, the younger men move up and down. In this way they take advantage of the water and grazing down by the rivers in the dry season, and move up to the savannah to avoid the floods and mosquitoes of the rainy season.

Cattle are at the centre of most Dinka activities. They are important for economic reasons as well as having social and religious significance. The Dinka see a parallel between the lives of men and the existence of the animals: they will imitate their cattle, each man imitating his own particular ox, in gesture and in dance. Each man sings songs to and about his ox, and in praising the animal he will praise himself. He takes the name by which he is known after his initiation, from the ox he is given at this time. The basic name is a straight description of the colour of the animal, but he and others addressing him will make many allusive references to the colour in referring to him. The word *kuac*, for example, means leopard, and a bull spotted in a similar manner will be called *ma kuac*. The same term is used for cloth with a spotted design, *alathnh ma kuac*.

The enormous vocabulary which the Dinka have for colours always involves the idea of cattle and cattle markings. To mention a man as being as fast as a leopard, when his ox is *ma kuac*, is the sort of allusion which abounds in Dinka songs. For social, aesthetic and physical purposes a man is identified with his ox; but for war, fighting and other occasions when leadership and virility are essential, he is identified with an uncastrated bull which represents these qualities.

Not only are social groupings named after the cattle-camp, but when a beast is sacrificed, the parts are distributed to relatives in a strict order, with particular parts of the animal being the right of a particular group; the sacrificer's maternal kin, for example, are given the rear right leg. But even cattle themselves have their own rights, second only to those of humans and of much the same

Each Dinka wife has her own house and cares for her own children. She takes turns, if she has co-wives, in cooking and caring for her husband.

The religious importance of 'Masters of the Fishing-Spear' has also lent them some political authority. Their shrines are revered, and a Master, when old and infirm, might ask to be buried alive to ensure the continued health and well-being of his people.

Peter Ibbotson/Robert Harding Associates

kind. They must not be killed wantonly, 'for nothing', and this would certainly include killing merely for food: they are sacrificed and then eaten, but always with respect.

In many social circumstances cattle are the equivalent of humans, and are consequently used in marriage payments and in compensation for homicide. They are individuals, each with a place in genealogy and society, and they serve as a mirror, a reminder and a record of social relationships and the changes which these have undergone in the course of time. The possession of cattle is a necessity: it marks the individual's place in society and his

Dr. J. F. E. Bloss

relation to his fellows. To be without cattle is to be truly an outsider: this is why the Dinka pity lesser, cattleless people. They are scarcely human, like many poor white people.

The Dinka year revolves round a cycle of movement which is dictated by the distribution of rainfall. The first rains of the year come in March and April, and by May they are regular enough to soften the ground for planting. At this time the Dinka are in their permanent homesteads doing the essential agricultural work, hoeing and planting, and the cattle are grazed nearby.

With the coming of the heavy rains in June and July, the depressions and lower parts of the land began to fill with water, rivers overflow their banks and large areas are flooded. While the older people remain in the permanent homesteads to look after the crops and continue weeding, the young men go with the cattle up on to the unoccupied savannah. There they build cattle camps, containing several related households, in which both the men and the younger animals are housed in mushroom-shaped shelters built on piles.

During October the rains come to an end and some of the herdsmen return to the homestead to help with the harvest. When the rains are well over and the harvest complete, the cattle will return from the wet season camps to eat the millet stalks. Preparations begin for the next year's agriculture, and as the season advances and the water recedes, fishing becomes possible. Several methods are used. Basketwork traps are left in the water into which fish swim and are unable to turn around to escape. Nets, special fish spears or harpoons are also used.

Autumn is the season when everyone is at home—it is the time for celebrations and ceremonies. Beer is brewed, religious sacrifices made, initiation ceremonies conducted, and marriages arranged. It is a time when the Dinka love of poetry comes into its own as a public art: songs of battle and of the ancestors underline and reinforce the solidarity and loyalty of local groups of relatives.

By January the grass near the homestead has all dried up, and the riverine pastures are free of floods. The animals are taken down, and the herdsmen live in temporary windbreaks and shelters until it is time to return for the planting with the coming of the 'little rains'.

The country of the Dinka is not well endowed with natural resources. There are few materials out of which permanent buildings can be made—little stone or iron and few tall or even straight trees. Possessions tend to last for a shorter time than the lives of their makers, so there are no distinctions of ranks based on material possessions and little sense of an historical development. Dinka society is egalitarian. In general, what a man owns is what he has made or obtained for himself. Hoes and spears, and beads for jewellery, are obtained from traders, and cloth and shoes are becoming more common. But for most Dinka, life still revolves round the traditional interests of the homestead and the family, and above all, cattle.

The homestead consists of a few—usually two or three—circular huts. They have conical thatched roofs and sides of wattle and daub. Each wife, if the man has more than one, has her own hut and her own mud screen to protect her cooking fire against the wind. Cooking pots rest on mud supports, and the whole cooking place is protected by a shelter which also serves to keep utensils out of the reach of animals or children. Household implements are few, but practical: clay pots for cooking and brewing beer, and for storing water, and various gourds and baskets.

The Dinka have few personal effects. The women have goatskin skirts, personal trinkets and sleeping-skins. There is little household furniture: headrests and the

Dr. Peter Fuchs

The Dinka accompany their songs with a wealth of gesture which is also characteristic of their lively reactions to each other—reactions which can, on occasion, extend to abuse or lead to violence.

occasional stool made from forked branches, and, in every household, the wooden pestle and mortar for pounding grain. Weapons include a variety of spears and a parrying shield of ambach wood of a very ancient type. In each settlement there is a set of dance drums, made and kept by an individual but considered as public property.

The basic food of the Dinka is a heavy millet porridge, eaten with a sauce flavoured with vegetables and spices, or with milk. Milk in fact provides an important part of the diet: soured milk or curds is the staple of the young men in the cattle camps, and is eaten by others when available.

Because the Dinka are only 'at home' for two short seasons of the year, at the height of the planting and the harvest, and given the fundamental importance of cattle in their lives and thoughts, it is understandable that they should conceive of their family and larger political relationships in the idiom of the cattle camp. The smallest of these camps is that of a man and his children with their own cattle. A number of these basic 'households' will come together on the basis of relationship, friendship or local association to form larger camps, and it is a number of these which are seen as constituting a sub-tribe. A number of these sub-tribes in turn constitute a tribe, which may contain anything from 1,000 to 30,000 members. These tribes in turn form the larger regional groupings, aggregations which are distributed over Dinka land.

Within each of these regional groupings, and running across them at all levels, there are a number of clans. Each of these clans has its own totemic symbol which is usually an animal. There are two types of clan: priestly or *Bany*, and commoner or *Kic*. And each tribe and sub-tribe contains many of these. It will be identified, however with one 'priestly' clan, which is said to 'have' the tribe's land in its keeping. It is from this clan, and particularly from its basic lineage, that the 'Master of the Fishing-Spear' will come. These men are primarily ritual specialists, but their peace-keeping and other ritual functions gave them the only kind of political authority which the Dinka recognize.

Dinka religious beliefs reflect their passion for the family. The idea of personal immortality for the Dinka is closely

As the area of water contracts after the rains end in October, it is possible for the Dinka to use their cane traps to catch the fish with which they supplement their usual diet of millet, vegetables and milk.

Dr. Peter Fuchs

bound up with the family and the necessity of having children: they have a number of institutions to ensure that a man will not be legally and morally 'childless' even if he dies without children. A levirate system ensures that a child is always born to his father's name: since a man has already paid the cattle in exchange for his wife, the rights of social paternity are established, and any children his wife bears, even long after his death, will be his.

Because the family, its relationships and responsibilities, and indeed the whole of the range of social obligation, is expressed through the idiom of cattle, they are naturally the vehicle for much religious sentiment and ritual. Cattle are the first choice of sacrificial animal, although in practice sheep may sometimes be substituted.

The Dinka treat their religion as an integral part of their social and personal life, turning to it for comfort and help in any situation of difficulty or trouble, illness or drought. They believe in a supreme being, called *Nhialic*. They also believe in a number of lesser divinities, *yath* and *jak*, whose multiplicity tends to obscure the essential monotheistic nature of their religion. But the lesser clan-divinities are of great practical importance to the Dinka, and it is often to these that sacrifices are made in times of need.

One of the most important features of the religion of the Dinka is the burial alive, at his own request, of any 'Master of the Fishing-Spear' who has become old and feeble. If he were to die a natural death, his people would be weakened, and the natural order of the world put at risk. His burial alive ensures that he is still in control: a symbolic action which maintains mastery of a world which is otherwise capricious.

Poetry and song rather than the modelling arts occupy the aesthenic sense of the Dinka. Songs are important in a wide variety of social and individual contexts: formal, as on festive occasions, or informal when an individual sings while working in the fields or looking after the cattle. All the activities of the Dinka especially war, initiation and other age-set activities are marked by and recorded in song.

Through their songs the people reinforce their identity, recall and praise their ancestors, and advertise the particular excellences of the group or its members. This last function is of particular importance since the Dinka are a lively, competitive and rather quarrelsome people: the songs provide a means of pursuing a dispute or a rivalry to a point just short of violence. This point is sometimes passed, and in fights, as in court cases, the antecedent song-battle can have played an important part.

Francis Deng, a Dinka author of a sensitive study of a number of songs he collected, points out that they also act as a means to make claims, particularly by the young, in a way which acts as a substitute for real control of the system, or as an outlet for dissatisfaction. Another aspect of this 'substitute' activity is seen in the fact that in song a man can mention things which he could never do in ordinary conversation: sexual experiences, his wealth or to sing his own praises.

Songs help to make misfortune acceptable, and they are a means to achieve honour. They enshrine the beliefs, the history and above all the values of the Dinka and their passions. It is not surprising that so many of them concern cattle:
'O Creator
Creator who created me in my mother's womb
Do not confront me with a bad thing
Show me the place of cattle,
So that I may grow my crops
And keep my herd.'

Dogon
MALI

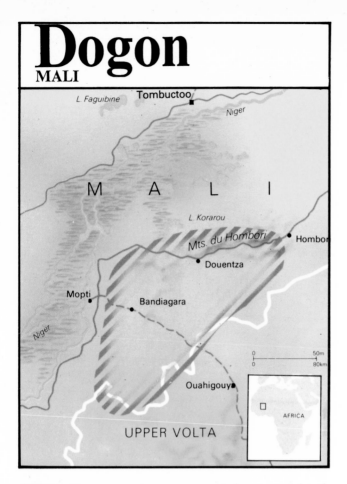

The Dogon people never accepted conquest by the great medieval empires which flourished around Timbuctoo on the Niger River to the north of them. These great empires, associated with the names of ancient Ghana, Mali and Songhai, rose and fell after each other, each ruler trying to extend the conquests of his predecessors. This centralized political structure, however, did not include the Dogon. Seeking refuge in the broken ravines and unscalable cliffs of their arid rocky plateau, they were able to defend themselves against attack and shield peoples to the south from the conquests and upheavals which characterized the history of the Songhai, Hausa and Mande peoples to the north, east and west. The Dogon are of interest for many reasons, but in particular because they may represent what many peoples of the Nigritic group were like before the development of the large Sudanic empires.

The Dogon, like most other peoples of the Voltaic subgroup, are relatively small in number (rather less than 250,000 people), culturally distinct, and have features of social organization which may be of very great antiquity. It is reasonable to speculate that it was the constant threat of attack from their powerful neighbours which stimulated in the Dogon a passionate adherence to their own traditions and their own view of the world. Like other peoples in Africa who took refuge in hills, they were probably always conservative: to them the acceptance of new ideas was as abhorrent as the idea of paying taxes to the conquerors. The need to resist outside threats evoked in the Dogon a passion for system, an almost neurotic insistence on the absolute necessity of ordering and organizing a cosmos which appeared too often to be shaken to its roots by political cataclysm.

The way they have sought to comprehend and impose this necessary order is by the use of myth—indeed by a vast panorama of myths. And while each of these myths explains one particular part of the universe, each one is also part of a wider structure. The myths explain the structure of the universe and the relationships of the physical and social worlds, by describing another 'structure'—a symbolic one, which relates to the moral and conceptual worlds. Reality and symbol constantly interact in the minds and the society of the Dogon. They do so to such a degree that the great French anthropologist, Marcel Griaule, to whom we owe most of our knowledge of this complicated set of beliefs, stated that the symbol and what it represented were, for the Dogon, reversible. In some contexts it is clear that they are not only interchangeable, they are almost indistinguishable.

The line between what we would consider reality and metaphysics, between the material and the immaterial, between the world and our perception of it, is less hard and fast, less sure and sometimes non-existent for the Dogon. Following the Western practice, we must describe the Dogon physical and social world as the reality and the myths as 'explanations' of it. But it is worth bearing in mind that this is probably a distortion. For the Dogon both are real, both 'exist' with the same degree of certainty.

Not everyone is familiar with all the myths. But all Dogon know some of them, even if many have only the 'superficial knowledge' of the better-known myths. Deep knowledge of the whole system is the property only of a comparative few who have made its study their special care. This is not to say that the myths are in any way secret or guarded: they are accessible to anyone with the patience, the intelligence and the maturity to understand.

It is because the knowledge is not esoteric, that we have access to it. This fact also underlies the story of how Marcel Griaule came to acquire it, which is worth relating

Foto Hetzel/Leimbach

M. Renaudeau/Top

(Above) The Dogon see their material and social worlds in terms of complex creation myths. They draw the primary vibrations of life and matter as a zig-zag, shown here on the front of a shrine, which represents the fertile combination of opposites.

(Right) This man is a Hogon, a spiritual leader who presides over religious and judicial ceremonies, and is distinguished by his red cap and woven tunic.

(Below) Villages are often sited for defence near high sandstone cliffs. The arrangement of houses and other buildings within the village represents a human figure lying on its back.

Naud/A.A.A. Photos

because it makes the Dogon attitude clearer. Griaule had been studying in Dogon and neighbouring Bambara country for nearly 16 years when one day he was summoned on a flimsy pretext to see an old man, a hunter who had been blinded by an exploding gun. After a little while it became apparent that the old man, well known for his wisdom, had a great deal that he wanted to tell. Griaule later learnt that Ogotemmeli had been specifically deputed by the elders to pass on this knowledge. They had accepted Griaule's sincerity and had decided to enlighten him. That this knowledge constitutes an important part of being Dogon, is seen in the fact that when Marcel Griaule died in 1956 he was buried with full Dogon funeral rights. In this way the Dogon showed not only their love for him, but their acceptance that he was 'Dogon'. The knowledge, the explanations, the myths, the words–these are the world, they are reality. They are truth.

There are several Dogon myths, partly variants of each other, which explain the creation of the universe. The origin of life is symbolized by the smallest cultivated seed (*digitaria exilis*) the fonio grain which the Dogon call *kize-uzi*, the little thing. Its life began as an internal vibration—a series of seven 'pulses' which are envisaged as expanding in a revolving spiral—until it broke its sheath and the life-vibration expanded to reach the ends of the universe. The spiral thus represents the infinite extension of the universe, and the conservation of matter and energy within it. Seen from the side, the spiral would look like a rising zig-zag, and this design appears frequently on Dogon houses and shrines. This *ozu-tonnolo* in turn represents the perpetual alternation of opposites (right-left, high-low, odd-even, male-female), which is the essential principle of 'twin-ness'. Life proliferates by the interaction and mutual support of opposites, and each individual has elements of both poles within himself.

Each individual is himself the product of these same seven vibrations. If we imagine them as a clock, the first and sixth pulses at eight o'clock and four o'clock are the legs. The second and fifth at ten and two o'clock are the arms, and the third and fourth, at eleven and one o'clock, are the left and right sides of the head. The seventh and strongest, at six o'clock, is the sex organ. If the whole symbolizes the individual, the universe and the smallest grain, the seven 'pulses' also represent the constituent parts, and the other seven seeds (millet, sorghum and so on) which the Dogon cultivate. The smallest thus implies the greatest, the parts imply the whole—and the individual comprehends the society of which he is a constituent part. The whole of creation is conceived in terms of this cosmic egg, *aduno tal*. It is the universe and the world, the infinitely large and the infinitely small, energy spent and conserved, unity, duality and complexity.

Once the creation included individuals and their individual wills, the process became more complicated. In one myth the creator-God, Amma, flung pellets of earth out into space to make the stars, and he made the Sun and the Moon by using pottery, the first craft invented although it was not known to Man till later. He took a further lump of clay, squeezed it and flung it down. It spread out as it fell on its top (the north) spreading towards the bottom (the south) and so formed the earth. It extended to the east and the west like a foetus in the womb, its members branching from the centre until the earth lay flat, spread-out like a woman on her back, her vagina an ant-hill and the clitoris a termite-hill. Amma approached her, and thereby introduced the element of disorder into creation. The termite hill rose up and prevented him achieving intercourse. He cut it off and penetrated her. The clitoris represents the male principal in the female and the Dogon still remove it. But the irregularity of this mating produced, not the desirable twin birth, but a monstrosity—a jackal.

Further intercourse was more successful, as the water (the divine seed) of Amma, entered the earth and produced twins. They were each both male and female, green, human down to the loins and serpents below. They had forked tongues and were called Nummo. Eventually they joined Amma in heaven and seeing their mother the earth lying there naked and speechless, they took the fibres of the eight plants and wove two strands to cover her before and behind. The coils fell from heaven in a spiral, the symbol of tornadoes, of water flowing, of Nummo in motion, the *ozu-tonnolo*. Nummo, speaking while forming the strands with their forked tongues, soaked the strands in vapour, in water, in speech. Spiritual and technical instruction are thus one. Speech is organization, mastery of the world.

The jackal tried to snatch the strands from his mother, the earth, in order to obtain speech. Using force he defiled earth with the woman's menstrual blood. So Amma, seeing that things were going wrong (evil and negative) decided to restore the balance (twin-ness) by creating more living things. He created twins, each of both sexes. The man's feminity resided in the foreskin which Nummo circumcized: the foreskin fell to the ground and became a lizard, *nay* (which also means four, the female number). The male-twin had intercourse with the female-twin, who bore the first of four sets of twins, the eight ancestors of the Dogon. The pain of birth concentrated in the clitoris which was detached, fell to the ground and became the scorpion. Its sting represents the pain, and by losing it, the female loses her male element.

Each of the eight ancestors (fertilizing themselves) gave birth in the anthill, became Nummo, and went up to heaven to receive instruction. It was the seventh (the sum of three and four, male and female, and so totality) who achieved particular mastery of this second 'instruction'.

He was thus able to be the instructor of the world, the 'saviour' of society. He took possession of the earth and his lips merged with the edge of the anthill: pointed teeth emerged, eventually 80 on each lip. He spat out 80 threads between the teeth of the upper lip and the same below: the odd and the even threads of the warp, which he alternated by opening and closing his mouth. Weaving the weft across with the stud in his lip, he wove a web in the vapour of his breathing, speaking as he worked, imparting knowledge to the cloth. Cloth is called *soy*, the spoken word, which also means seven, the number of perfection and totality. Men began to imitate the anthill in the form of their houses and to weave. There is therefore interaction between technical and spiritual matters, between mind and matter.

The eight ancestors were each given knowledge and each

M. Renaudeau/Top

received one of the eight grain-seeds. On coming to earth each pair became the founders of one of the four Dogon tribes. The four male ancestors were called Amma Seru, Dyongu Seru, Binu Seru and Lebe Seru. Their tribes are the Arou, Dyon, Ono and Domnu. They shared the universe between them, taking the four elements, air, fire, water and earth, respectively, each one standing at a cardinal point of the compass, east, south, west and north. They each also took on particular social functions. Arou took chieftainship, medicine and divination. Dyon took agriculture. Ono and Domno both took trade and crafts, because by combining only three 'functions' with four tribes, one gets the number seven. Twin-ness of two pairs gives four, which is femininity, and represents the 'given', status, the unchanging—the 'raw material' of the universe. Three represents masculinity, the 'obtained', achievement,

These masked dancers at Sangha in Mali are celebrating a funeral. Belonging to the Dogan Society of the Mask, they dress in tall, elaborately constructed and painted masks and brightly coloured straw skirts.

the changing—the force which manipulates the universe. The world and work, society and its functions, female and male, thus combine to make totality: seven, perfection and the symbol of complete order.

The creation and ordering of the universe is reflected, not only in the social order, politics, the roles of the sexes, weaving and the plant kingdom (and incidentally the animal kingdom which was also distributed in order around the cardinal points), but in the organization of the land itself, its settlement and its houses.

The centre of an ideal lay-out of fields is represented by

B. Leidmann/Bavaria Verlag

(Above) Dogon women look after gathering, while the men are responsible for hunting, fishing and caring for livestock. Both share in the agricultural work, which is traditionally done communally.

(Below) Weaving was the first craft taught by the Seventh Dogon ancestor to Man, and also symbolizes the combination of opposites like male and female and the fertilization of the earth by water.

M. Renaudeau/Top

Georg Gerster/Rapho

M. Renaudeau/Top

The Dogon are mainly farmers. Surplus grain was once stored in granaries built in a shape which reflects the creation of the universe. Although some is still stored, most surplus grain is now taken to market.

three ritual fields, and subsequent fields are placed in a spiral, ranged along the four sides of a square. The first are laid-out in a line going south, then turning east, and then north and west. The second turn of the spiral begins by running down to the west of the first line, going south, and then turning east, south of the first 'circle', and so on. Clearing should proceed with the back to the line of the field already cleared, and the front edge of each field longer than the back to represent the opening-up of the infinite universe.

Among the Dogon, each extended family should have eight fields, grouped in pairs on each side of the square, facing the four cardinal points, and each associated with one of the eight seeds. Cultivation in each field goes back and forth (zig-zag), and the hoe is changed from hand to hand (left-right, male-female) at each step. Each line of grain is eight feet long, and a patch should have eight lines. The whole method is like weaving: the insertion of the grain into the land, fertility and sterility, wet (Nummo) and water combining with dry (the jackal, Ogo or Yurugu).

A Dogon village too represents the primal vibration of the cosmic egg. It is sited, ideally, in the centre of the spiral of fields. It may be square, like the first plot cultivated, or the first cloth woven. Or it may be oval, like the egg, open at one end for the exploding germination. It is a person, the smithy representing the head; shrines at the other end represent the feet, and the huts of the menstruating women, off to the sides at east and west, represent the hands. The group of family houses in the centre is the chest, and the cone-shaped shrine at their southern end is the penis. The hollowed stone nearby on which the fruit of *lannea acida* is pressed for oil, represents the female genitalia—because both the male and female principles are in a proper being. Villages are built in pairs, an upper and lower, water and dry, heaven and earth, Nummo and Yurugu. Districts too have upper and lower sections. The chief or Hogon resides in the upper, and the open space in front of his house is round, like the sky which it represents. The shrine to Lebe at the centre is the Sun, and the eight ancestor-grain shrines surround it. They are also the eight ancestors bringing down to earth a new world, word and knowledge.

Individual houses also reflect the pattern. The great central room is the belly; the kitchen at the north end is the head; the two hearths the eyes; the two lines of store rooms on each side the arms; and the two towers at the ends, and either side of the stable at the south end, are the hands and feet. The grinding stones in the centre are where fresh grain is crushed, the resulting liquid representing semen which is carried along the narrow passage to the west (the penis) and poured on the ancestor shrines to represent fertilization.

Parallels could be multiplied infinitely. The chief, the family, marriage and social organization, all express the same symbolic system. Society and all activities are part of the same scheme which the myths organize and explain. The individual is part of it and *is* it. In himself, he holds the dual forces, the balance of good and evil, male and female, the zig-zag spiral *ozu-tonnolo*, the smallest seed and the totality of the universe. ☐

Dogon women carry their agricultural produce to market. There they trade with Fulani pastoralists.

(Next page) The day houses in a Dogon village.

Ewe
GHANA

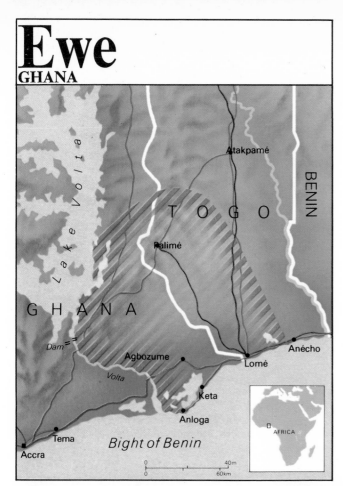

Atakpamé

BENIN

T O G O

Palimé

Lake Volta

G H A N A

Dam

Agbozume

Anécho

Lomé

Volta

Keta

Anloga

Tema

Accra

Bight of Benin

AFRICA

0 — 40m
0 — 60km

The Ewe people live on the West coast of Africa in an area divided by the present Ghana-Togo border. It is a region which falls into three physical zones: on the densely populated coastal zone of sand-dunes and lagoons, fishing is the chief livelihood of the people; behind this lies grassland savannah which is becoming important as a cattle rearing area; and to the north are the uplands of the forested Togo hills where cocoa farming is important.

Old men today look back on a way of life that was very different. Change has been rapid, but the vitality of the ancient culture of the Ewe (pronounced evay) is still visible beneath symbols of modernity.

In pre-colonial times, each family produced its own material needs on land provided by the lineage group to which it belonged. Tools were so simple that any man could make his own. Differentiation of occupations and social roles, and such division of labour as there was, did little more than define the tasks performed by a husband, wives and children. For larger tasks such as harvesting, a man could call upon members of his lineage for help. The head of the lineage was responsible for the economy and welfare of all the families in the lineage group. Every member of that group could look to the lineage for his material well-being. In these circumstances, trade and exchange remained limited to purchasing slaves, kola nuts and gold from northern tribes in exchange for cloth, fish and salt from the coast.

Today, only in the most isolated areas has this system

The Ewe believe that God can only be known to men through his children, who are known as Voduwo. Men may worship these spirits by joining a cult-house—like the Yewe cult, shown here, which is devoted to Vodu Hebieso, the god of thunder.

survived. It has been changed by the influence of several centuries of European commerce on the coast. Most Ewe farmers now produce a cash-crop of onions, cocoa or palm-oil, with the crops for their own consumption. They need the money to pay for the education of their children, to pay taxes or to buy modern goods such as radios. In the wealthy farming areas, land can be bought or sold, despite the ancient tradition that land is a gift from the ancestors to those who are not yet born, and must never be sold. Ewe preachers have good reason to sermonize on the theme that 'Money is the root of all evil'; for it is destroying the traditional family economy and upsetting the natural order. Children no longer have the same respect for their fathers, nor wives for their husbands, and sons quarrel over their inheritance.

Ewe fishermen today supply a vast market. The scale of production has changed completely, with expensive nets requiring a labour-force of 50 men to operate them. These men are no longer kinsmen as they used to be, but labourers employed by the net-owner for a cash-wage.

In growing towns such as Agbozume, ancient crafts like weaving are no longer cottage crafts but are now carried out in small factories. Urban markets provide expanding opportunities for women to earn cash.

With changing conditions, parents have made their children's education a major investment. The Ewe have great respect for education and the power and influence it brings—civil servants and teachers are useful kinsmen.

But Ewe society has never been static. It was probably the search for new farmland which caused the migration of the Ewe in the mid-17th century from Benin to their present homeland. Migration caused changes in their system of government. The Anlo-Ewe tell the story of how they fled from the tyranny of the ruler of Notsie under the leadership of their hero, Togbi Sri, later the founder of their ruling dynasty. In their haste, they forgot 'The Stool', which was the symbol of royal authority. Togbi's son refused the dangerous mission of returning to collect it, but royal honour was redeemed by the bravery and cunning of the King's nephew. In gratitude, Togbi declared his nephew heir to 'The Stool', and since then the descendants of the son and nephew have formed two royal clans, Adzovia and Bate, which hold office in alternate generations.

On the coast, the Ewe came into contact with European slave traders. Since they were accustomed to using war captives as domestic slaves and as a form of currency, the Ewe became suppliers of slaves to the Europeans in return for arms, cloth and alcohol. But the demand for Negro slaves to work in the New World colonies was insatiable and led to a great increase in warfare between the Ewe sub-tribes and the Ada and Ga peoples. After a series of wars with the Anlo-Ewe, the Danes won a monopoly over the trade in 1784, which they enforced by building Fort Princestein at Keta. In face of continual Ewe opposition and the collapse of the American slave market, the Danes abolished slave-trading in 1803.

A new trade developed to supply raw materials to the factories of industrializing Europe. Ewe traders were appointed by the trading companies to purchase copra, palm oil and rubber, and to sell manufactured products. The British, who had virtual control of the coast as far as the Volta River, resented the ease with which the politically independent Ewe were able to smuggle goods across the border. Determined to stop what they regarded as unfair trade, the British moved to extend political control over the Ewe.

In 1850, Britain purchased Fort Princestein from the Danes and used it to enforce their rule on the local population. For 50 years, through five major wars, the Anlo-

George Rodger/Magnum

(Above) An Anlo-Ewe woman waters her field of onions. The most important cash-crops are shallots, onions, cocao and palm-oil, and are grown alongside crops like millet which they use themselves.

(Below) Ewe women and children wait on the beach for the men to bring in the day's catch. The women's task is to sort and dry the fish, which they then trade in the central markets.

Ewe resisted colonialism; but the major towns were burnt to the ground, markets were pillaged and the chiefs were reduced to a state of subservience.

While the Anlo area was being annexed to the British Colony of the Gold Coast, the Germans conquered the Northern Ewe people from their base at Lomé. When war broke out between the Imperial Powers in 1914, Eweland became a remote battlefield in a world conflict. The Germans were rapidly forced to capitulate by the colonial armies of Britain and France; after the peace of 1819, German Togoland became a French and British protectorate.

After the Second World War, as the Gold Coast neared independence as the new state of Ghana, the United Nations sponsored a plebiscite in British Trans-Volta. The Ewe were given the choice of becoming part of Ghana or rejoining their brothers in French controlled Togo; since they chose the former, the old border became the state's new boundary, splitting the Ewe people between Ghana and Togo. Even today, the border remains a very sensitive political question for the Ewe. Periodically, secessionist movements develop in what is now the Volta Region of Ghana. One of them, the Togoland Congress, was violently put down by the late President Nkrumah of Ghana.

Economic change has brought a new individualism to Ewe society. In the past, the interest of the kinship group as a whole predominated over that of its members. Even today, two strangers in conversation will politely question each other on their ancestry.

Clans are composed of many lineages, that is, extended families living in compounds surrounding an original ancestral home. Lineage members are able to trace their ancestry back over eight generations to a common grandfather. His descendants are economically interdependent since they all have rights to the ancestral land. They must show great respect for the oldest male of the senior generation, who is the head of their lineage.

Since a girl must marry outside her own lineage, intermarriage has created links between the different lineages of the villages. Marriages are traditionally matches arranged by the elders, not individual contracts. The best match is between first cousins, since it limits the claims which can be made on lineage property by heirs. The marriage ceremony is in reality a protracted ritual of negotiations between the families concerned; the groom's family transfers gifts to the bride's family in return for her domestic and procreative functions.

On marriage the son is given land close to the ancestral compound. He should build a homestead of rectangular huts surrounding a courtyard, one for each of his wives and their children, and one for himself. Depending on his wealth, he may also accomodate his grandparents, and his brother's and sister's families.

Children are brought up to be dependent on the lineage. A baby is breast-fed by its mother until it can walk. After weaning, the child is circumcized and initiated into an age group of its peers. Under the authority of older children, this group learns through play and work the skills of adulthood. At puberty girls undergo initiation rites which

(Below) A Ewe woman prepares akple—a mixture of maize and cassava flour. Akple, mixed with a fish or vegetable broth, forms the staple diet of the Ewe.

signify their readiness for marriage. Young men reach adulthood only at marriage, and women at the birth of their first child. The older the parents and the larger their group of descendants, the greater becomes their social prestige.

Within the family, men excercise strict authority over their wives and children. Husbands and wives never eat together; they have different friends and follow different occupations. Wives are expected to support themselves and their children through trade. Children see their fathers and his male relatives as authoritarian and punitive, and their mother and her relatives as warm and indulgent.

Today, the Ewe are citizens of remote and impersonal nation states and their total population is about 700,000. In the past the lineage was a small organization in which everyone could influence decision-making. A man's first loyalty was to the oldest male descendant of the founder of his patrilineage, who was the keeper of the 'family stool', and the guardian of lineage property. The junior family heads within the descent group formed a council

of advisors who had to be consulted on all decisions. Within the village, the head of the founding lineage would be regarded as *Dufia*, or town chief, and he would consult with an advisory council of village elders, (some of whom were women, although they took no part in politics until they were past childbearing). At the apex of this family system was the council of clan heads who advised the paramount chief of the whole kingdom. Unlike the neighbouring Ashanti, the Ewe were never politically united into one state. They were fragmented into 10 chiefdoms or *Dukowo*, which were politically independent but culturally united.

The *Awoamefia*, paramount chief of the Anlo-Ewe, was a semi-sacred figure who lived in seclusion from his people. Even today he is the final judge of cases involving customary law. His jurisdiction over criminal matters, which sometimes involved sentence of death, has passed to the Ghanaian judiciary. In the past he would have conducted all foreign negotiations, a function now conducted by the state authorities, but he continues to

Tim Megarry/Robert Harding Associates

Ewe fishermen pull their long fishing net into the sea. In the densely-populated area of sand dunes and lagoons on the west coast of Africa, fishing is the Ewes' chief form of livelihood.

participate in regional government.

In wartime, the Anlo-Ewe armies were organized into three sections each commanded by a distinguished warrior. Over the years these war chieftainships became hereditary offices. Each town fell under the jurisdiction of one of these chiefs who acted as state officials and advisors to the *Awoamefia*. In each village the young warriors formed a group, the *sohe* which acted together politically. The military organization thus tended to balance the political system based on age and kinship. If a chief became too autocratic he could be 'de-stooled'. A popular saying sums up this principle: 'It is the people who rule, not the chiefs.'

The chiefs were not aristocrats, and they were owed nothing except the respect and trust of their people. Colonialism destroyed this democracy. Chiefs who led their people's resistance were replaced by chiefs who were officials of the colonial government. The new chiefs enriched themselves and abused their power and there were many attempts by the people to oust them.

Today, as a result of missionaries' work in education and medicine, nearly half the Ewe are Christians. They have transformed the new religion to bring it closer to traditional beliefs. These have their roots in the lineage, which consists not only of living individuals but also of the ancestors and those who are not yet born. The ancestors are thought to have great power over the conduct of the living. This they exercise from the sacred realm of *Tisiefa*, the other world, which seems to mirror the organization of the living world very closely. Each compound has its shrine devoted to the house ancestors, and the lineage head acts as family priest on major ritual occasions.

On the death of a member, all the relatives in the lineage gather for a series of funeral rites which last over a year. After the death, the purpose of these celebrations is to free the two souls of the deceased; the life-soul returns to God for judgement and the personality-soul to the ancestral lineage in *Tisiefa*. Those who die honourably will eventually return to the land of the living, reincarnated in the body of a newborn child. Seven days after birth, a baby is presented to its kinsmen in a ceremony known as *Vihedego*. Libations are made to thank the ancestors for their generosity and *Afa* divination is used to determine which of the ancestors has been reincarnated in the child. It is this that determines a child's destiny. In addition every child embodies the breath of *Mawu*, or God. This is the sacred life-soul, or conscience, which gives the freedom of moral choice.

Unlike the Christian God who can be worshipped and known, *Mawu* is hidden from his people. He has no church and no priests. Like the *Awoamefia*, *Mawu* is secluded, aloof from the world he has created. *Mawu* can be known to men only through his children, *Voduwo*. Natural objects such as lakes, trees, and streams are homes to these spirits who can be worshipped by joining a cult devoted to a particular deity. The *Yewe* cult, for example, is devoted to the *Vodu Hebieso*, the god of thunder. Each cult-house has a hierarchy of priests and a lay membership. Victims of misfortune will consult a diviner who will read the signs and advise them to seek the protection of a tutelary *vodu*. Initiates to the cult undergo a series of expensive rites and are then given a cult name, taught the cult's secret knowledge and required to observe certain behavioural taboos.

In Ewe belief, all material things have an occult energy within them which can be controlled for good or evil by men. If illness has physical causes, it is because an enemy is directing occult powers against mind and body. Thus, the sick consult a *Bokor* who is a magician, diviner and herbalist.

Witches are said to be old women who have unconsciously inherited the powers from their mothers. When asleep, the personality-soul of witches leaves the body and flies in the form of a nocturnal bird to night-time witch-meetings where they feast upon the souls of human victims. All manner of disasters are attributed to witches. Though the fear of these 'people of the air' is very real, and many cults offer protection against their misdeeds, there are no organized witch-hunts and nobody is ever publicly accused or punished for the offence.

The traditional beliefs of the Ewe still play an important part in their lives and are a powerful unifying force. But the pressures of over-population are forcing many Ewe to migrate seasonally in search of new fishing grounds, and those who do not settle return with alien beliefs and customs. It will be some time before the effects of this new mobility and the absorption of alien customs in the Ewe society can be fully appreciated. □

Falasha
ETHIOPIA

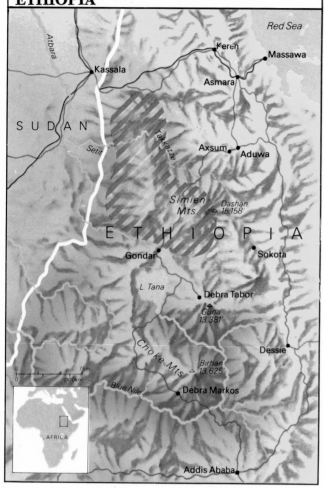

The Falasha live high in Africa's Simien Mountains, a region bordered by the Takkazze River on the north and east, Lake Tana and the Blue Nile to the south and the Sudanese frontier on the west. For centuries these 'Black Jews of Ethiopia' have obtained a precarious livelihood on the dry, bare rock slopes of the 'roof of Africa'.

The origins of the Falasha are lost in antiquity and this has inspired many diverse theories on where their ancestors came from. One suggests that at the time of the Exodus of the Hebrews from Egypt, some drifted south through what is now the Sudan to settle in what was then called Abyssinia. There is also the view that after the first destruction of the Jerusalem Temple in 586 BC, or after the second destruction in 70 AD some Jews arrived in Abyssinia having travelled through Egypt. Another more romantic theory suggests that when Menelik I, the son of Solomon and the Queen of Sheba, returned to the country of his mother he brought with him some of his Jewish warriors. The intermarriage of these Jews with the indigenous population is believed to have given rise to the present-day Falasha.

Perhaps the most acceptable theory says that Jewish traders from Saudi Arabia crossed the Red Sea to Ethiopia and converted people on the coast and along the trade-route to the highland capital at Axum. Ethiopian chronicles show that Judaism was widespread before the spread of Christianity to Axum in the 4th century.

Those faithful to Judaism were persecuted in the wave of Christian conversion and compelled to retreat into the mountains. The Ethiopians also raided Arabia and in 525 AD, King Kaleb met the Jewish king of Saudia Arabia, Pinchas Dhunewa, in battle. The latter was defeated; many Jewish prisoners were taken and settled in the Simien mountains, reinforcing the population there which already followed the Jewish faith.

It is difficult to distinguish the estimated 19,000 Falasha of the present day from their neighbours. Their clothing does not differ from that of the other Ethiopians. The men, who invariably carry a stick, wear cotton trousers which are wide above the knee and tight from the knees to the ankles. They also wear a rectangular cloth, *shama*, which they wrap around themselves in various ways. The women wear a long dress which reaches down to the ankles and wrap a *shama* around the upper part of their body. The priests are the only Falasha to wear headdresses: all others go bare-headed.

In the past, the Falasha spoke various dialects of Agau one of the central Cushitic group of languages. However today, apart from some outlying locations where one can still find a few Agau-speaking people, the national tongue of Ethiopia, Amharic, is most commonly used. It is not clear whether the Falasha ever had a knowledge of Hebrew or Aramaic. And ironically children are now being taught Hebrew in Falasha Schools.

The Falasha base their religion entirely on the first five books of the Old Testament – the Pentateuch or Torah—which were given to Moses by God on Mount Sinai. A number of apocryphal books such as Tobit, Judith and the Book of Baruch and the Books of Enoch and Jubilees are also sacred texts. But the Falasha are ignorant of, and often unwilling to accept what they know of, the Talmud and the Jewish oral law.

It is the early form of the religion of the Falasha, ignoring all that came after the Pentateuch, which distinguishes the Falasha from most other Jews. Further, the Torah of the Falasha is a translation which was not made from the original Hebrew text—as is the text used by conventional Jewry—but from the much later 3rd century BC Septuagint. This is also the translation accepted by the Ethiopian Church, which suggests that both peoples experienced the same Semitic influence at this period, at least, even if the Christian also accepted a later period of teaching as well. There is no evidence that the Falasha ever possessed a different version which was closer to the original Hebrew Torah.

The Falasha have priests (*cahen*) who claim descent from Aaron. In practice, however, every Falasha who is of good character and is from a respected family can assume the priestly function if he is well versed in prayers and the bible. In each region the priests elect a high priest from their midst which results in considerable ecclesiastical bickering. There are still a few Falasha monks who live a life of abstinence and dedicate their lives to God, but there are no longer any nuns among the Falasha people.

Life in a Falasha village on the Jewish sabbath, Saturday, has many features similar to those described as contemporary in Biblical times. Preparations for the sabbath begin on the Friday at noon when all work comes to a halt and members of the community make their way to the river to wash themselves and clean their clothing for the next day. It is mandatory that the Falasha live close to water for this ritual; other Ethiopians jest that the

(Right) A Falasha woman and her children. Although the Falasha base their religion on a translation of the first five books of the Old Testament, they differ from conventional Jews in that they do not accept the Talmud and the Jewish oral law.

Marcus Brooke

(Above) The farmland which these Falasha ploughmen are working is typical of the barren Simien Mountain region where they live. The poor quality of the soil accounts for the poverty of the people.

(Right) Amharic, the national tongue of Ethiopia, is the main language of the Falasha. But children, like these at Wuzaba, are being taught Hebrew in schools —indicating the growing influence of Judaism.

(Below) Two Falasha priests sit reading a prayer book in a Mesjid, or synagogue. The prayers are written and spoken in Ge'ez – the Latin of the Coptic Church which few Falasha understand.

Marcus Brooke

(Above) During their menstrual periods, Falasha women live in the 'blood huts' or 'huts of malediction' and do no work. Women also give birth in these huts and afterwards remain there for many weeks.

Marcus Brooke

Marcus Brooke

Falasha smell of water.

On the sabbath itself no work is done, no fire is lit and everybody remains in their village. The words *Sanbat salam* (good sabbath) are on everyone's lips. However, very few Falasha attend the *Mesjid* which is their house of prayer, or synagogue, because the prayer book is written in Ge'ez—the Latin of the Ethiopian Coptic church. In most cases this is merely a round mud house (*tukul*) with a thatched roof or occasionally a stone structure with a tin roof. They are topped nowadays by the *Maeen David* (Star of David).

Few Falasha wear shoes, but those who do remove them on entering the *Mesjid* for they believe they will thereby avoid crushing some of the thousands of angels that throng the floor of the synagogue. The biblical explanation for this practice states that God said to Moses '. . . put off thy shoes from off thy feet, for the place whereon thou standest is holy ground' (Exodus, 3:5).

Great stress is placed on every seventh sabbath (*Lengeta sanbat*). The third 'seventh sabbath'—that is to say the sabbath of the 21st week of the year—is the most important of all and is designated *Barba sanbat*. These 'seventh sabbaths' are celebrated with chanting and prayers from sunset on the Friday all through the Saturday until dusk accompanied by the drinking of much *tallah*, or lightly fermented barley.

The Falasha determine their festivals by means of a calendar which differs from the Ethiopian calender and resembles more the Jewish one. Their year consists of 12 months of 30 days and a 13th month of five days; every fourth year is a leap year and the last month is then six days long. The year begins with *Nisan* which occurs in the spring. In addition to the festivals prescribed in the Pentateuch, and which are celebrated by Jewry throughout the world, there are a number of unique Falasha festivals.

The most important of these is *Sigd* which is held on the last day of the ninth moon. This festival commemorates the return of the Exiles led by Ezra and Nehemiah from Babylonia. On *Sigd*, the priests, carrying their holy books, circle the summit of a high hill and the villagers, each with a stone on their back, mount the hill. At the summit they throw away their burden which symbolically represents their sins. Another custom at the *Sigd* festival is the feeding of grain to the birds, each grain being a remembrance for one dead person; this practice is also carried out on *Yom Kippur*, the Day of Atonement.

Stones play a major symbolic role in the life of the Falasha as they do in the lives of other central Cushitic peoples. To patch up a quarrel, each antagonist lifts up a stone and places it upon his back. Then, they hurl away the stones, kiss each other, and the quarrel is resolved.

The Falasha live in small villages of round huts with conical thatched roofs. These villages usually occupy the summit of a hill and lie near a river. In addition to the *Mesjid* each Falasha village has several other huts which set it apart from the villages of its neighbours. These are the huts of malediction or the blood huts. Here, during their menstrual period, the women are confined for seven days and do no work. At the end of this time they wash in the river and then re-join the community.

Formerly, in addition to the malediction hut, each village had huts for childbirth. Eight days after the birth of a boy—that is to say at the time of his circumcision—the mother would leave the hut of malediction, where she had gone at the onset of labour, and enter the hut of child-birth. At the conclusion of her 'days of uncleanliness' —40 days if the child is a boy, 80 days if it is a girl—the woman shaves the hair off her head, immerses herself and washes her clothes before returning to her home. The hut of child-birth would be burnt. Now, in many villages, there are no huts of child-birth and the mother remains in the malediction hut for 40 days in the case of a boy and 80 in the case of a girl—a period similar to that allowed to pass by the Amhara before their children's baptism.

The practice of clitorodectomy, or female circumcision, which is widely prevalent in Ethiopia, is rare among the Falasha as is venereal disease – a common ailment among other local people – and they forbid sexual intercourse on a Friday night. Since the Talmud suggests that this is the best time for sex, this is another illustration of the way in which the Falasha differ in custom from Orthodox Jews.

The Falasha, noted for their cleanliness, their honesty and their industry, are skilled weavers, superb potters and also the best blacksmiths of Ethiopia. Like other blacksmiths in Ethiopia, they are both feared and despised because of beliefs which associate the blacksmith's art with occult powers. They were called *tabib* which, in Amharic, means both smith and sage—both of which they are. But the term also has the pejorative connotation of wizard and it was believed that they could turn into hyenas during the night and prey upon humans.

Primarily, the Falasha are agriculturists and much of their poverty can be traced to the shortage of farming land and to the poor quality of the little of it there is. Like most Ethiopians, they do not own the land they farm.

Making clay pots is an important occupation of Falasha women, who are also expert weavers.

Because of the shortage of good farming land, some Falasha have been moving in recent years to the Setit-Humera area along the nothern part of the Sudanese-Ethiopian frontier. There the soil is composed of a rich black clay which does not require additional fertilizing. It provides excellent crops of cotton, sesame and sorghum. The contrast between the traditional Falasha homeland and the Setit-Humera region is dramatic; subsistence farming is replaced by cash-cropping. Tiny rocky fields on steep hillsides have become vast flat fields stretching to the horizon. Instead of mountain showers there are hot dry days and torrential downpours, and the Falasha are finding the adjustment difficult.

It is doubtful whether the Falsaha will manage to maintain their identity as a people for much longer. It is being eroded by missionaries and by Jews coming from abroad; many are now eager to emigrate to Israel which is still the Promised Land to the Falasha.

For more than 100 years an organization called The Christian Ministry to the Jews has determined that not only will the Falasha recognize Jesus but they will change their ways and abandon their rituals and customs. A combination of religious, social and economic pressures has meant that the population of the Falasha has declined from nearly 250,000 in the 19th century to less than 20,000 now. There is however, the Falasha Welfare Organization which is trying to improve the medical and educational facilities available to the Falasha and to prove to them that world Jewry has not forgotten them. ☐

Loading sugar-cane on to feluccas on the River Nile.

John Moss/Colorific!

Fellaheen

EGYPT

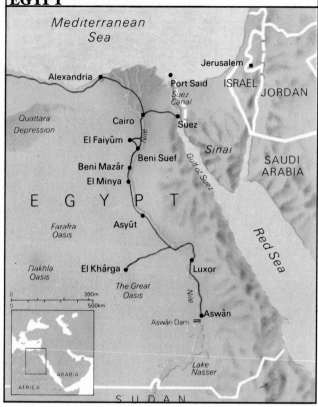

Gamal Abdel Nasser, remains the 'true' Egypt.

It is fairly certain that the Fellaheen are the descendants of the Ancient Egyptians—a people who produced one of the world's earliest civilizations. By 4,000–3,500 BC a settled way of life had already emerged in the Nile Valley based on irrigated agriculture, with a well-established pattern of villages and towns. Over the centuries that followed the Fellaheen changed their masters, their religion, their language and their crops, but not their way of life. The glimpses of their daily lives which emerge from Pharaonic tombs, the Arab historians, the early English explorers or the travellers of our own day seem to form one single sequence. All these scenes—the villages, the work in the fields, and family life—although separated by centuries, appear only to repeat and confirm the same pattern. Assimilation of other groups, especially Arabs and Negroes, has taken place, but the Egyptian facial type has remained dominant.

The Fellah is of average height, sturdily built though rarely stout. Skull and face are broad with a narrow forehead, dark eyes and curly black hair. The great majority of the Fellaheen are Moslems, but a small Christian minority belonging to the Coptic Church does survive. Copts and Moslems live together in the same villages, each following their own faith.

Before the revolution in 1952 which initiated a new political, economic and social order in Egypt, the mass of the Fellaheen lived in ignorance and isolation, hunger and servility beneath the sway of a few hundred landowners

Egypt is a land of contrasts. The marked difference between the fertile Nile Valley and the waterless deserts on either side is no less striking than the huge gulf which separates the towns and cities from the countryside.

During the 20th century, modern trade and industrialization have stimulated rapid urban growth – in 1978 at least 45 per cent of the population of Egypt were urban dwellers compared with only 25 per cent in 1937—a development which has sharpened traditional contrasts between town and countryside. Socially, the new occupations and the new knowledge from the West have driven still deeper the rift separating the urban-centred élite from the rural masses, the Fellaheen (from the Arabic verb *falaha* which means to labour, toil or till the earth).

Cairo and Alexandria, by far the most important urban centres, are the two largest cities in Africa. Together they contain more than half of the urban population of Egypt. The Greater Cairo region, with a population of over eight million, is one of the world's great conurbations. In these centres a high level of industrialization has already been achieved; incomes tend to be higher and social services superior to those in the countryside. Nevertheless, some three-fifths of Egypt's 40 million inhabitants still live in rural areas, and agriculture remains the leading sector of the economy. It employs over half the country's active labour force and earns, mainly through cotton exports, most of the country's foreign exchange. The Egyptian peasant, in the words of the late President,

Fellaheen women fetch water from the public fountain. In the past, drinking-water drawn from ditches or from the Nile was a source of disease, but most villages now have a piped water supply.

who controlled the wealth of Egypt and ruled it for their own ends. In 1938, Father Ayrout in his book *The Egyptian Peasant* wrote 'This misery, compounded of poverty, ignorance and disease, has its roots in a divorce. In fact a separation more striking than that between the white desert and the black soil, or between the Delta and the Said, has occurred between the upper and lower classes between the city and the countryside, between them and us.' Eloquent testimony to this division is provided by Hassan Fathy the famous Egyptian architect who writes: 'My father avoided the country. To him it was a place full of flies, mosquitoes and polluted water, and he forbade his children to have anything to do with it. Although he possessed several estates in the country, he would never visit them, nor go any nearer to the country than Mansoura, the provincial capital, where he went once a year to meet his bailiffs and collect his rent. Until my 27th year I have never set foot in any of our country property.'

Today the gulf between town and countryside in Egypt remains wide, but a number of very real material improvements have been made by the government since 1952 affecting at least some aspects of the daily lives of the Fellaheen. Mental attitudes, however, change more slowly, and in spite of some impressive advances more progress is made on behalf of Fellaheen than is made with their active co-operation. Government intervention, although aimed at reducing inequalities of the countryside and narrowing the gap between town and country, has in fact produced new tensions within the rural community.

Egypt is truly the gift of the Nile. The Nile Valley and Delta support 99 per cent of the total population on less than four per cent of the land area. Population densities average 360 per square mile, rising locally to above 460—rural densities here are among the highest in the world. The many villages are situated on the least productive plots of ground, on rocky out-crops or where sown land meets the edge of the desert, in order to avoid wasting valuable agricultural land. The great majority have between 1,000 and 5,000 inhabitants.

Approaching a village the clusters of low dwellings come into view, separated from one another by narrow, winding, unpaved streets. The traditional type of dwelling usually has walls two or three feet thick constructed of unbaked bricks made with Nile mud and straw. The use of cement blocks is now increasing, but its effect on local styles of architecture is often unfortunate. The only entrance to the traditional home is a large wooden door, usually closed for privacy, which opens on to a roofless, dirt-floored courtyard. During the summer months one corner of the courtyard is used as a kitchen where cooking is done on a kerosene or wood-burning stove. Opening off the courtyard are one or two dark rooms which the family sometimes shares with its animals.

Most homes are poorly furnished one-storey structures. Many have no furniture except mats made of straw, or blankets spread on the floor. Roofs are made of rough wooden beams covered with sticks and straw overlaid with mud, and are frequently used as a drying area for both clothes and agricultural products. Many houses still have no latrines, and the people use open places, especially near the irrigation canals. New dwellings, resembling urban houses in structure and design, are beginning to appear in villages near some of the larger urban centres in Lower Egypt, and their number will no doubt increase in the future. A considerable variety of livestock can be seen everywhere—camels, donkeys, goats, sheep, cattle, and water buffaloes. Everywhere in the narrow streets and alleys, and frequently inside homes, there are chickens, ducks, turkeys and pigeons.

In the villages the principal garment for the men is the

Threshing grain in the Nile Valley, where in some years three crops can be grown. For the farming people of the Valley, life has remained substantially unchanged since the days of Ancient Egypt.

Picou/AAA

jalabiya, which resembles an ankle-length nightshirt. It distinguishes the Fellaheen from the peasantry in most other Moslem countries. The winter *jalabiya* is made of flannel or heavy cotton while the summer one is more lightweight. It is worn over a cotton undershirt and knee length shorts which is usually all they wear when working in the fields. A small cotton or woollen skull-cap is also worn, especially by the older men. A black *jalabiya*, together with a shawl for covering the head, is considered the only appropriate dress for the village women who also use local cosmetics such as *kohl* (eye make-up), and *henna* to tint the hair and to cover hands, feet and fingernails at the time of marriage and for the great festivals. Many men and women still walk barefoot, but shoes and sandals are becoming increasingly popular.

Until recently the Felaheen brought their drinking water directly from the Nile or from the nearest irrigation canal. Today, the government has provided thousands of villages with piped drinking water and it is a common sight in the villages to see women and girls carrying jars on their heads going to and from the public fountains. The fountains are also places where the village women congregate to exchange the latest gossip while they wash their clothes and kitchen utensils. Rural electrification is also going ahead very rapidly under government plans to provide electricity for over 3,500 of the 4,000 villages of Egypt.

Before the Second World War the Fellaheen suffered appallingly poor health and Egyptian death rates were among the highest in the world. Because of the dense network of irrigation canals and ditches, water-borne diseases such as bilharziasis and malaria affected a high proportion of the rural population. Ankylostomiasis (hookworm) and trachoma, which results in partial or total blindness, were also widespread, together with tuberculosis, bronchitis and various heart diseases. Although some medical centres were established in rural areas before 1952, the most important developments have occurred since then. In 1952, there were only 289 medical centres of various kinds in rural areas, compared with 1,750 in 1969. The health of the Fellaheen is improving, but only slowly.

As long as the physical conditions essential for good health are lacking, this situation is likely to continue. The majority of villages are still unhealthy and depressing places. The unpaved streets are dusty during the summer

(Above) An old man sells beans in a village market. Beans and other pulses make up for the lack of protein in a diet based on agricultural produce. Meat and fish are only available during Islamic festivals.

(Right) The saqia is an ancient design of water wheel which lifts water to the level of the irrigation ditches. The fertility of the Nile Valley allows it to support a very dense rural population.

and muddy during the winter, making it difficult to keep homes clean. The absence of a sewage system encourages the villagers to dump their dirty water in the streets; and the village canal is used to dispose of all manner of waste material. But equally important, in spite of recent improvements, the villagers' diet is still mainly a starchy one, with little protein, fat or sugar. About 80 per cent of the rural population's calories still come from the maize of millet bread, *aish*, the rest of the diet being made up of a variety of vegetables. Cheese, dates and melons are sometimes available but meat and fish only on rare occasions. During certain Islamic festivals richer Moslem families are expected to kill sheep and goats, and distribute the meat to the poor.

Until 1933 educational opportunities in rural Egypt were extremely limited, and if there was a village school it was the *kuttab* at the mosque where the *shaik*, or religious leader, taught the pupils to read and write as he instructed them in the principles of Islam. Although free secular education for all boys and girls between the ages of seven and twelve was made compulsory after 1933, many villagers never accepted the new state system. The level of school attendance was low, especially during irrigation and harvest periods when there was much work to be done in the fields.

Since 1952 many new elementary schools have been opened in the rural areas and much progress has been achieved, but so rapid is the population growth that the number of illiterate people is actually increasing. Nonetheless, the Fellaheen's attitude to public education is changing significantly and there is now a growing awareness of the importance of formal education. Parents frequently refer with pride to the fact that their sons are

attending school, for a pupil's educational attainments reflect favourably on his entire family.

After centuries of isolation, the Fellaheen's horizons are beginning to expand beyond the village community thanks to the mass media, and especially the radio. Transistor radios can be seen everywhere in the villages; agricultural workers wear them on their belts as they work in the fields; most shops and stalls have them playing to entertain their customers. The radio is particularly effective because it overcomes the barrier of illiteracy. It brings the Fellaheen information about life in the cities and about events in other countries. It is also used by the government not only for political purposes but for the promotion of social reform programmes such as family planning.

These improvements in the quality of village life during the last two decades have been accompanied by equally important changes in the structure of land ownership in the Egyptian countryside and in the farming methods of the Fellaheen. Land reform laws of 1952, 1961 and 1969 have stripped the rich landowners of the bulk of their estates, and the expropriated land has been divided into small plots and given to landless labourers and smallholders. But this has still left millions of peasants without land, or with only very small holdings, for there is just not enough land to go round. It is important to remember that some 95 per cent of all landowners own less than five acres.

Each new peasant proprietor, as a condition of his land grant, is required to join one of the newly formed co-operatives, and the co-operative system has been extended to villages outside the land reform areas. The co-operatives provide credit, and technical and practical advice for the

Fellaheen; they arrange for the marketing of produce and generally supervize farm production. Their most striking impact, however, has been through the introduction of a three-yearly crop rotation system to increase crop yields.

Under the traditional system, farms consisted of several strips of land scattered throughout three or more large blocks of land, and individual farmers could grow any crop they wished on their own strips. Today in many areas this chequerboard of small plots has been replaced by vast fields of 70 or more acres, with each field under one crop, for example *berseem* (Egyptian clover), cotton or maize.

Under the new system the lands of the village are divided into three large consolidated blocks, each assigned to a particular crop.

Today, as for centuries past, the Fellaheen depend entirely on the Nile to irrigate their crops. Since 1969 the High Dam at Aswan has retained all the water of the Nile, bringing to an end the annual flooding of the Valley north of the dam. Nile water is now released on a controlled annual pattern throughout the year. Although various technical problems have emerged, the new arrangement is making possible an expansion of perennial, or gravity-flow, irrigation. With this form of irrigation crops can be grown all the year round in the three growing seasons—winter (*shitwi*), summer (*seifi*) and autumn (*nili*)—and much land now produces two or three crops a year. Not only do the Egyptian Fellaheen farm their land intensively, but they also achieve some of the highest yields in the world per acre for most of their main crops.

In the midst of the many marked changes in the lives of the Fellaheen, continuity with the past nevertheless re-mains; especially in family and kinship organization, and in religious observance. The extended family—husband and wife, their married and unmarried sons, and their unmarried daughters—functioning within the clan structure, still remains the basic social and economic unit. Obedience and respect to father and elder brother as well as to the clan head and clan elders, and loyalty to close relatives and clansmen, are the basic rules of social life. Marriages between members of the different clans which make up an Egyptian village are rare. Instead marriage to a close relative, especially to a paternal first cousin, is generally preferred. Both girls and boys marry early in life, and there are strong economic incentives to have large families. A married woman normally lives in her husband's family home where she plays a role subordinate to both her husband and her mother-in-law. A wife with grown sons, though still subordinate to her husband, exercises considerable authority in bringing up her children and in supervising the household activities of her sons' wives.

Weddings, births, circumcisions and deaths remain the most important social events for both Christian and Moslem Fellaheen. Moslems also celebrate the major religious festivals, the '*Id il Fitz* (little feast) which comes at the end of the fasting month of Ramadan, the '*Id il Adha* (big feast) and the *Mawlid an-nabawi* (birthday of the Prophet) and Islam continues to play a major role in their daily lives. Even a simple question will receive the reply *In sh'llah* (whatever God wills). The use of charms for the prevention of illnesses and protection against the evil eye is still widely practised in rural Egypt.

Even though the power of the great landlords over the Fellaheen has now been broken by the land reform laws, other forms of social tension have appeared within the rural community. As a result of the government's agrarian policies a modest improvement in the income of small landowners, especially the beneficiaries of land re-distribution, has occurred since 1952. It is these richer peasants and their families who control the new co-operatives and who have now acquired the political and economic influence to dominate the rural areas. Tenant farmers, whether operating under cash rents or share-cropping systems of tenancy also appear to have made some gains from the reforms. But the most unfortunate group among the Fellaheen remains the landless labourers who have actually suffered a loss of income as a result of the reforms. This group represents the majority of the rural population, and their number is increasing.

In the future, in spite of an extension of the cultivated area through desert reclamation schemes and an increase in productivity, continued rapid population growth in rural areas, at least for the remainder of the 20th century, will make it extremely difficult to maintain, let alone increase, the Fellaheen's standard of living. The percentage of the population living in rural areas will no doubt continue to decline as many of the Fellaheen continue to leave for the cities. Nevertheless, absolute numbers will continue to increase, and by the end of the century the already overcrowded rural areas might have to support at least another 15 million people.

The Egyptian government is committed to a family planning campaign, and advice is available in the newly established rural health centres. Unfortunately the campaign has had little impact, and even greater efforts must be made to reduce natural increase in rural areas. Greater numbers must be absorbed in agriculture, and new labour intensive industries need to be established in the villages. Given the existing tensions among the Fellaheen, the consequences of failure to cope with the expanding population could be explosive. □

Andrew Baring

Fon

BENIN

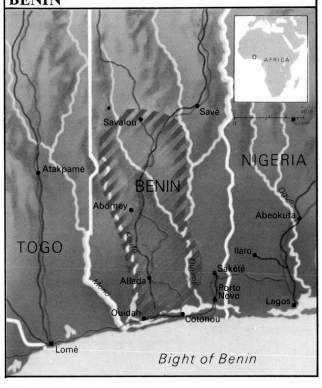

Few other West African people have exercised a greater fascination over the minds of Europeans than the Fon of Benin (formerly Dahomey). The reason for this fascination is not hard to find. The kingdom of Dahomey had features which appealed to all the feelings of mystery with which the Victorians viewed 'Darkest Africa'. Each year, for example, at the King's Annual Custom the royal lineage paid tribute to its ancestors, and human sacrifices would be made by the score if not by the hundreds. Then, at the death of a king, even more victims would accompany him to the next world. The King's Court was spectacular with its great officers, its eunuchs and its famous regiment of female warriors, the 'Amazons', who played a leading role in Fon wafare. The kings did their best to keep Europeans out and the mystery surrounding these customs was maintained until the conquest of Dahomey by the French in 1894.

The power of the king came to an end with the French conquest and the sacrifices of human victims had to cease. But the vigour and dynamism which made the founding of the kingdom possible still exists. For the Fon, the beliefs which sustained the state were the same as underpinned their whole social and family structure, and they were influential in all the people's daily lives. These beliefs, in fact, describe the whole view of the world held by the Fon, and it is essential to understand them if we are to understand the people.

With a population of more than a million, the Fon are the largest of the peoples speaking languages related to Ewe. These are part of the Twi branch of the Kwa sub-family of languages spoken by most of the peoples of

Distinguished by their umbrellas, these are Fon chiefs from Abomey in southern Benin. In their past such chiefs, like the kings of the whole Fon State, would maintain an elaborate hierarchy of ministers.

Ghana, Togo, Benin and western Nigeria. Presumably, like the rest of these peoples, the Fon once cultivated the crops of what is called the Sudanic Complex—akee, ambary, cotton, cow- and earth-peas, various pumpkins and gourds, guinea-yams, millet and sorghum, okra and oil palms. These crops are still grown, but they are only of major significance in the north of Benin. In the south of the country, where the savannah breaks through the tropical rain-forest to reach the sea, the crops of the so-called Indonesian Complex are of much greater importance. These were originally imported from the Far East, and include Malaysian yams and cocoyam, which grow extremely well in the more humid areas of West Africa and were the basis upon which the forest peoples originally prospered.

But with the coming of the Europeans, and particularly during the period of the slave-trade in the 17th and 18th centuries, many plants were also brought back to Africa from the Americas. These included maize, manioc, peanuts, peppers, squash, sweet potatoes, tomatoes and cocao, and have become an important source of food for the Fon. Cocoa and palm oil have become the main sources of cash, and the Fon also keep a number of animals—sheep, goats, cats and dogs, pigs, chickens, guinea-fowl, ducks and pigeons. Cows are kept for meat, but are not usually milked; horses are used for transport, although less so than in the past when they were an important part of the king's armoury.

The Fon live in compact towns and villages which are divided into quarters and compounds, usually occupied by members belonging to one patrilineal clan, a group of people related to each other through male ancestors. The

But although descent and succession usually follow the male line, there are a number of other forms of marriage, some of which do not require the normal payment of bride-price by the husband to the family of his wife. The result can be that children of these marriages will be affiliated with their mother's rather than their father's lineage. This system of choice as to the affiliation of children is found in many other societies along the West African coast and makes for complex forms of family organization.

The organization of the Fon state was very complex, and it may help to understand it if we first see how it came into existence. The original inhabitants of the area were organized in small local groups, with no overall loyalty to a king. Each town would try to guard its own independence, and perhaps gradually tried to extend its influence over its neighbours. But none of the states which had emerged up to the beginning of the 17th century were very large. Savi and Whydah on the coast did achieve some importance, as did Arda in the interior near Allada. But between 1600 and 1625 one band of warriors left Arda and succeeded in conquering much of the region to the north around where Abomey is today. And this laid the foundation of the Fon kingdom.

The first king of the new dynasty built his palace over the body of the king he had defeated, and this idea was reflected in cult practices which continued up to the coming of the French. The great King Agadja reigned from 1708 to 1732 and greatly extended the kingdom, conquering the original home-state of Arda, and pushing Whydah back to a narrow strip along the coast. When the Fon came into direct contact with European traders, they had access to arms which enabled them to embark on still further conquests. They cut out all other middlemen and eventually controlled the very profitable slave-trade in all of the interior of what became known as the Slave Coast. The powerful 19th century Fon kings, Ghezo, Glele and Behanzin extended the kingdom from Savalou to the coast, and from the Koufo River in the west to the Ouémé in the east. King Glele was visited by the famous English explorer Richard Burton, and it was Behanzin who was finally defeated by the French in 1894.

The Fon kings maintained a brilliant court, a large standing army and a strict military organization. This enabled them to keep up the lucrative flow of slaves to the coast, and one of the army's most striking features was the corps of perhaps as many as 2,500 Amazon warriors which so fascinated the Europeans. Court ceremonial was elaborate, and the king was treated with great awe, absolute monarch that he was. Anyone approaching him had to prostrate himself on the ground and throw dust on his head. One of his sons, not necessarily the eldest, was singled out as heir apparent, but the rest of the royal family were deliberately kept powerless to reduce their chances of effecting a coup. The royal princesses, particularly, lived a life of freedom and irresponsibility and were noted for their profligate and self-indulgent characters.

The administration of the Fon state was also organized in a very elaborate manner. There was a strict hierarchy of ministers with clearly defined functions, who were always commoners, and appointed and removed at the king's pleasure. At the head was the *Minga* who was Commander in Chief of the Army, Prime Minister and Chief Executioner. The *Meu* was the guardian of the royal princes and princesses, chief of protocol and chief collector of taxes. The *Yovoga* controlled the port of Ouidah, and was charged with controlling relations with the Europeans —a sort of foreign minister. The *Adjaho* supervised the affairs of the palace and headed the secret-police and espionage organization. The *Soga* commanded the cavalry and was overseer of the large number of the king's own

Access to such a huge variety of crops—including many from both the Far East and America—resulted in the frequent trading and exchange of food from different areas. This market system has made it easy for the Fon to adapt to a cash economy.

C. Bryan/Robert Harding Associates

ultimate ancestor is usually a supernatural being, a *tohwiyo* who was the offspring of one human and one animal parent. The animal is the totem of the clan, and its members never eat its flesh. There are other ceremonies which unite the members of the clan and so help to maintain the social structure of the Fon as a whole.

Each family, within the clan, will build its compound near the others. Compounds usually consist of rectangular houses with walls of wattle and daub or dried mud, and gable roofs which are thatched or covered with corrugated iron. The houses are built round an open rectangular space in which there are shrines to personal, family, clan and national gods and spirits. Fon men can have more than one wife and each one will have her own house. Marriage itself is encouraged between cross cousins (the children of a brother and sister, but not the children of two brothers or two sisters), and it is permissible for a man to marry a second wife who is the sister of the first. This, it is thought, helps maintain peace between them, since co-wives in a polygynous household are prone to quarrel. Marriages also tend to take place within the local group.

A man will usually take his wife to live near his father's compound, where he will eventually inherit property.

slaves. The *Tokpo* supervised markets and agricultural produce and acted as a kind of minister of the interior, while the *Benazo* was treasurer and looked after the palace and its dependents. The chief eunuch, *Totonu*, looked after the king's women and personal attendants. Each official also had a kind of 'double', a female equivalent who actually took formal precedence over him at court functions—just as, technically, the King himself was outranked by the Queen Mother.

The principle of this strict and clearly defined hierarchy, along with the military overtones of much of the system and the absolute power of the king, all clearly owed much to the history of the Fon State. It grew up, just as the neighbouring state of Ashanti did, partly in response to the presence of the Europeans on the coast and partly because of the slave-trade. Its success was largely due to the way in which it managed to manipulate the situation and to satisfy these needs—the slaves were sold for weapons with which more slaves were obtained, and so the Europeans and the Fon state prospered together. But these principles are also evident in other areas of Fon belief: they go deeper than mere political expediency. The fact that they survived shows that they did work in those particular historical circumstances, but their survival now that the circumstances have changed shows that they are fundamental to the Fon way of looking at the world. Even the principle of balance and equality between male and female is one which is built into Fon religion and cosmology.

According to Fon belief, the universe was originally partitioned by the creator-god *Mawu*, who is herself usually seen as female, and representing the moon. But she is also described as having both male and female characteristics. And so she was able, alone, to give birth to a son, *Lisa*, the Sun. *Mawu* and *Lisa* are generally combined as the King of the Gods. *Mawu* gave the other gods, who are

(Above) Fish fences at a coastal village in Benin. This part of what was once called the Slave Coast was drawn into the Fon State in the 18th century, and gave the Fon full control of the slave-trade.

(Below) Fon women are renowned for their freedom and independence. In the past many Fon princesses were permitted complete self-indulgence, and the free acceptance of lovers was a fashionable habit.

Foto-Hetzel

Independence Day celebrations in southern Benin. The strict organization of the Fon State was destroyed by the French conquest in 1894. But even with Benin's continuing contact with Europeans, and Independence in 1960, the Fon's traditional sense of order and hierarchy has endured.

her sons, their special powers and defined their spheres of operation. The method of succession and the separation of the various functions parallels both the political organization of the state and present-day social organization. Each god has a cult devoted to him, whose followers make up a clan. They worship him only, even though they do not deny the existence of other gods and the importance of their cults for their followers. The system has many features in common with that of Ancient Egypt, and we may guess that it is similarly the result of the combination of separate cults into one overall mythology as people combined into a state. The success of the state is a measure of the success of this combination process.

Mawu is thus the chief god (which, incidentally, the Fon call a Vodu and is the origin of the word Voodoo as it is used in the West Indies), and the other Vodu who have their own cults are her sons. The eldest is *Sagbata*, who is the god of the Earth-cult. A younger brother of *Sagbata* is *Xevioso* the Thunder god. There are thus three major cults, related but separate, headed by the Vodu of the Sky, Earth and Thunder. But there is a hierarchy, like the court within each cult.

Within the Sky-cult, for example, further sons of *Mawu* are ranked like ministers. *Gu* is second to *Mawu*, and is the god of metal and war: he gave men tools to build houses,

to hoe, to cut trees and to make boats. 'Thanks to *Gu*', say the Fon, 'one can cut off heads'. He is the god of iron-working so his shrines are found out of doors. Next comes *Age*, the god of the bush, animals and birds. The third is *Dji*, who is also called *Aido-Hwedo*, the rainbow who helped the Thunder god to come down to earth. The twins *Wete* and *Alawa* are guardians of their father's possessions and another pair of female twins perform the same service for *Mawu* herself. The youngest son of *Mawu* and *Lisa* is *Legba*, the trickster and reconciler. He is cunning, and it is he who enables men to manipulate their fate, so he has his own cult, as well as being part of *Mawu's*. Each cult has its priests, *voduno* and *vodunsi*, cult initiates or 'wives' of the gods and a complex of temples and cult houses. Those of *Mawu* were located within the palace, another parallel with the monarchy.

To most Fon the cult of *Mawu* was less important than that of *Sagbata*, which may indicate its greater antiquity. *Sagbata* was the eldest son of *Mawu*, but on being sent to earth was greedy and tried to take everything with him. Overloaded, he could not carry fire and water, and people were likely to starve for lack of them. A reconciliation was effected, however, between *Sagbata* and his brother *Xevioso*, who agreed to supply the desired water by rain which comes with the fire of lightning. The two gods share the right to administer supreme justice which they do by fire and thunderbolts, or, in the case of *Sagbata*, by smallpox and other skin diseases for the wicked. This is why smallpox itself has a cult.

Under *Sagbata* there is a similar hierarchy of gods to those subordinate to *Mawu*. *Suvinengge*, the vulture, for example, is the messenger of the gods and carries sacrifices up to them. *Alogbwe*, the many-handed, guards and distributes riches, lights travellers on the road, opens doors to let out illnesses and arrests those who must be stopped. He is a master of forests and fish, and like all other junior gods, he must render proper duties to his parents. But while *Sagbata* is the greatest king on earth, two kings cannot rule in one place, and so the Earth-cult shrines are outside the limits of the town which is the sphere of the king and *Mawu*. This perhaps is further evidence that *Sagbata's* is the cult of the original inhabitants of the region in which the Fon held power.

Even with the cults of supernatural ancestors belonging to the various clans, the variety of cults among the Fon is not exhausted. They also believe that each person has three 'souls', and they must be cared for by further religious activities and by diviners known as *Bokono*. *Legba* too has his own cult, as does the serpent *Da*, and there are many spirits and semi-divine creatures in the forest who are worshipped by individuals or by secret societies. There is a magic charm *gbo*, which will protect against *Sagbata* in his form of smallpox. Within the compounds of every Fon village, in the village itself and even outside there are thus many shrines to various gods and spirits.

The parallels between the methods of organization on the religious, social and political levels accounts for the great coherence of Fon society, particularly since its historical origins might have made for division rather than fusion. Yet as the functions which the system supported have changed, so has the system. War and slave raiding are no longer important, but the family and the ancestors are. And the assurance which this organized view of the world gives to the Fon is a source of great strength when they come to face the problems of the modern world. The diversity of their cults is lessening: their world is no longer peopled with such a variety of supernatural beings. But something of the ideas of hierarchy and separation of function remain and help to define, for the Fon, a world which is changing rapidly. □

Fulani
SUDANIC AFRICA

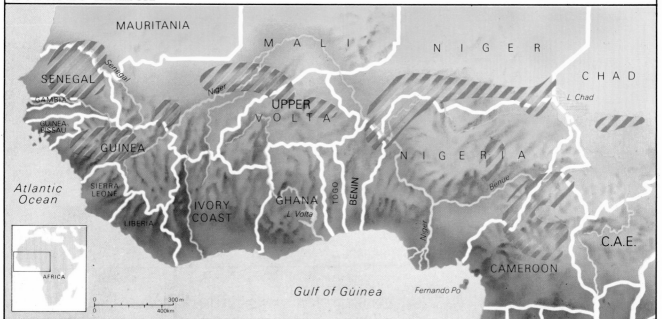

The beautiful appearance and elegant gestures of the Fulani have long made them attractive to other peoples, African as well as European, who have come into contact with them. But their elusive nomadic life, their independent warrior values and their reputation for skill in both beneficial and harmful 'medicine' have also made them objects of suspicion.

Some theories about the Fulani have been highly speculative and their origins have been widely disputed. In fact, there need be little mystery about them. Their language, Fulfulde, is related to a number of languages found in the extreme west of the Sudan belt, and it is reasonable to assume that it developed there. As the Fulani spread eastwards, different dialects developed— the main ones being those of the Fouta Senegalais and Fouta Jalon, of the central Niger region, of northern Nigeria, of Adamawa and Cameroon and of Bagirmi in Chad.

The Fulani who moved further east into the Republic of the Sudan, are greatly mixed with the Arab cattle-herders, the Baggara, and they speak Arabic. But the Fulfulde language is now classified, with general agreement, as one of the West Atlantic family and most ethnographers accept that this area was their original home. Their particular appearance (and also, incidentally, their similarity to many Ethiopians) is accounted for by their assumed ethnic origin as a people of mixed Caucasoid and Negroid ancestry.

Most of the inhabitants of the savannah among whom the Fulani live are settled agriculturalists, and the Fulani are principally distinguished from them as pastoralists. For the Fulani, cattle products such as milk, butter, cheese and blood, are the main means of food supply. It was the use of dairy techniques which enabled the Fulani to rely completely on their animals for subsistence, because

it is not possible to live exclusively on pastoralism otherwise. Nevertheless, while this did enable the Fulani to utilize marginal lands on the southern edge of the Sahara desert, where rainfall and water supplies were too slight for agriculture, it is probable that they have always had access to agricultural produce in exchange for their animal products—hides and meat as well as dairy foods.

The importance of pastoralism as the essential characteristic of their society is seen in the legends of the origin of the Fulani. The first Fulani to own cattle acquired them after he was driven out from his original home village. He wandered in the bush, suffering greatly, until a water spirit helped him by sending him cattle. In one version the cattle were the last of many animals he was forced to water on the spirit's instructions, and he was given them as a reward for his hard work—but only on the condition that he light a fire for them every night. This would keep them in the camp—without it they would leave and return to a wild state.

For over 1,000 years, Arab writers have reported the existence of the Fulani, but for the first few centuries after they acquired cattle their numbers do not appear to have expanded very fast. An important exodus of Fulani from the kingdom of Tekrur in Senegal occurred in the 11th century, and gave them the name Tekruri, by which they are still known in the eastern Sudan. They had reached northern Nigeria by the late 12th century and there were considerable numbers there by the 13th century. Penetration was peaceful and gradual. The 14th century saw the arrival of Islam in some of the Hausa cities of this area, and it is possible that the Fulani were also participants in this early conversion. But the Fulani states further to the west were generally hostile to the new religion. The Fulani kingdom of Fouta Jalon in the 10th century, for example, and that of Fouta Senegal in the 16th, both persecuted Moslems.

But once the Fulani had been converted to Islam the states which they built up or conquered became strong, even fanatical, centres of Moslem evangelism. The highlands of the Fouta Jalon had seen considerable immigra-

A Fulani Bororo woman uses calabashes - the hardened outer skins of gourds - as containers for milk. The butter churns of the Fulani are made from goatskins.

Andrew Baring

tion of Moslem Fulani during the 17th century, and in the 18th century they declared a Holy War or *Jihad* against the pagans and succeeded in conquering and forcibly converting a considerable area. A second kingdom was established in Fouta Toro, and in 1776 Moslem Fulani replaced the previous pagan Fulani dynasty. The same thing happened a little later in Macina. But the most important Fulani *Jihad* was that led by Uthman dan Fodio at the beginning of the 19th century.

In the course of little more than a quarter of a century he established an Empire that covered nearly all of northern Nigeria and parts of what are now the Republics of Benin, Niger and Cameroon. Uthman dan Fodio took the title of *Serkin Musulmi*, Commander of the Faithful, and settled the succession of the title and the eastern half of the Empire (with the capital at Sokoto) on his son Bello, and the western half (the Emirate of Gwandu) on his younger brother Abdullahi. The rest of the 19th century saw a great deal of strife within the Fulani Empire, and against non-Fulani who were conquered. The people of Bornu in northeastern Nigeria managed to resist the Fulani, but in most other areas their forces were victorious.

This success profoundly changed the nature of Fulani society. Up to this point the people had been mainly pastoralist, and for most of their history they had been at a disadvantage in relation to their settled neighbours on

the savannah. The Fulani were despised by many of the more sophisticated inhabitants of the cities as primitive bush-dwellers, uncivilized, dirty and untrustworthy. They may occasionally have been useful as suppliers of dairy produce, but they were often a nuisance when their cattle destroyed standing crops. They were also feared as sorcerers, and the guarded and rather precarious tolerance with which they were treated as long as they behaved themselves could often change to violent hostility.

Today, this is still the attitude of some settled peoples to those Fulani who remain uncompromisingly pastoralist. The largest and most clearly defined group of these are the Bororo who live across the border between Nigeria and the Niger Republic. They still prefer to lead a very traditionalist life. They only come into the towns for their dances, or to make use of markets to sell their produce and to buy what they need in the way of food supplies and small manufactured goods. But the Bororo still would not dream of living in towns. They despise agricultural work as fit only for slaves: for them the life of a gentleman is the life of a pastoralist. The important things are cattle, family, personal appearance and skill at dancing and poetry. It is around these matters that their lives still revolve.

Even the severe droughts of the early 1970s, which brought starvation and death to many of their animals, and to the Fulani Bororo themselves, have not altered their basic values or belief in this style of life. They are transhumant—

life revolves round an annual cycle of seasonal movements. The wet season, *dungu*, begins late in June and lasts to the beginning of October. It is a time of hard work, but it is enjoyable because the Bororo can see their cattle becoming sleek and fat on the lush grass. They keep on the move to avoid the fouled and soggy ground and too many flies which result from staying too long in one place. Moving enables them constantly to choose the best grazing—and to avoid the tax collector.

From the end of October to the end of December is the hot dry season after the rains, *yawal*. It is an intermediate period when the herds begin to move south, eating the stubble of early-harvested crops towards the end of the season. Cattle have to be carefully controlled to prevent them damaging standing crops. These are harvested during *dabunde*, the cool dry season of the Harmatan wind which lasts from December to February. The herds eat the remaining stubble, and in return manure the fields for the next season's cultivation. Pasture declines during this period, and by the end of it, the herds have to be moved frequently to find what grazing remains.

(Left) Umbrellas are used by the rulers of many West African states. Here, the Emir of Zaria is greeted by the late Sir Ahmadu Bello, a descendant of the founder of the Fulani Empire, Uthman dan Fodio.

(Right) The mixed racial origin of the Fulani is seen in the appearance of these two women who have come to Potiskum for one of the ceremonial dances which are an important part of Fulani life.

(Below) The Fulani were originally nomadic pastoralists who were able to expand with their herds of cattle in areas not used by the surrounding cultivators. Many Fulani attitudes still reflect pastoralist values.

Andrew Baring

M. and E. Bernheim/Susan Griggs Agency

(Above) On 'Salah' day at the end of the sacred fast of Ramadan, a crowd of brightly dressed Fulani women watch the procession of their hereditary prince —the Emir of Katsina.

Cheedu is the hot season after the cool Harmatan and lasts a couple of months from March to April: it is the worst time of the year for the pastoralists. Grazing is bad, water is scarce, the heat tries everyone's patience and quarrels and ill-temper are common. Everyone greets the onset of the 'small rains', and the windy period just before the rains recommence in June, with relief. Grass springs up rapidly, and the herds are moved northwards away from the farmland, before the planting begins.

The effects of the *Jihad* and the establishment of the Empire meant little change, therefore, in the life-style of the more nomadic Fulani. Their status in relation to the Hausa, for example, improved, but they still remain largely 'outsiders' preserving their own individualistic way of life. But for the settled and partly settled Fulani conditions changed considerably.

There are several kinds of partly settled communities amongst the Fulani. Some result from the loss of cattle wealth and the consequent need to supplement food resources by agriculture. Where this mixed subsistence is pursued, the 'home' area of the house and the farmland is often the focus of a wider area used for transhumant, seasonal, grazing of cattle. Herds are smaller than those owned by the pastoralists, and the area over which they move is more restricted. To some extent the Fulani themselves have taken over the role played by the Hausa agriculturalists in the lives of the Bororo. Very often the household is split, with the family head remaining at the home, while the younger married and unmarried sons move with the herds while the crops are growing. Kinsmen may be employed to do the herding, and paid labourers may be hired to work the farm, depending on the individual circumstances of each family.

In some cases, particularly on the Jos Plateau, a type of semi-settled existence has been adopted—not because cattle have been lost, but because this offers a better way to keep them. The high land is freer of tse-tse fly and other pests and, by settling, the Fulani have been able to protect their grazing grounds from the encroachments of other settled cultivators. The cattle had to move smaller distances, because the grazing was of good quality, while their numbers could still increase. Those Fulani who established permanent settlements could still move when they wanted to, and could employ paid labour to tend the gardens of maize and pulses round the settlement—thus having the best of both worlds.

The fully settled Fulani are at the same time the poorest and the richest sections of the people. The poorest are those who have lost all their cattle and have been forced to become agriculturalists in order to survive. They are greatly despised by their more fortunate fellow-tribesmen, for cattle have far more than economic value to the true Fulani, and to be without them is the greatest misfortune a man can suffer.

At the other end of the scale are the Fulani who have become the rich and powerful rulers and the aristocrats in the Hausa towns which the Empire incorporated. They are often members of the clan of Uthman dan Fodio, the Toroobe. They may, like the poor, have forgotten the Fulfulde language and adopted Hausa, but they can afford to remain in the town, without loss of 'face', because they hold political offices which carry status.

These men are often rich enough to be able to maintain their herds away from the town, and to pay other Fulani to look after them. Many are descended from the more distinguished generals and Holy Men of the period of the *Jihad*, and they represent the upper class of the Fulani whether this class difference is measured by descent, inheritance, education, wealth or occupation.

Between these two extremes, however, there are a number of more ordinary middle-class communities of settled Fulani. The main ones are the Toucouleurs of Senegal, the Upper Niger community of the Khassonke at Kayes, the Fulani of Wassulu also on the Niger in Guinea, and the Fulanin Gida or houseowner Fulani of northern Nigeria and Niger. Some Fulani Holy Men, local-government officials who live permanently in towns, and scribes literate in Arabic, also come within the range of comfortable middle-class settled Fulani. Many are men of great scholarship, and are the foundation of the sophisticated Moslem intelligentsia which has been a feature of the major towns on the southern edge of the Sahara for many centuries.

The Fulani thus include a number of diverse communities with a wide range of life-styles and occupations. They are held together by a common language, to some extent, although this has been lost by the Fulani at the extreme ends of the scale—the rich and the very poor. Religion also plays an important part in their lives. But it is their common background and history which is really their strongest cultural possession. Many suffered greatly in the droughts which afflicted the southern edge of the Sahara in the early part of the 1970s. But even when Fulani are forced to settle, many of their attitudes to life, their beliefs, and much of the social structure acquired as pastoralists, survive. Few Fulani now undergo the whipping-test of manhood, the *sharo*, which marked an important stage in a young man's life, and was a necessary part of his initiation into adulthood. But the ideal of manliness, and the ability to bear pain and suffering without complaint, is still part of what it is to be Fulani. □

Philip Stevens

(Above) A Fulani man cuts strips of meat from a specially slaughtered cow and smokes them over an open fire. The pieces of meat will later be eaten as a delicacy at a naming ceremony.

(Below) The Fulani assemble in the towns to conduct their initiation ceremonies and their dances. As the young men begin to dance the girls approach and join in opposite the man of their choice.

Andrew Baring

Galla
ETHIOPIA

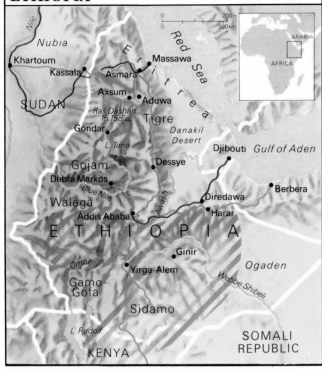

The Galla of Ethiopia are one of the most numerous peoples of the African continent. While the total population of Ethiopia is estimated at 26 million, approximately half are believed to be of Galla origin. Their language is one of the Cushitic sub-group which also includes Somali, Afar, Konso and Darassa. They live in an extremely varied environment ranging from the well-watered highlands of Wollo and Wallaga, to the coffee-rich forests of Jimma, the luxuriant rain forests of Jamjam, the arid expanses of the Awash Basin and the savannah pastures of Bale and Sidamo.

Most of the Galla share a common culture, language and set of social institutions. However, at no point during the past four centuries have they been politically unified, and after they began expanding into the Ethiopian highlands they became fragmented into warring tribal units.

The religion which is common to most of the Galla is centred around the concept of *Waka* (God). *Waka* is a kindly figure and the Galla pray to him and offer sacrifices, but there are no excessive exhibitions of humility and prostration. *Waka* is associated with the sky; he rewards mankind with rain and punishes by withholding it. Two kinds of rituals are performed to propitiate *Waka* directly or through his intermediaries. These are water rituals and the rites of fertility.

Galla attitudes towards fertility have always been ambivalent. On the one hand they regulate and restrict child-

(Left) Bringing scarce water to the herds.

Galla women fill water containers, known as gerber, which are made from whole goatskins.

birth more rigorously than any other people in Ethiopia; on the other hand they love children and desire to have as many as possible. Sacrificial offerings are therefore made from time to time to encourage fertility in women, at least during those stages of the life-cycle when child-bearing is allowed.

The rites of passage are another type of ritual practised by the Galla. As in most African societies, birth, circumcision, marriage and death are celebrated; but the Galla have gone further to develop an extremely elaborate complex of transition rituals covering the entire life-cycle. The ritual calendar governing transitions is a form of esoteric knowledge that men of learning study throughout their adult lives. In all these ritual activities, human intermediaries—*abba jila*—are asked to supervise the proper performance of rites and to mediate between men and God. Any knowledgeable person who has mastered history (*gada*), time-reckoning, divination (*raga*), or the rules of ritual (*jila*), can serve in this capacity. However, hereditary specialists such as the *kallu* and *bokku* have the responsibility of overseeing the most important rites, called *muda* and *butta*, which are attended by great numbers of pilgrims from large areas of the Galligna speaking community.

The entire religious system has survived to this day among the Borana and other pastoral Galla in southern Ethiopia. Moving northwards, however, much of the ritual appears to be modified or simplified. The rites of passage have been abridged or replaced by the corresponding Christian or Moslem rites. The traditional time-reckoning system has been abandoned and replaced by the Ethiopian or Moslem calendar. The disciplined and restrained ritual life of the pastoralists has given way to more ecstatic forms of religious behaviour.

The *kallu* institution in particular has proved very resilient and it is as important among the Macha of the central highlands as it is in the south. Indeed, the institution has become more pervasive and more central in

(Above) A Galla man ploughs a field with his team of longhorn zebu cattle. Skilled agriculturalists, the Galla cultivate grain crops and coffee as well as herding cattle, sheep and horses.

(Below) A Galla man and child wash newly born lambs in the shallows of Lake Abiata. Traditionally the Galla feared large expanses of water, believing them to be inhabited by evil spirits, 'borenticha', which required propitiatory sacrifices.

Marcus Brooke

Smallwood Photography

John Moss

community life and has passed on to Christian and Moslem Ethiopia in the modified form of the *Kallicha*, or possession, rituals.

Both Islam and Christianity have had considerable impact on the agricultural Galla. The Galla of Harar, eastern Arussi and Kafa were the earliest converts to Islam. In these areas, the shrines of Moslem saints have become the centres of pilgrimage and the rallying points for Galla peasantry. On the whole, the spread of Islam was not the work of organized missions. Believers, traders, pilgrims and self-taught *mallams* spread the faith from community to community. Only in some established congregations, mainly those of Harar and Jimma, is there a tradition of Islamic education.

Christianity was introduced by north Ethiopian colonists. Most of the war chiefs who led the imperial conquests were accompanied by clergymen; they built churches and put pressure on their new subjects to accept Ethiopian orthodoxy. Church schools attracted a few converts and taught them to fast, to read and to chant in Ge'ez, the classic language of the church. In some areas Protestant missions successfully created an effective educational system. In Wallaga, for example, self-supporting Christian communities have emerged, and these have played an important role in the growth of Ethiopia's bureaucracy.

The central institutions of the Galla have undergone radical change in some parts of Ethiopia. The original political system shared by all the Galla was based on the *gada* system—a democratic institution in which successive genealogical generations assumed political power. The

(Above) In the areas of Ethiopia which are isolated and untouched by outside influences, Galla women still wear traditional clothes and ornaments, and painstakingly plait their hair into tiny strands.

institution survives today only among the pastoral Borana and Guji, although most of the agricultural Galla also continue to perform fragments of *gada* ritual. In the pastoral societies, political power is widely distributed.

In Borana, the leaders or *hayyu adula* are elected by a large assembly of clan delegates who represent the entire population. They do so under the supervision of the two hereditary leaders called *Kallu*. After several months of debate three councillors are elected by each half of the tribe. The most senior of the six councillors becomes the *Abba Gada*, or father of the *gada* council.

The councillors are elected 21 years before their term of office. In the interim they lead their own *gada* class as it passes through two stages of warriorhood. Should they fail in this leadership, they are removed before their investiture in a formal impeachment ceremony called *bukkisu*, or 'the uprooting'. If they succeed, they take power and govern for a single term lasting eight years. Just before they take power 14 junior councillors are elected to assist them. The two councils jointly constitute the *gada* assembly, called *ya'a arbora*, the whole of which is ordered by seniority. If a member is killed in war or removed from office, his immediate junior succeeds him. The Gada assembly is responsible for the resolution of major crises between clans, camps and age groups.

Warfare as a means of relieving the expansion of population was dependent on the mobility of semi-nomadic life, on the availability of horses and a readily transportable food supply. The Galla have always been highly skilled in hunting, tracking, locating underground water, digging wells and dams, regulating pastures and exploiting the natural vegetation. As they migrated northwards, they avoided the densely populated and intensively cultivated regions of the Sidama, Kafa and Gurage.

The greatest initial expansion was along the rift valley pastures stretching from central Kenya to the Eritrean border. The Galla settled in the open grasslands and gradually adopted mixed agriculture—cultivating grain crops as well as keeping cattle. Later they began their slow penetration of the densely peopled regions of southwest Ethiopia. The most extreme changes occurred in this region as they adopted the intensive agricultural techniques of the western Cushites including terracing, irrigation, and the cultivation of the *ensete* or 'false banana'. Coffee became their most vital cash crop.

The *gada* system was closely tied to the pastoral way of life and the effective operation of the institution depended on the ability of the people to co-ordinate their movements to make periodic wars and large-scale popular assemblies possible. The adoption of agriculture and sedentary village life was inevitably followed by political fragmentation and

Galla love children, but their attitude to childbirth is ambivalent. While they exercize more rigorous population control than other peoples in Ethiopia, they also make sacrifices to encourage fertility.

Sarah Errington/Alan Hutchison

the emergence of chieftaincies and kingdoms. The Galla became enmeshed in the feudal networks of the very populations they conquered.

Political change was the force which transformed the way of life of the Galla in Shoa, Wallaga, Wollo, Harar, and the Ghibe kingdoms. In the face of protracted wars against organized states, their own military leadership became more permanent and the *abba dula*, or chiefs, assumed more extensive powers. In the 17th century, the Wollo Galla were perpetually at war with the highly organized kingdoms of Amhara. They responded by developing the same kind of military administrative organizations as their adversaries and eventually evolved into fully fledged kingdoms.

During the 'Era of the Princes' the Wollo dynasty brought the Gondar emperors under their control and came close to taking the Imperial crown itself. Similarly, in the 19th century, Wallaga was constantly at war with Gojam and Shoa. Two families of warriors, the houses of Jote and Bakare, finally emerged as hereditary rulers. They intermarried with the expansive central aristocracy of Ethiopia and became an integral part of it. Below them a class of native landowners called *abba lafa* was established by the combined aristocracy. They were given the title of *balabbat* and, like feudal lords, had privileged access to farm lands and labour in exchange for their loyalty and administrative military service.

The most highly developed Galla kingdoms emerged along the borders of the state of Kafa in an area which was most unlike their traditional open grassland territory. The five Ghibe kingdoms—Jimma, Limmu, Gomma, Guma and Gera—were partly modelled on Kafa and partly developed uniquely Galla administrative bureaucracies. From Kafa they borrowed their complex defensive system which consisted of trenches dug along the more vulnerable borders, drawbridges, toll gates and frontier guards. The kings ruled through a hierarchy of governors, market overseers and tax collectors, whom they appointed, transferred and demoted at will.

This despotism was alien to Galla culture, and even here the tradition of government by assembly continued at the level of local community organization. In keeping with Galla tradition, they also absorbed the conquered populations and elevated the ablest and most loyal among them to positions of political authority. They never developed into the rigidly stratified caste society of Kafa.

Where the Galla had a well-developed monarchy or chieftaincy, their leaders and landed gentry were readily absorbed into the central feudal state of Ethiopia, and they aided the Emperor in his conquests of other Galla territories. Galla generals such as Ras Gobana and Ras Makonnen Guddisa played a critical role in Ethiopia's wars against Italian imperialism.

Where the traditional democratic institutions were preserved, however, incorporation into the Empire was violent. The Arsi, for example, fought a protracted and costly war against the combined Amhara-Galla forces of Menelik. Their population was decimated, their land was expropriated, and colonies of highlanders were installed as their rulers. The traditional leadership was abolished, and the population became stratified into an alien class of landed soldiery charged with administrative responsibility and another class of landless tenants stripped of all political power.

This unstable situation continued for seven decades until it erupted in the 1960s: the Arsi of Bale province armed themselves with modern weapons and staged a successful rebellion that altered the power balance and installed Arsi leaders in the local administration for the first time since their incorporation into the Empire. □

Hausa
NIGER AND NIGERIA

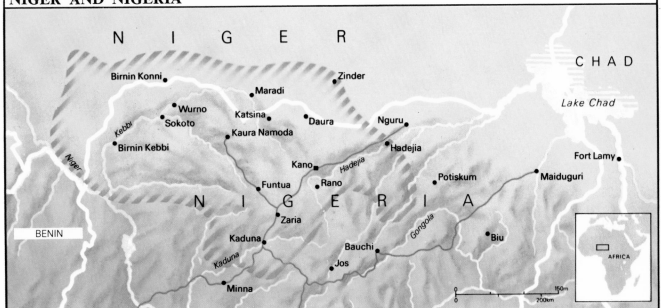

The Hausa have a passion for proverbs. One says, *Zamma wuri uku shina da anfani: zaman makaranta da zaman mahauta da zaman fada*—there are three places in which it is profitable to live: a school, a slaughter-house and a council—and this neatly illustrates some of their most abiding interests. The idea of profit and the desire to maximize gain in many areas of social activity is common to all dynamic societies. But it is the particular directions in which the Hausa seek this profit that are interesting.

School and learning for the Hausa now mean Islamic studies—such knowledge is intimately connected with the way a Hausa Moslem sees himself and his relationship with the world and society. It is also an important part of how society sees him, since status and religious distinction are closely interwoven. The slaughter-house in the proverb represents economic activity. (Characteristically, this means the activity of the middleman rather than the original producer or manufacturer, as the Hausa are skilled and passionate traders.) The council, of course, represents political power. Status derives, then, from knowledge, wealth and power and although the proverb may be Hausa, the message is universal. It is partly this community of understanding which makes the Hausa so sympathetic.

It is also typical of the Hausa that the three places in the proverb should mostly be found in towns, although this might appear odd since the majority of Hausa are peasant farmers, living in villages and hamlets. The image of the Hausa, however, is essentially that of the townsman. It is the townsman's view which travellers report since it is in the towns that history is made, and certainly where it is written.

For the countryman himself, the towns represent a wide range of social, psychological, economic and political attractions. But it is the values of the village which have probably contributed most to the Hausa view of the world. The big cities may be glamorous, but the earth abides. Power and the powerful may be sought and admired, but they have their limits; or as the Hausa put it, *Ko a Kworra da tsibiri*, 'even the great River Niger must go round an island'.

Hausa culture, like the Hausa language, is best seen as the result of the 'fertilization' of a peasant society by ideas emanating from towns situated, in most cases, at the southern end of the trade routes which cross the Sahara desert. The desert acted like a sea, channelling political and religious ideas, inventions and imported goods to specific 'ports' on its southern shore. The cities served as collecting points for the goods the caravans took northward in return: gold and slaves, ebony and ivory, ostrich feathers and fine leather. Much more significantly, from the Hausa point of view, the cities were dissemination points from which new ideas and technology spread out, under Berber and Arab influence from the north. This process is one which has been going on for a very long time. Kano, the largest Hausa city, central to the whole Hausa area, was probably well established by 1066, when William the Conqueror headed the Norman invasion of England.

Berber influence on the inhabitants of the southern savannah region also resembled the Norman invasion in that the existing population far outnumbered the new-comers. The genetic effect of this immigration has, there-fore, been slight and the original Hausa inhabitants prob-ably looked very much as the Hausa do now—tall and well built, with rather dark skins. The developing towns may have controlled the countryside immediately around them, but they were not organized into large states and the powerful states of Songhai to the west, and Bornu to the east, prevented the further expansion of the Hausa.

The Berber language has been of great importance in the formation of Hausa, which shows the consistency of this process and the long period of time over which it has been taking place. Hausa is, as a result, a composite language, just as Hausa is a composite culture. This is probably the main reason why it has been so successful and has expanded so widely. Hausa is easy to learn, at least in the initial stages. But real mastery, especially of the subtle tonal differences which define the variant mean-ings of some words, is harder to acquire. Many foreigners are caught out by the differences in tone which separate

John Moss/Colorific!

Ancient dye-pits in the city of Kano. Indigo dye and dyed textiles have been traded across the Sahara for many centuries and were one of the principle commodities on which Hausa prosperity was based.

the various meanings of the word *kashi* for example; it can mean a fight or a beating; to be rain-soaked; gambling; or a small heap or pile. But it can also mean excrement, so care is necessary to ensure the intonation is correct.

This example reflects the process which formed the language. The simple grammar is the product of the inter-action, while the difficult tonal elements reflect the Sudanic base before simplification by contact with outsiders. A similar development was taking place at roughly the same time in England: both Anglo-Saxon and Norman-French were more grammatically complicated than the English which resulted from their mixture.

Hausa is spoken today by nearly 20 million people as a first language and perhaps by as many more as a secondary one. This makes it the most widely spoken African language, with between five and 10 million more speakers than Swahili, the next largest spoken language. It is interesting that Swahili, spoken by about 25 million people in East Africa, is also a composite language: this suggests that there is something particularly useful about such languages. A notable feature of Hausa is the great degree of homogeneity it possesses: it varies very little over the area in which it is spoken, from Senegal to Chad and even into the Sudan.

Hausa legends about their origins also reflect this mixing process. It is recounted that the inhabitants of the town of Daura (which is now on the border between the two most important 'Hausa' countries, northern Nigeria and Niger) were suffering greatly from the oppression of a *serki*, a snake. It lived in their well and would only allow them to draw water on one day of each week and required sacrifices as well. A young nobleman (said to be a son of the Caliph of Baghdad, though this is perhaps a later addition under the influence of Islam) slew the snake by cutting off its head. Many of the townsmen claimed that they had liberated the town from the *serki's* oppression,

but only the young nobleman could produce the head, and so the Queen, also called Daura, married him. He was given the title of *Makas-serki* 'The Snake-Killer' and since then the chiefs of Hausa towns have been called *Serki*. He had seven sons, who became the chiefs of the original seven Hausa cities, the *Hausa Bakwai*. The actual lists of these vary but the most generally accepted one includes Biram, Kano, Rano, Katsina, Zaria, Gobir and Daura itself. This still represents the Hausa 'heartland'.

As Hausa culture, language, and conquest spread, so other city states came to be included, on a slightly lower level of prestige, as the 'Bastard seven', the *Banza Bakwai*. These were Zamfara, Nupe, Kebbi, Gwari, Yaure, Koro-rofa and even Yoruba. Many of these are not Hausa at all and their inclusion probably represents an intermediate stage in Hausa expansion, later reversed as historical forces vered in a different direction. The presence of the Europeans on the coast, for example, turned the focus of Yoruba trade to the south rather than to the north, across the desert. It was the northward trade which underlay Hausa economic success and it is probable that if the Europeans had not arrived, many more peoples to the south of the Hausa would have been drawn into their orbit.

Relations between the Hausa states were probably always highly competitive: mastery of the towns at the ends of the more important routes across the Sahara was a valuable prize. By the end of the 16th century there were six leading states, Kano, Katsina, Gobir and Zaria from the original 'seven', and Zamfara and Kebbi from the *Banza Bakwai*, while Daura and Yaure were of minor importance. The whole historical process was one in which the fortunes of the towns varied, as did their relative importance. Throughout the period, however, the process by which each city extended its influence over the surrounding countryside continued. The towns, and the more sophisticated and complex culture which they were developing, gradually became the Hausa 'norm'—certainly they represented the growing part of a dynamic society.

It is curious that this process did not proceed further. The towns, after all, controlled the surrounding peasantry and extracted taxes from them, establishing themselves as socially and economically dominant. Communication between them, as in most of the Sudanic belt of Africa, was easy. Why did they not develop into the larger empires, and ultimately nations, that grew up to both the east and the west of the Hausa cities? And why were they so often controlled by these other states, like the Songhai Empire to the west or Bornu to the east?

The answer may lie partly in the relative equality of the power of the various cities and their resources, although this still begs the question of why one city did not succeed in gaining at the expense of the others. There were many of them it is true, but they remained fairly evenly matched. A further limit on the growth of empire was the difficulty of administering large areas without the facility of writing. Perhaps most significant was the absence of any overall ideology which could unify the various states into a large unit. Perhaps also, the heterogeneous origins of the city-states and of the Hausa people themselves, help to account for this fragmentation.

It was not until the coming of Islam that the vital unifying factor made its appearance. Islam had reached Kanem, near Lake Chad in the east, as early as the 11th century and may have begun to filter into Hausa lands at the same time. But most of the immigrant Berbers were probably hostile initially to the religion of the Arabs, who had driven them out from their homes across the desert, and it was not until the 14th century that Islam made any serious headway in the Hausa cities. The Kano Chronicle mentions kings with Moslem names from this time, and states that the new religion was introduced from the west by Mandingoes.

By 1500 AD, Islam was dominant in all the main Hausa courts and in most towns, but had reached few rural areas. Its strength waxed and waned for the next 300 years. The beginning of the 19th century, however, saw the great Jihad of Uthman dan Fodio. He managed to use the many Fulani who lived and moved throughout the Hausa lands to conquer the cities and to establish Fulani princes in place of the Hausa kings. All the Fulani owed overall loyalty, and paid tribute, to the 'Leader of the Faithful' in Sokoto, and in this way the first effective unification of the Hausa peoples came about.

In spite of a certain amount of internecine squabbling after the death of Uthman, the Fulani-Hausa empire remained powerful for nearly a century until the British placed the whole area under their control. The existing system, however, was retained by the British and they confirmed the position of most of the existing Emirs. The British also removed those individuals who proved uncooperative, and gradually increased their control over the administration of those they allowed to remain. The present states in the northern part of Nigeria reflect the history of the Hausa cities and of the Fulani Empire, and both these are important determinants of the present-day Hausa sense of identity.

The Hausa cities are no longer independent, of course, but each is still the focal point of the surrounding countryside, and the source of learning and religious knowledge. Islam religion and law are closely interwoven, so the towns are also the location of the upper courts. They are centres of administration for the government, and in spite of the larger realms of political power which exist beyond them, they are the focus of intense local political activity. Above all they represent wealth, not only to those who live and trade within them, but to the rural peasant who either sells his produce there himself, or through a middle-man. The Hausa still go to the town to find the council, the school and the slaughter-house.

Differences of status are much more marked in the town than in the country. One writer has described their social

For most Hausa the market is a major focus of interest. Traders travel widely and often become rich on the long-distance trade for which they are famous.

Uthman dan Fodio's Holy War in the early 19th century gave the Hausa cities Fulani rulers. In speech and dress they are now indistinguishable from their Hausa subjects such as the do-gari or guards who are protecting this Emir.

structure as consisting of a number of overlapping strata based on occupation. The Hausa try to advance their status and have a fine sense of behaviour appropriate to a given level: the lion, they say, however debased, will not play with a pig. At the head of the hierarchy are the royal families in each town and the official nobility, followed by a class of learned Moslem intellectuals, the lawyers, preachers, teachers and scribes.

Today however, these overlap with high government officials and those with educational qualifications obtained from outside the purely Islamic world—university teachers and doctors, for example. Next, but also overlapping this class come the wealthy merchants, especially those who specialize in long distance trade. They are often very wealthy indeed. Next come the lesser traders and the crafts-

(Above) Hausa boxers bind their right hands into 'clubs' and try to knock out their opponents. Boxing and wrestling reflect beliefs in the holiness of strength and the fertility cults which were widespread in Sudanic Africa before Islam.

(Below) Typical Hausa architecture reflects influences from the Near East which spread along the North African coast and across the Sahara. Mud is the most practical building material as it evaporates moisture from the air inside the house and keeps it cool.

men. This last group is numerous and skillful and includes the leather workers, the weavers and dyers of cloth, the tailors, carpenters, skilled builders, and lower down the scale, the blacksmiths.

In the past the bottom of the social scale was occupied by the slaves and by the eunuchs who were attached to the harems of the rich. These, of course, no longer exist, but there are still individuals who attach themselves as clients to richer men as a way of obtaining financial backing for trade, or to obtain grain for planting. This is an important aspect of the Hausa sense of involved mutual obligation which gives great cohesion to the society.

This sense of mutual obligation and co-operation is probably stronger in rural areas than in the towns. Social stratification is much less marked in the villages, where the notion of 'class' hardly applies at all. There are, however, distinctions. The Village Head, the *Mallam* (religious teacher), or any paid government official such as a teacher or a veterinary inspector, is given automatic respect. Farmers who are noticeably successful, or traders who become richer than their fellows, acquire a correspondingly greater influence.

Village life centres on agricultural activity, and so is largely controlled by the two main seasons: the wet and the dry. The rains are concentrated in the months from May to September, and are preceded by the hottest and driest time of the year. During January and February the prevailing wind comes southward across the Sahara and brings with it a mass of fine, sandy dust. The Harmattan is a period of comparative cold, the sand gets into everything, the eyes are irritated and the lips crack. Fortunately, it comes between harvest time, at the beginning of the dry season from October to December, and the main preparation for planting in March and April.

The dry season is also the time for other activities such as the craft production for which the Hausa are famous, for trading, clearing new 'bush', and for ceremonial activity such as marriages. It is also the best time to make the Pilgrimage to Mecca, and the Hajj, and many Hausa also travel away from home to seek paid employment at this season. In the past, the dry season was also the time for war, and particularly for slave-raiding, which, although it has now been abolished was once important to the Hausa economy.

Trading is one of the most important dry season activities. Local produce is traded in weekly markets and is also taken to the nearby towns: there are several cash crops including cotton, tobacco and groundnuts. The last is most important and is the foundation of a considerable industry in Kano. The nuts are exported, and oil and peanut-butter are prepared from them. The great pyramids of sacks at Kano are a remarkable sight as they await transport or processing.

More important to many Hausa is the long-distance trade. The caravans travel, as they have done for centuries, between the various Hausa towns, to Ghana and across the Sahara. Long journeys, says another proverb make most money: *Tafarkin Gwanja ga nisa ga riba*, 'Road to Gonja (Ghana), far and rich'. This trade was an important element in forming the Hausa sense of community and identity, and is closely connected with another basic passion, the hearing and telling of 'news': *Ba bako ruwa ka sha labari*. 'Give a stranger water and listen to the news'.

The rainy season, and the months immediately before and after it are devoted mainly to agricultural activity in the village. Much of this is done on a co-operative basis under a system called *gandu*, in which the sons of a family are obliged to work a certain amount on the *gandu* land controlled by their father, and in return the father is

obliged to provide them with seed and equipment. He also allocates them other land which they work in their own time, using the produce themselves. After the father's death, this co-operation system may continue among brothers, but it usually breaks up as new generations set up their own *gandu*.

The Hausa are very skilled farmers whose main means of cultivation is the hoe. They grow a wide variety of crops, including millet, sorghum, maize and a certain amount of rice for food, apart from cash crops. The grain is pounded in a mortar to a flour and boiled to make a thick porridge called *tuwo*. This is eaten with a sauce, usually of vegetables such as onions, tomatoes and *okra*. It is flavoured with meat in rich households and on special occasions like the Moslem festivals.

The Hausa also keep animals. Cattle are often owned by the rich, and looked after by paid Fulani herdsmen. Many keep sheep and goats which are generally looked after by the younger children. Chickens and guinea fowl are also common.

A notable feature of life in the village, or in the scattered homesteads in which many rural Hausa live, is the contrast of egalitarianism with the hierarchical social structure of the towns. The explanation lies partly in the fact that wealth does not endure for long. The son of a poor man can become rich, if he is fortunate and works hard. Hard work, indeed, is greatly admired and many proverbs relate to it: *Zomo ba ya kamuwa daga zaune:* 'A hare is not caught by sitting down'. But work must be directed to a reasonable end: *A shakara saran ruwa sai tambatse:* 'A year of cutting water only makes spray'. Opportunity is equal for most in the countryside and a rich father does not necessarily have rich sons.

The focus of the Hausa family is the father, and inheritance and succession pass in the male line. A man may have several wives, but the first has greater status: under Moslem law he should share his time equally between them. Any favouritism shown, for example, to the newest, will produce acrimony. Each wife has her own house and is responsible for feeding her own children. First marriages are ideally made between first cousins, and the father is expected to help his son find the necessary bride-wealth. After the first marriage, a man must rely on his own resources. Children are greatly desired, for 'birth', say the Hausa, 'is the answer to death'.

In spite of all the glitter and sophistication of the Hausa cities, there is a very earthy, peasant, even cynical, feeling in most Hausa attitudes. They seem to rejoice in the discomfiture of the great. Wealth always wins, in the end: 'The good-looking man is kind', they say, 'if a rich one is not near'.

What counts is wealth, and wealth comes from hard work. The Hausa feel that if work is to be done at all, it must be done seriously, for as they put it, *Su babu tsaraka wanka ne*—'fishing without a net is bathing'. The Hausa are also cautious and prefer to see the end of a course of action before they begin: 'Before you tie up a hyena think how you are going to let it go'. There may be Emirs and princes, with all their great officers in the courts of the cities, but the countryman is independent and self-reliant. It is this independence which is perhaps the most basic characteristic of the Hausa, and it may explain, in part, why the Hausa cities never formed a larger empire.

But the process of integration was incomplete when the British arrived, and it continues today. Religion, economics and political power are the basis of national unity everywhere and Hausa consciousness is still spreading. They are already the largest culture-language group in Africa and may well be the focus in the future of an even wider unity.

Wendy Watriss/Susan Griggs Agency

Ibo
NIGERIA

The mammy-waggon—a battered truck, piled high with market goods and shrieking children perched precariously on duck-board seats, racing desperately along the winding forest roads—is a common sight in the East-Central State of Nigeria. This is Ibo country, where most of the Ibo-speaking people live, and the hurtling mammy-waggon, daubed with some hopeful slogan like 'In God we trust', could serve almost as a symbol of the people. The vitality, the readiness to share, and the casual assumption of terrifying risks are characteristic. Turning a sharp bend it is not uncommon to find the shattered wreck of a mammy-waggon that was driven too hard.

An Ibo saying has it that 'he who is too careful of his life will be killed by a falling leaf'. The qualities of energy and resourcefulness are particularly valued. Yet the Ibo also have an unusually strong sense of community; another saying has it that 'older succeeds, younger succeeds' and there is a powerful tradition of mutual assistance. A clannish system of intense, integrated loyalties, allied to an almost obsessive determination to succeed, makes the Ibo one of the most progressive and forward-looking peoples in Africa.

Yet for two years, from 1967 to 1969, their very survival as a people seemed in doubt. Western newspapers carried appalling stories of apparent genocide by the Nigerian Federal Government after the former Eastern Region, dominated by the Ibo, announced its secession from the Federation as the new state of Biafra. At least 600,000 Nigerians died in the course of the civil war, a large

Many thousands of Ibo suffered terrible injury when Biafra tried to secede from the Nigerian Federation in 1967. The Civil War claimed over 600,000 lives and caused massive damage: millions of pounds have been spent on reconstruction.

Keystone

(Above) Local market trading is traditionally left to Ibo women, who bargain long and aggressively. Their other major economic role is preparing palm oil—until recently Nigeria's main export.

(Left) The Ibo regard education as vital to their material advancement, and have built many schools. Villagers will often save communally to send their brightest children to high school and university.

Romano Cagnoni

proportion of them Ibo, for the Biafrans mounted an astonishing resistance in the face of overwhelming odds.

Their sufferings in the war won the Ibo world-wide sympathy, particularly when starvation ended so many of their lives. But the intensity of their resistance, their almost suicidal refusal to submit, was a mark of the steely determination in their character. Since the surrender the Federal Government has spared no effort to reconcile the Ibo with their former enemies, notably the Hausa and the Fulani, and hundreds of millions of pounds have been spent reconstructing the shattered country.

Yet one side-effect of the war is worth noticing—in the horrors of the fighting a new unity was forged among a people who had previously been categorized as 'Ibo-speaking' rather than Ibo. Anthropologists, for example, generally classify the Ibo into five main divisions and 14 sub-divisions. Their colour and even their physical size varies considerably: most are short and muscular, but the Ibo of Nsukka are lean and tall. Linguistic differences are similarly striking: although all the dialects are related, many are mutually unintelligible.

Most of the Ibo live in the heavily forested area between the River Niger to the east and the Cross River in the west: a tableland which rises northwards from the mangrove swamps of the vast Niger delta. Although the soil is poor, restricting the range of crops that can be grown, the forests are densely populated. The Ibo have no common myth of migration from another land, and ancient sculpture discovered at Igbo-Ukwe suggests that they have lived in their present surroundings at least since the 9th century.

Contact with Europeans first came in the mid-15th century, when Portuguese traders came ashore on what would soon be known as the Slave Coast. Shipping slaves to the West Indies soon became a lucrative business and the arrival of the Dutch in the 17th and the British in the 18th century accelerated the trade. At the port of Bonny alone about 16,000 Ibo were sold during each of the last 25 years of the 18th century.

With the abolition of the slave trade in 1807, however, European exploitation of West Africa entered a new phase as the trading companies pressed deep into the hinterland for raw materials: palm products, timber, elephant tusks and spices. The British Niger Company claimed administrative control of the area until 1900, when the Protectorate of Southern Nigeria was proclaimed and responsibility passed to the British Colonial Office.

The arrival of missionaries—the first mission was founded at Onitsha in 1857—was a crucial element in the European penetration of Ibo territory. The bush schools, set up both by Protestants and Roman Catholics, provided an educational impetus that the Ibo were quick to exploit.

(Right) Anxious Ibo refugees seek shelter during the Biafran War. Hundreds of villages were destroyed, and the disruption of food supplies was a steadily increasing cause of starvation.

Their enthusiasm for learning was soon apparent and has not abated: the Ibo today have the highest literacy rate in Black Africa. And many of the Ibo leaders who emerged when Nigeria finally won independence from Britain in 1960 received their earliest education at mission schools.

With Nigeria's emergence as a modern state, and particularly with the wealth she has drawn in oil revenues—the country is, in fact, the world's eighth largest oil-producer – many Ibo have inevitably been caught up in the technology and lifestyles of the Western world. The influx of bicycles and motor-cars, together with western clothes and fabrics, is immediately obvious to the visitor; on the other hand, rural communities continue very much in the traditional ways.

The village economy is still based on subsistence agriculture, with yams and manioc (from which cassava is made) together with many varieties of coco yam, the staple crops. In the tropical climate—the average temperature is about 80°F (25°C)—only one crop per year is possible. The farming year starts in February, with planting. The rainy season lasts from April to October, and a brief drought occurs in August, accelerating the growth.

Ibo men are responsible for cultivating the yams. They plant the seedlings in small 'yam-hills' about six feet apart; then the women are allotted their own plots, on which they grow maize, manioc and coco yams, as well as melons, okra, pumpkins and beans. This system of 'intercropping' —growing several crops on the same soil—is a valuable protection against soil erosion.

The density of the Ibo population puts great pressure

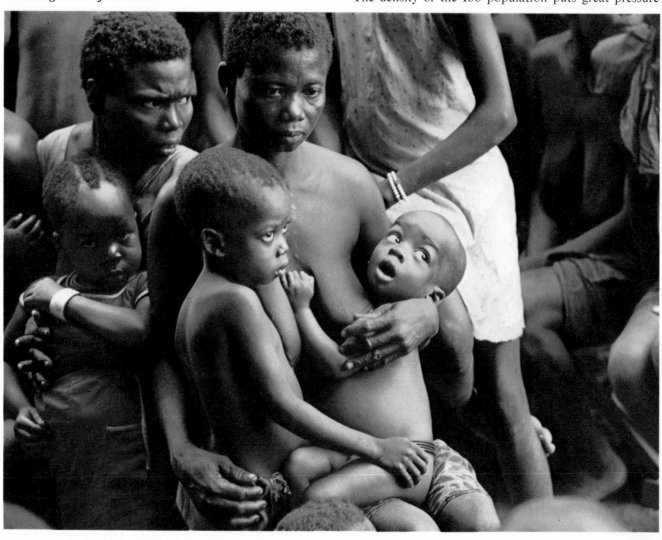

Keystone

A side-attraction at an Ibo market: the hair-dressing booth. Markets play a vital social role, particularly in rural areas, by providing a network of meeting places for traders, friends and relatives, and strengthening the sense of community.

on land for agriculture and every acre has an owner. Since Ibo women always marry outside their villages, they rarely own land; but male children are made responsible for a part of their father's land and inherit a share of it when he dies. The Ibo put great emphasis on the virtues of cultivation and owning land is a symbol of being born free—a mark of real dignity for a people who suffered so greatly from the slave-trade.

The two major economic roles of Ibo women are the preparation of palm oil (formerly Nigeria's most important export) and trading at the market. Palm oil is prepared by crushing the nuts and soaking the kernels: the oil then belongs to the man and the kernels to the woman. But it is at the market that the women really come into their own. A central part of Ibo life, markets, great and small, are held nearly every day. Bargaining is intense, noisy, often long drawn-out, and everyone is determined to make a profit—so much so that Ibo children make a 'market wish' every time their mothers prepare to leave home with their wares: 'Mother, gain from market people; market people, lose to mother.'

The markets also have a vital social function, particularly in the rural areas, for they are attended by everyone and provide regular opportunities for meeting. This is especially valuable to the women, who would otherwise find leaving their villages on marriage a far more traumatic experience. Since they usually marry into neighbouring villages, market days serve as reunions for parted friends and relatives.

The intense competitiveness fostered by the markets, together with the community feeling they generate, is fundamental to the Ibo character. They are a highly self-reliant people, committed to improving themselves, but they also have powerful loyalties and the spirit of co-operation is marked. Most Ibo villages, for example, operate credit associations—voluntary savings organizations that force their members to pay regularly or lose what they have already saved. In this way an individual Ibo can both save quickly and, on occasion, borrow considerable sums of money from his association.

Another notable characteristic of the Ibo is their intolerance of imposed authority. Their own leaders do not inherit their power but must earn it. They are held firmly responsible to the community and can easily be replaced if they fail in their duties. This trait confused the British Colonial Office when they attempted to control Iboland through 'native' authorities, because they unwittingly regarded the more opportunist and forthcoming Ibo as established leaders and appointed them 'warrant chiefs'. Their lack of community support did little to promote good relationships with the British authorities.

The determined independence of the Ibo was illustrated most strikingly in 1929. The previous year Ibo men had been taxed for the first time in their history, after a general census of their property. When the authorities turned next to make a survey of women's property, the Ibo mistakenly assumed that they too were to be taxed and resistance was spontaneous. The Women's War (or Aba Riots, as the British government termed the uprising) left 32 women dead and 31 wounded; but it exposed the weaknesses of the system and speeded up reform.

Ibo society is essentially a 'grass roots democracy'. They have a saying that 'no-one knows the womb that bears the chief', plainly expressing the fluidity of their political system. The largest political unit used to be the village—even clusters of neighbouring villages co-operated only when it was convenient—and the village is still the strongest social unit. Each village community impresses on its members the importance of 'getting up', or advancing itself as a unit. Villagers will save communally to send their brightest children to high school and even to university; later they will expect them to return, or at least make a donation, to help the village improve itself.

This local pride and ambition has some incongruous results. Social amenities become status symbols and each village wants its own hospital, post office, school, church and market place. This inevitably results in unnecessary expenditure and over-production, but it is a trait so deeply ingrained in the Ibo character that even the Federal administration seems unlikely to hold it back. Community pressures are so strong that they affect personality at the most fundamental level: introspective or quiet Ibo are regarded as anti-social, failing in their duty to play a full part in the affairs of their village.

Yet the Ibo permeate almost every level of modern Nigerian life. As pressures on the land make agriculture a less likely way for a young man to 'get up', so more and more travel away from their villages and into the cities. Ibo are found in every trade and profession, and at every level. In 1966, when the corrupt and traditional leaders of the Nigerian Government were killed in an army coup, almost 50 per cent of the army officers were already Ibo.

Their qualities of great energy, determination and ambition combine with a fascination for administration and bureaucracy. Journalists in Biafra during the civil war were astonished to find administration dutifully being carried out even in the most severely damaged areas of the secessionist state. As the Federation's willingness to bind up the wounds of the past continues, and as the Ibo themselves learn to integrate their own qualities into the needs of a large political unit, Nigeria may well emerge in the last decades of the 20th century as the giant of Africa. □

Karamojong

UGANDA

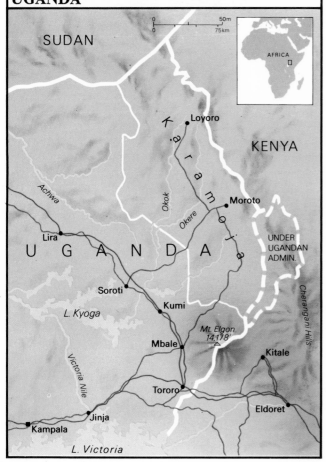

SUDAN

KENYA

Karamoja

Loyoro

Achwa

Okok

Okere

Moroto

UNDER
UGANDAN
ADMIN.

Lira

U G A N D A

Soroti

Kumi

L. Kyoga

Cherangani Hills

Mt. Elgon
14,178'

Mbale

Kitale

Victoria Nile

Tororo

Eldoret

Jinja

Kampala

L. Victoria

50m
75km

AFRICA

K aramoja is one of the last unspoilt wildernesses in Africa. It sprawls across the northeast corner of Uganda, bordering Kenya and the Sudan: wild, semi-desert, jagged with blue volcanic ranges, and crossed by wide, empty riverbeds of sand which proclaim that the countryside receives rain for only a very small part of the year.

Karamoja is occupied by five tribes, collectively known as the Karamojong. They are the Dodoth, the Jie, the Bokora, the Matheniko and the Pian—all physically very similar. They are all Nilo-Hamitics, which means that their ancestors came down from the north and may have had some connection with the peoples who once lived in ancient Egypt.

The chief occupation and the passion of the Karamojong is raiding. All the tribes are dedicated to raiding each-other and, when that palls or proves unprofitable, their Kenyan neighbours—particularly the Turkana and Pokot.

The purpose of Karamojong raids is always the same: to steal cattle. The actual pattern of warfare within the five tribes of Karamoja is very complicated. In the far north, Dodoth raid southwards, fairly lightly, against Jie and, of course, into Turkana country to the east. The Jie in turn steal cattle from Bokora and Matheniko, who also

Although spears are now illegal, most Karamojong still possess them—many of the weapons of these Napore tribesmen were made from government ploughs. As late as the 1960s, 500 deaths by spearing were recorded each year in Karamoja.

raid them. And the Matheniko generally raid their nearest neighbours over the Kenya border, the Turkana. The Pian, southernmost of the Karamojong, go raiding mainly against non-Karamojong neighbours.

Raiding might almost be described as a Karamojong national sport. Under British rule, many attempts were made to 'civilize' the territory and spears were made illegal, with fines imposed in money and cattle. Although money means very little to the Karamojong, cattle mean everything. They are cattle people, viewing their cows not only as wealth but as objects to be venerated with almost religious fervour. But fines, even when made in cattle, made very little impression. After several hundred head had been confiscated from the Pian and the Bokora by the British—as compensation paid to the Pokot for 106 of their tribe killed in raids—Karamojong warriors were heard to say: 'The Pokot have fertile grazing. We'll let them fatten up our cows for a month or two. Then we'll go and steal them back again.'

What has happened to the Karamojong in recent years is impossible to say. Even in the days of British rule in Uganda it was hard to get permission to travel freely in Karamoja because of the constant inter-tribal warfare.

With the coming of *Uhuru* (Independence), it became even more difficult. There was a very definite drive by former President Milton Obote to put these 'Stone-Age' people 'into long trousers'—a fairly common reaction to primitive, especially naked, tribes in emergent African nations. And stories filtering through concerning the tactics of President Amin's régime in Uganda suggest that, as far as the Karamojong are concerned, conversion to more modern ways has been at gunpoint. The stories of genocide remain to be confirmed, but what can be said with certainty is that the days of the proud Karamojong warrior are limited, if not over.

As with warrior pastoralist tribes, the traditional social organization of the Karamojong contains two completely separate life-styles—His and Hers. 'His' is a life of dandyism and, to a large degree, idleness. 'Hers' is one of childbearing and work. As among similar peoples, such as the Masai or Turkana, it would be beneath the dignity and station of an adult Karamojong male to be seen hewing wood or carrying water. Work is for women.

However, the women of Karamoja enjoy a definite status and the respect of their menfolk. They are by no means chattels. It is simply that they have a different way of life to pursue.

The homestead is predominantly the place for the women, the children and the old. A typical Jie homestead, for example, is like a small walled town. The seven-foot-high walls, perhaps 200 yards in circumference, are built from stakes driven into the ground and protected by thorn bushes. Before nightfall the milking cows and goats are driven into a thorn *boma* inside the main *kraal*. The narrow entrance in the outside wall is blocked with a dense tangle of thorn bushes.

Life in the homestead starts as soon as the sun is up and before the clouds of flies can worry the milking cows. Nights are often bitterly cold; the little children sleep on the hard earth under a single cow-hide cover. It is common to see these shivering children run on awakening to the first cow that lifts its tail, and stand beneath the cascade of steaming urine to warm their bodies.

Once the cows have been milked, the women shake the milk in gourds until it separates. The skim is either drunk or mixed with sorghum to form a crude form of porridge. The fat—called ghee—is kept for rubbing into their bodies or for mixing with fine black sand to ornament their hair.

Each woman has a small patch of land near the homestead, the senior wives reserving the closer allotments.

111

KARAMOJONG

Younger women often have to walk a mile or so into the bush to till their plots with primitive hoes made by the smiths who live away to the west in the Labwor Hills. Sorghum, the main crop, provides the Karamojong with flour and, when fermented, beer. They grow millet as well. The women also gather wild greens and roots. But they can only do this after the rains have brought the dry bushland briefly to life.

The children mind the few cows kept for milking. They also herd the goats, drive the stock to water, fetch water in large gourds and, when the crops ripen, stand all day in the sun on rickety wooden platforms, clapping their hands and cracking whips to drive the marauding doves away. Despite all this work, Karamojong children seem happy, laugh a lot and play when work allows. One of the favourite games for the boys is hurling wooden spears at wooden hoops bowled along the ground.

Most homesteads have a termite hill nearby, which is 'owned' by one of the women. Cooked termites are considered a great delicacy by the Karamojong. When the first rains fall, the winged insects emerge through the many holes in the heap to make their nuptial flights. The women cover their termite mounds with cowhide, held down by mud, and build a mud trap with only one exit through which the termites can see the light. The women drum on the cowhide to simulate the patter of rain. The termites hatch, fly towards the light and fall into the trap, whence they are scooped out by the handful. They are then fried in their own fat, and shaken on a sieve until the wings fall off. The cooked bodies are ravenously eaten, and are an important source of protein.

A warrior hands out gourds of 'pombe' or millet beer in the celebration before a wedding. Karamojong men are inveterate dandies and spend most of their time decorating themselves; their hair-styles sometimes take more than three days to complete.

Photographic Library of Australia

(Above) While Karamojong women and children take care of all domestic tasks at the homestead, the men are part of another world. Theirs is a nomadic life with the tribe's herds of cattle, travelling where grazing or water dictate.

(Below) In a small village near Moroto, a girl grinds millet into flour for cooking. The grain is stored in the raised granary in the background.

F. & H. Schreider/Photo Researchers

Inside the homestead, each wife has her strictly personal area which she builds and maintains herself, thatching the roofs with grasses, which are plentiful after the rains; or, in the dry season, plastering them with cow dung which lasts until the rains bring a fresh growth of grass. A wife's household consists of a hut for herself, another for the children, several granaries raised on stilts as protection against rain and animal thieves, and a kitchen that may serve as anything from a nursery to a goat house. The kitchen walls are not packed with mud but left open so that the smoke can escape. All this is usually confined within its own separate stockade.

The man's world is completely different. From the age of about 15 he belongs with the tribe's cattle, out in the bush, living a nomadic existence, moving when lack of grazing or water dictates, herding the cattle inside a rough thorn *boma* at night. This is also where he sleeps, on the ground, his head propped on a low wooden stool.

The basic diet of the Karamojong warrior is blood and milk. The blood is obtained from the jugular vein of a cow or ox. First its neck is bound with a leather thong to make the vein stand out. Then a special blunted wooden arrow is fired from close range, with the minimum power required to penetrate, into the vein. Blood rushes out into a gourd already half-filled with milk. When the gourd is filled, the thong is removed and wet mud plastered over the wound to stop the bleeding.

The Karamojong warrior is a tremendous dandy and indeed spends most of his time decorating himself. As an uninitiated man he wears his hair matted with red pigment and grease and sewn together with string made from a local wild sisal called *sanseveira*. This hair-do protrudes from the back of his head like an enormously elongated fez. In the past, initiation meant that a warrior had to kill an enemy and run the gauntlet of spears with sticks. Today the first requirement has been modified to spearing an ox in a ceremony to which only the men are admitted. Running the gauntlet has been ritualized to a light tapping with sticks by two or three of the elders.

After initiation, the young man assumes the full Karamojong regalia of painted clay head-dress, which often takes the hair-dresser three full days to complete. The first day's work is to pack the hair into a hard bun with a forked needle. Into the bun are worked wire tubes in which ostrich feathers will be stuck on ceremonial occasions. The second day consists of working the coloured clays into the bun. As the hair-dresser does not provide these, the client has to bring them with him.

Between sessions the client rests his head on his two-legged stool. On the third day the clay has dried and is ready for painting with coloured pigments and brushes made from ostrich feathers. Often a separate clay fore-piece is worn on the brow. Head-dresses among the five Karamojong tribes are very similar, but colour schemes vary. Quite often the older men, on going bald, save up enough hair-clippings to make a toupee.

Even before Independence came to Uganda, it was a comparative rarity to see a six-foot tall Karamojong armed with the long spear, without which the warriors look almost 'undressed'. Although spears were confiscated in order to try to cut down deaths in inter-tribal cattle raids, they always seem to make a miraculous appearance when needed, not only when raids are contemplated but when other tribal rites are performed.

Removing spears is but one symptom of an attempt to 'civilize' these warrior peoples. Another, and possibly more practical scheme, had a delightfully paradoxical effect on the armament industry of the Labwor—the metal-workers who live west of Karamoja. The British introduced a Karamoja cattle scheme to try to persuade the tribes to

With a gourd ready to catch the blood, a warrior aims a special blunt arrow at the jugular vein of an ox. A drink of half blood and half milk is the basic diet of the Karamojong men.

become ranchers and to sell their surplus cattle. With the money they got for their cattle, they were urged to buy modern steel ploughs. At first, government agricultural officers were delighted with their success. Ploughs appeared to be just what the Karamojong had always wanted. But then the truth dawned. The ploughs were disappearing westward into the Labwor Hills where the smiths re-forged the good steel and turned it into spear blades, perhaps the clearest instance on record of turning ploughshares into swords.

A major factor in the high incidence of cattle-raiding among the Karamojong is the high bride-price. To marry may cost a man 50 head of cattle and as many goats. Since no Karamojong warrior has riches of that order during his early manhood, the simplest way to equip himself is to go raiding across the tribal border.

A Karamojong betrothal is long. The period from betrothal to final marriage may be as long as five years. By the time she is finally married, a girl may have borne her betrothed four children, with her parents' knowledge and approval. Her style of dress reveals the stage that her courtship has reached. A young marriageable Jie girl, for example, wears a leather skirt over her buttocks and a short apron in front made of heavy chain.

If a girl bears a child when not officially wed, she builds a hut of her own within her mother's compound. If all the parties in both families, and the elders agree, she may then become 'engaged' to the father of her child. This is the point at which the bridegroom usually makes a down-payment of, perhaps, five head of cattle. Once this is done,

he has marital rights over the girl, though he is expected to complete the full payment as soon as possible. If he cannot raise the down-payment, then he just has to wait until he can. In the meantime, anyone else more rich or suitable may marry the girl. Very few young men are ever capable of raising the full bride-price themselves, usually they gather 20 or 30 head of cattle over a period and rely on friends or relatives, who are interested in seeing the union completed for reasons of blood ties or increasing the family herds, to provide the rest.

Early on in the courtship, the young man visits his girl's family *kraal*, bringing with him male friends and relatives in full regalia and driving ahead of them some of the best of their oxen or cows. This ceremony, which is called *Akimuj* among the Jie, is designed to impress the bride's family. The bridegroom's party advance, posturing and making mock battle charges in the direction of the women, including the bride, who come out to greet them. The cattle are then driven into the *kraal* and everyone sits down and drinks milk and beer just as at any other engagement party.

Once the initial payment of cattle has been made, the girl changes her dress to a bulky apron of bamboo grass. Later still, when she achieves full marital status, she changes this for the more elaborate leather apron and full skirt of a married woman.

The tragedy of such people as the Karamojong is that they have gained nothing from the so-called improvements brought to them by 'civilization'. Instead they have lost a way of life – indeed, with political developments in Uganda, many of them are likely to have lost life itself. Even without the damage inflicted on them by direct violence it is doubtful whether peoples like the Karamojong can be integrated, except as a curiosity, with the needs and pressures of a modern society. ☐

Kikuyu
KENYA

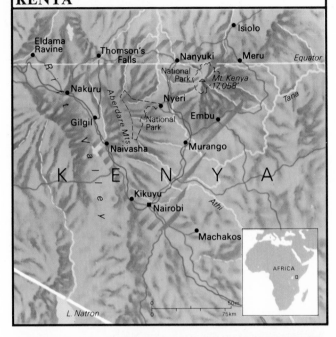

There was once a great medicine man among the Kikuyu, whose name was Mogo wa Kebiro. Widely revered for his mystic powers, he came to make an astounding prophesy. One night in a vision Mogo saw strangers with skin like that of a pale frog, who came into his land carrying magical sticks which spat fire; behind them came a huge iron snake, with legs like a centipede, which was indestructible.

This nightmare experience was profoundly shocking. Mogo woke up trembling and covered with bruises. Only after the tribal elders had sacrificed on his behalf could he be coaxed into speech. And when he did finally speak, he warned the elders of what was to come, of a fate they would be powerless to resist. His fears were justified some years later, towards the end of the 19th century, when the first White men were seen in the Kikuyu homelands; soon afterwards a railway from Mombasa to Lake Victoria brought the first of many 'iron snakes' into their country.

This story is related in a book called *Facing Mount Kenya*, written in the 1930s by a determined Kikuyu student who called himself Jomo Kenyatta. Twenty years later this same man emerged from a prison camp in the desolate village of Lokitaung in northern Kenya to lead the tribes of his country to independence. The struggle with the British colonial authorities, which had lasted for more than half a century, was led by the Kikuyu —Kenya's largest tribe.

Britain had laid claim to Kenya during the European 'scramble' for Africa of the 1880s; the railway which would carry the imperial apparatus from Mombassa to the Ugandan Highlands had reached the papyrus swamp called Nairobi before the turn of the century. This happened at a time when the fortunes of the Kikuyu were at a low ebb—famine and small-pox had depleted the tribe in the years 1897–9, and forced them to retreat from their boundaries.

The railway had a decisive impact on the Kikuyu. Nairobi was used as a supply station and expanded rapidly, soon to become the administrative centre for a new colony. Then the authorities started encouraging British citizens to come out and settle, to stimulate the growth of the Colony. They were drawn by the splendid plateau rising north of Nairobi towards Mount Kenya—which seemed strangely empty – and the authorities began to advertise vast tracts of the land for farming.

In 1905 there were perhaps 150 white settlers in Kenya, but a slow trickle built up into the torrent which had brought 20,000 to an African 'land of opportunity' by 1948. As they moved further into the White Highlands, so they took more and more land from the Kikuyu, confining them to a tribal reserve.

The effect of this confinement was inevitably destructive. The Kikuyu farming methods required large amounts of land, for they did not rotate their crops. The new confinement forced them to plant repeatedly in the same soil, exhausting its natural richness; as their population grew, poverty became common and many young men were forced to leave the reserve to seek work in the White community.

Off-reserve Africans were subjected to the degrading 'Kipande' system of registration, and forced to carry identity certificates. At first they were hired as servants in Nairobi, or as labourers on the settlers' farms, but as small industries were set up, many more were taken on by

Kikuyu women meet at a local market. The Kikuyu today number more than 2 million, and are Kenya's dominant tribe. They control the government and many of the strategic institutions in the country, including the Central Bank and the police force.

John Bulmer

the factories. These industrial workers were often obliged to live in appalling housing and separated from their families.

The indifference of the settlers to the damage they were doing, however, and their failure to understand Kikuyu society, meant that they had little prospect of getting their rule accepted by the tribes they sought to govern. And it was the Kikuyu, with their homelands so temptingly close to Nairobi, who suffered most severely. For the colonists had stolen the very source of their social organi-

zation—the land itself.

The earth has a mystic value for the Kikuyu and many of their rituals emphasize this fact. Unlike their Masai neighbours, who are nomadic and live almost entirely off the meat, milk and blood of their livestock, the Kikuyu have always been cultivators. Their traditional social system, therefore, was directly related to the land and the demands of agriculture. Even children were encouraged to farm small plots of land. In rural areas today, life continues in much the same way: the main crops being

only when the offender showed repentance by providing a feast.

The Kikuyu also place great emphasis on the family. Traditionally, an expanding family meant increasing wealth, for with each new wife a Kikuyu would be able to farm more land. Modern conditions have inevitably altered things—greater industrialization and a cash-economy provide alternative routes to wealth—but many Kikuyu attitudes and beliefs still relate to the value of a large family. For example, a strong sense of communion with the ancestors is a stimulus to family life. It is considered vital to continue the line, so that the continuum of existence may not be broken.

Each time a man marries, his first duty is to provide a home for his new wife; here again, communal help is called for in the rural areas. Kikuyu believe that the hut must be built in a single day—though preparations may be made over a longer period—and so friends and neighbours assist. Huts are round, with wooden walls, and grass-thatched roofs: the men dig the trenches and build the walls, the women thatch the roof.

But if their agricultural life itself encourages social cohesion, Kikuyu tribal organization is further streng-

(Left) Kikuyu in ceremonial dress wait to greet President Kenyatta during a visit to their village. A rich traditional life is still maintained, particularly in the country areas, despite rapid industrialization since the Second World War.

(Below) Kikuyu women pick amongst the wares at a market near Nairobi. Increasing population density, and the consequent shortage of land, has encouraged the formation of a large urban proletariat which now poses serious problems for the Government.

John Bulmer

Marion Kaplan

maize, beans, sweet potatoes and vegetables, while coffee and European potatoes have become increasingly important to the economy. In some areas yams, sugar-cane and bananas are also grown.

Agriculture normally demands communal labour, and the Kikuyu have always laid great stress on mutual help. When a man wants to dig or weed his field, he calls on his neighbours to help him and, in turn, he will assist his neighbours whenever requested. To ignore a request for help is to invite social ostracism, which would be overcome

John Bulmer

The exceptional fertility and beauty of their home-lands helps to explain the mystical attachment the Kikuyu feel for the earth. Unlike their Masai neighbours, the Kikuyu have long been farmers, and keep cattle mainly for prestige.

thened by the life-long process of initiation undergone by the men. The four most important stages are circumcision, marriage, fatherhood and the circumcision of the first son. The strength of this system lies in the principle of age-grading: each Kikuyu is born into a particular age-set within which strong bonds are developed, particularly at the stage of circumcision. The traditional practice was for both girls and boys to undergo circumcision in ceremonies held annually. Periods of preparation and celebration surrounded the ceremony and it was then that the young Kikuyu were initiated ritually into adult membership of the tribe.

The practice of female circumcision was the subject of bitter controversy in the 1920s, when the Christian missionaries, considering it a barbarous and unnecessary act, launched a propaganda campaign against it. They did not understand the value attached to it by the Kikuyu as a foundation of their social organization, marking both the graduation of a child into adulthood, and providing each age-set with a shared experience which could bind them together with exceptional loyalty.

The impact of Christianity was powerful, nonetheless, and many Kikuyu were converted from their tribal belief

in *Ngai*, the founder and creator of all things. The missionaries also opposed the tribal custom of oathing—taking ritual oaths at times of great solemnity, which it was unthinkable to break. Sometimes accompanied by the sacrifice of a sheep, these oaths were regarded as blasphemous.

The success of the missionaries, particularly through their schools, brought a reaction from Kikuyu who preferred the traditional ways. During the 1930s they set up many independent schools to provide an alternative education, and these quickly became identified with the pressure groups which had begun to push for more political power in the colony.

Demands for better treatment from the settlers grew throughout the 1930s, but the drive for African independence gained its decisive thrust from the events of the Second World War. Thousands of Kenyan Africans, many of them Kikuyu, were conscripted by the British. They were to have the salutary experience of helping one colonial power dislodge another, for they were part of the army which restored Haile Selassie to his throne in Ethiopia.

The soldiers returned to Nairobi at the end of the War to find that the colony was again calling for settlers, and offering alienated lands to ex-servicemen—but only Europeans. For the landless Kikuyu there was the prospect of more unemployment and housing shortages. In 1946 another significant event took place—the return from Europe of Jomo Kenyatta.

Political activity within Kenya had grown during the War years, notably with the foundation of the Kenya African Union. The leaders of Kenya's largest tribes had realized the need for unity if they were to achieve their common goal, but Kikuyu dominance in the party was marked. In Kenyatta, however, they all saw a man who could transcend tribal differences.

Though an elder of his tribe, his position was by no means easy. Kenyatta's authority was based on political skills, not on traditional status. Yet he remained committed to the traditional ways, so far as he thought possible. Furthermore, Kikuyu society was deteriorating badly, with a considerable amount of crime and violence. Younger men were turning towards militant action as the route to freedom, dividing the tribe.

The culmination of this unrest was the Emergency, declared in 1952, when 'Freedom Fighters' went to the forests which skirt the Kikuyu territories to carry out a guerilla campaign under the name Mau-Mau. Only 32 Europeans were killed during the Emergency—about the same as died in road accidents in Nairobi during the same period—but nearly 15,000 Africans were killed in fierce fighting between the Mau-Mau and the 'loyalists'. The KAU was banned at the very start of the fighting, and Kenyatta himself convicted of leading the Mau-Mau. After a dubious trial he was sentenced to 8 years imprisonment in the north of the country.

The Emergency convinced the British government of one thing: Kenya proceeded to majority, and therefore African, rule. KANU, a new political party, was formed in 1960, based on an alliance of the Kikuyu with the Luo, Kenya's second-largest tribe. Kenyatta was immediately elected president—he had completed his sentence and the Government was forced to accept him. Elections to decide who would rule the independent country went overwhelmingly in KANU's favour. On December 12, 1963, the official ceremonies marked the end of colonial rule.

Harambee, the Swahili word for 'pull together', was Kenyatta's slogan for independence, and the problem he faced was plainly to preserve the unity of the different tribes which had enabled them to win their freedom. By

Jomo Kenyatta, President of Kenya since Independence in 1963, has a charismatic appeal for nearly all Kenyans. The country's unity depends on his ability to transcend tribal differences.

Christianity is one of the major legacies of British rule in Kenya, and white weddings are common. But as early as the 1930s many Kikuyu set up independent schools to combat the missionary influence.

appointing the Luo leader Odinga Vice-President of Kenya, he went some way towards that goal. But events since 1963 suggest that the stability for which Kenya is admired may not survive her first president.

The fundamental problem is the tribal rivalry. Despite Kenyatta's olympian posture, the smaller tribes fear Kikuyu domination. The Kikuyu are the best educated tribe and the most experienced politically, as well as the most numerous. Inevitably, their hold on the top political posts is out of all proportion to their numbers. In 1970, for example, 6 of the cabinet of 22 were Kikuyu. The tribe provided 9 of the 22 Permanent Secretaries in the Civil Service, as well as heading the police, the Central Bank of Kenya and the University of Nairobi. Yet in a Kenyan population of about 13 million, the Kikuyu number only just over 2 million.

A constant source of grievance has concerned land-ownership. As the new government took back alienated land, the question of its redistribution became all-important. The government has accepted the principle that market forces should govern redistribution, but the radicals object that rich Kenyans, among them several cabinet ministers, have managed to buy up large estates, while the number of unemployed and vagrant Africans in Nairobi continues to grow. The radicals demand controlled re-settlement in the reclaimed areas and the creation of a prescribed limit to individual holdings.

The pressure for greater regional autonomy—which would effectively mean greater tribal autonomy—has been resisted by the ruling KANU party. And although Kenyatta has refused to legislate for a single-party state in Kenya's constitution, attempts to form opposition parties have found him such an uncompromising opponent that they have crumbled.

The danger is clearly that a multi-party system might encourage tribal division, even if designed only to allow opposition. In 1966 the former Vice-President, Oginga Odinga, founded the KPU to provide a radical opposition party; in 1969, however, it became the focus for Luo tribal activity when Tom Mboya, a leading Luo member of KANU, was assassinated by a Kikuyu. Rioting broke out and 11 people were killed when Kenyatta visited the Luo homelands; soon afterwards Odinga was arrested and the KPU banned.

The Kikuyu cannot, of course, return to their old methods of social organization—they are part of a wider community and the conditions of their society are irrevocably changed. The demands of a technological society make talented men of any age more valuable than the traditional elders. Nevertheless the paternalism of the older order remains deeply ingrained, and the fierceness with which loyalty is demanded poses a severe threat to the harmony of the Kikuyu themselves.

In March 1975 Josiah Kariuki, a strong critic of the establishment and a leading contender for the succession to the Presidency, was found murdered in a forest near Nairobi. There was considerable suspicion of government collusion. Many people believed that Kariuki had been assassinated not just because he opposed the establishment, but because he came from the northern area of Kikuyu territory—not, like Kenyatta, from Kiambu, the 'spiritual home' of the tribe.

With growing industrial production, the Kikuyu are increasingly faced by the conflict between their traditional ways and the ideas of the outside world. Some of the leaders, and Kenyatta in particular, seek a middle way, an adaption which can enable them to maintain their tribal identity without losing their unity. The difficulties of living in a post-colonial era may prove even more testing than the struggle for independence.   □

Kongo
ZAIRE, ANGOLA

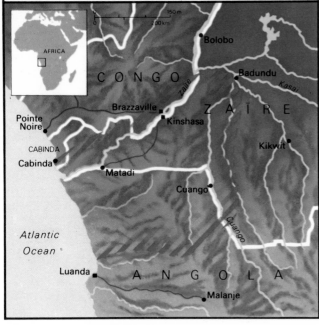

(Left) *A Kongo carving of a supernatural being.*

This small settlement stands on the north bank of the Zaire River which divides Kongo territory.

In the last 200 miles before it reaches the sea, the mighty Zaire River (once known as the Congo) passes through a series of spectacular rapids known as the Livingstone Falls. On either side of the Zaire was the territory of the once-powerful African kingdom of Kongo and today it still forms the homeland of the Kongo people.

The first contact between the Kongo and the Western world took place in 1482 when the Portuguese navigator, Diego Cam, landed in the estuary of the Zaire River. He was told of the royal capital of Kongo, which lay some 150 miles inland. Three years later Cam returned to the area bringing with him envoys from the King of Portugal in order to make contact with the Kongolese court. On Cam's homeward voyage, Kongolese envoys journeyed with him to Lisbon.

The Portuguese found in Kongo a strong centralized state, ruled by a king with the aid of a council of ministers and other political functionaries. Legal and judicial institutions were also well developed. The king's power had both a spiritual and temporal base, as he was the religious leader of the kingdom and also the head of a standing army. Taxes and tribute financed the structure; slavery provided the labour force.

For the next 80 years relationships between Kongo and Portugal flourished. A succession of Kongolese kings embraced Christianity, seeking help from Portugal and later the Vatican to convert the population. Craftsmen, artisans, schoolteachers and priests were invited to help modernize the Kongolese capital. Portuguese soldiers helped consolidate and extend Kongo's political supremacy along the coastal regions.

In return the Portuguese secured exclusive trading rights in the region—slaves being the principal commodity. At one time every European in Kongo was exclusively

John Moss/Colorific!

to be published in an African language was started amongst the Kongo.

The Kongo people no longer form a centrally organized political unit, but rather a loose federation of autonomous tribes. Their feeling of group identity is, however, very strong and this is grounded above all in their claims, real or imagined, to originate in the 15th century state of Kongo. The Kongo live in permanent village settlements —an average-sized village containing about 300 people. Kongo villages are laid out on a grid pattern with houses in neat rows. Most houses are rectangular in shape and constructed of brick either sun-dried or fired in the village kiln. Many are nowadays roofed with tin, although straw and palm thatch are still common.

The social structure of the villages is governed by two main principles—kinship and land ownership. In regions where the original migrating family group remained intact, all the villages are linked in a kinship relationship. Each village is composed mainly of close kinsmen and their dependants. Leadership, whether at village or regional

(Left) Kongo steel-erectors at work on the new railway bridge across the Zaire River. The expansion of road and rail communications is providing an increasing number of jobs for Kongo men.

(Right) A young boy helps his mother with the household chores. The Kongo live in rectangular brick buildings with roofs of thatch or tin. Villages are usually laid out in rows, on a grid pattern.

(Below) Ancestor-worship forms the basis of Kongo religion, and the Kongo rely on ritual specialists like this man to intercede with the ancestors on their behalf.

engaged in the trade. In their ruthless pursuit of slaves, the Portuguese made use of different factions in the kingdom, turning one against the other and undermining the position of the king. Soon relationships between Kongo and Portugal began to deteriorate.

Finally Portuguese interest shifted away from Kongo altogether, leaving the kingdom seriously divided. In this weakened state the Kongo fell easy prey to an invasion of warriors, known as the Jaga, who emerged from the deep interior. The break-up of the kingdom of Kongo marked the beginning of a gradual migration northwards across the River Zaire into the territory beyond. These migrations took place on a broad front and the Kongo today occupy a broad block of territory, bounded on the west by the Atlantic Ocean and on the east by a line which runs roughly north to south, embracing the major cities of Kinshasa and Brazzaville.

Formerly known as Leopoldville, and once the capital of the Belgian Congo, Kinshasa is the administrative centre for a vast area of central Africa, the Republic of Zaire, while Brazzaville on the opposite bank is the capital of what was once the French Congo. Both these cities are transfer posts for the large amount of trade travelling along the River Zaire and its many tributaries—to avoid the impassable Livingstone Falls, all goods must be taken the last 200 miles to the coast by rail.

The Kongo have not been slow to take advantage of the economic development of their territory; many have found work in the cities and the Kongo have become prominent in the national affairs not only of Zaire, but also of Angola, where they were closely involved with one of the liberation movements. Their territory is well served with government and mission hospitals and schools. The standard of literacy is high and one of the first magazines

Richard Diamond/John McCallin

level, is governed by seniority in the kinship system. Elsewhere, however, where groups of unrelated people have come together, leadership is granted to the 'owners of the land'—in other words, the original settlers of the territory.

Power among the living is very closely linked to power among the dead, and ancestor-worship forms the core of Kongo religion. The world of the dead is the mirror image of the world of the living and the ancestors of the Kongo are believed to retain a strong interest in the land where they once lived. In order to succeed in any enterprise, a Kongo must obtain the blessing of his ancestors and maintain their goodwill through the correct performance of his duties.

Intercession with the ancestors takes place at different levels. Each household, for example, will have its own shrine where the household head prays and makes offerings to the ancestors on behalf of the family house. At village level the headman undertakes duties to the ancestors on behalf of the whole community. Regional chiefs will likewise intercede on behalf of the wider social grouping under their control.

The subjects of the Kongo chiefs are nowadays a farming people. Although a great variety of crops are grown, manioc can be considered the staple. Both the root and the leaves of the plant are eaten; the leaves are boiled to make a delicious nutty-flavoured dish which looks like spinach, but the roots need more preparation. They must first be scraped, soaked for several days, then laid out to dry before being pounded into flour. The flour is then boiled to make an elastic dough known as *fou-fou*. Groundnuts, maize, rice, various kinds of bean, peas, tomatoes, aubergines and peppers are also commonly grown. A species of hot pepper known as *pili-pili* is

widely used as a flavouring and relish. Cultivated items are supplemented by a great variety of herbs, roots, wild fruits, honey and such products, which are foraged from the countryside, while no village is complete without a grove of oil-palms from which palm wine is made and oil is extracted for cooking.

As in many other tribal communities in Africa, Kongo women are responsible for agricultural production, the men only assisting in heavy work, such as tree-felling for land clearance. There are, however, a few crops which are male responsibilities—these include sugar cane, tobacco and Indian hemp.

Although much of the Kongo region is suitable for grazing, few cattle are raised on the farms. Domestic animals receive little attention and wander freely around the village and its environs. If there is danger from wild animals, leopards in particular, then livestock may be penned in at night. Meat is chiefly provided by hunting and fishing rather than from the slaughter of livestock. Hunting is an exclusively male activity although women may take part as beaters on communal hunts in the savannah regions. Fishing, on the other hand, is not confined to either sex, and groups of men and women work together to net the variety of fish which abound in the rapids of the Zaire River.

Among the Kongo there is no distinct class of hunters, as is the case with some neighbouring tribes. However, the many specialized skills required for successful hunting—such as training dogs, making and maintaining weapons (including magnificent flintlock rifles), making traps and snares and the knowledge of animal behaviour and habits—effectively limit this activity to a few men in each village who undertake to provide meat for the whole community.

Most surplus produce is traded through a large network of weekly local markets. Marketing is mainly a female activity and it gives the women a fair degree of economic independence from the men. The markets are well-organized affairs where goods of all kinds are traded for agricultural produce. In some areas, however, the more enterprising men group together to purchase a lorry which they then use to transport goods directly to and from the major urban markets.

Each Kongo market place is controlled by a 'chief of the market' who has a kind of police force at his disposal. In some of the major regional markets, which attract people from many miles around, it is essential to guarantee the safety of all those taking part. Everyone is free to buy and sell in the markets, but anyone who comes bearing arms will be refused access unless he surrenders them to the officials. To denote the neutrality of the market place a rifle is ceremonially buried. The religious character of the markets is symbolized by a sacred tree planted, it is said, over the grave of a criminal who was buried alive. Many important initiation ceremonies, and sometimes also courts of justice, are held at the markets. In the old days the penalties for breaking any of the rules of the market place were very severe and the death penalty could be exacted for such offences as fighting, theft, or spreading scandal.

The traditional systems of law-making and justice among the Kongo have now largely been superseded by the judiciaries of the three countries whose borders divide their territory—Congo, Zaire and Angola. The two large cities of Kinshasa and Brazzaville similarly dominate Kongo trading and business life, providing employment for many but further changing tribal life-styles. Yet despite these new developments, the Kongo retain a deep sense of unity which gives them great strength in shaping their future. □

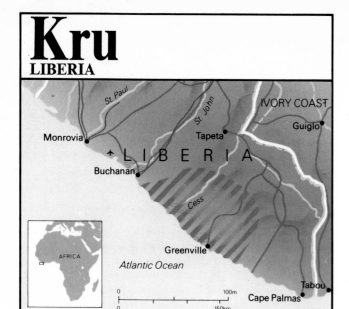

Kru
LIBERIA

Palmas, and extending to the northeast border of the Republic and neighbouring areas of the Ivory Coast. Their lands are sparsely settled—they number about 400,000, a quarter of Liberia's population—and the home territory of the Kru proper, who number about 85,000 in Liberia, stretches along the coast from Grand Cess to River Cess.

Despite their renown as seafarers, Kru traditions say they came from the interior, possibly from the source of the great Niger River. They were probably in their present territory by the 16th century; by the 18th century they were already working on the European ships. This was during the period of the notorious slave trade, when the Kru are said to have extracted a promise from the European traders that Kru should not be taken as slaves. In return, they permitted slaves from the interior to be brought across their territory. The traditional Kru facial tattoo—a vertical line down the centre of the forehead, said to represent a ship's mast—was adopted at this time so that Kru could be identified by the slavers.

During the second half of the 19th century, when sail gave way to steam, ships called more frequently and regularly along the Kru coast, using surf-boats to load palm-kernels, palm oil, pepper and ivory, and also taking on gangs of men. The traders considered the Kru tough, loyal and dependable. They worked as able-bodied seamen, and also at discharging and loading vessels along the coast, to spare the White seamen prolonged exposure to the African sun and the fevers of the mangrove swamps. Kru were invaluable as coastal pilots, providing crucial information about safe anchorages and convenient watering places. By this time their favoured employment was on the British mail-boats, which had regular sailings and guaranteed a not-too-distant return to the Kru coast.

The Kru people of Liberia are famous as mariners. For centuries they have served aboard European and American trading ships as sailors, cooks and interpreters, and ashore as lightermen, dock-hands, warehousemen and shipyard artisans. Life at sea is still a normal part of growing up for large numbers of Kru men, even for those who later find other occupations. There are few among those who today are civil servants, teachers, doctors and politicians whose fathers, uncles or grandfathers never sailed on the ships plying up and down the West African coast.

The Kru are one of a group of people which includes the Bassa, De, Grebo and Krahn. Between them, they occupy more than half the territory of the Republic of Liberia, encompassing the coastal area from Monrovia to Cap

A Kru fisherman steers his canoe out to sea. There is no coastal road through Kru territory, and many journeys are still made by dugout canoe—which can often be hazardous in bad weather.

Ian Berry/Magnum

Travellers on the coastal steamers of the 19th century give graphic accounts of recruiting on the Kru coast. As a steamer cast anchor off-shore, a fleet of canoes would launch towards it dancing like corks on the surface of the water. A crowd of men would invade the ship, offering their services. The captain would choose a headman from among them—perhaps a man he already knew—whose job it would be to select the number of men needed. Several young boys were usually taken on, as well as adults, to serve as 'rice-choppers'. They received no pay but were responsible for preparing food for the men during the voyage and, on the way home, for looking after the stores of cloth, guns, gin and utensils which the seamen acquired *en voyage*.

Some gangs travelled with the ships as far south as Luanda, a trip which could take many months. On the vessel's return voyage they would usually disembark at their home towns, but a few sometimes went on to Europe or America, replacing White seamen who had fallen sick on the journey. A migrant's return home was an occasion for great rejoicing, not least because of the gifts which he would bring to his family and to the town elders. After a period at home, spent carrying out rough work on the farm or fishing, a man would sail off again. Commonly he would spend his life from early youth, when he might make his first voyage as a rice-chopper, to middle age journeying down coast every other year and sometimes staying to work at trading depots ashore, before retiring to join the company of elders.

The Kru home territory stretches inland from a long and beautiful sand-dune beach, interrupted from time to time by rocky outcrops and by the estuaries of the rivers which run from the interior uplands towards the coast. These rivers are not bridged at the coast, and there is no road connecting the Kru townships which nestle among the palm-trees behind the shore-line. Communication between them, or between them and Monrovia or Cap Palmas, used to be made on foot or by sea, sometimes in simple dug-out canoes—a dangerous journey taking them 12 to 15 miles out into the boisterous Atlantic. Today a road connects Greenville with Monrovia, but it follows a long and circuitous route through Zwedru in the interior.

The population of Kru townships varies from a few hundred to several thousand. In the past each township (with its outlying hamlets) was independent, under the authority of its own chief (the *koloba* or 'father of the town'), and the elders of the various clans, or *pantons*, which made up the community. There was no political authority above the *koloba*, although groups of towns were linked together, by dialect and by traditions of migration, from the interior, to form *dako* or sub-tribes.

Today, the towns are part of the Republic's administrative system. Many have both a traditional section where farmers and fishermen live in rectangular houses with mud or plaited mat walls and thatch or corrugated iron roofs, and a newer 'municipality' where houses are modern and more elaborate, often with several stories. Government and municipality employees normally live in this section. Many of the larger houses were built in the 1930s, when foreign firms—English, German, Dutch and Swiss—were opening stores and building warehouses along the coast, employing local Kru as buyers, store clerks and checkers.

The degree of prosperity enjoyed on the Kru Coast declined when a new deep-water port was constructed at Monrovia during the Second World War. It had already become common for Kru men to join ships in Freetown; more recently many gangs have been taken on in Monrovia. Few foreign traders returned to the Kru Coast after the war, and trading ships no longer anchor off-shore. Recent economic developments in Liberia—the expansion of iron-mining and the construction of a new major port at Buchanan—have by-passed the Kru Coast, which is now

Market women greet the return of a fishing fleet to Greenville. The Kru are renowned as fishermen, and paddle up to 10 miles out into the Atlantic to catch snapper, barracuda and shark.

Ian Berry/Magnum

one of the most isolated parts of the Republic.

There is little wage employment locally. Transport difficulties hamper the development of large-scale cash crops. Because of the absence of most of the young men—at sea, at school, or at work in Monrovia or on the Firestone rubber plantation at Harbel—the bulk of the work on family farms is carried out by women. They grow rice, cassava and peanuts and keep a few goats and chickens.

Formerly, the Kru seamen were eager to return to their home towns after travelling abroad. But since the 1930s, a great many have settled abroad where wage-employment is more easily found, and they have been joined by their wives and children. Indeed the *kpafoka* (those who have settled abroad) are almost certainly more numerous now than the inhabitants of the Kru Coast.

Monrovia contains the largest of these 'colonies', as the Kru call them. When the Americo-Liberians arrived in 1821 there was already a small community of Kru fishermen and seamen at the foot of Cap Medurado. Today, Kru people in Monrovia follow many occupations and live, interspersed with other ethnic groups, in most parts of the city. Those who continue in maritime employment naturally choose to live near the port area, where several 'Krutowns' have grown up.

With characteristic adaptability, the Kru have developed a new form of organization to suit urban life. They have grouped themselves in a 'Kru Corporation' which acts from time to time as labour union, keeper of law and order, and provider of social services. At its head is the Kru 'Governor'—the term is borrowed presumably from

The Kru governor sits below a photograph of President Tubman. Liberia was the first independent Black African state, but has always depended heavily on American investment—the national flag is based on the 'Stars and Stripes'.

British colonial practice. In Monrovia, he is assisted by seven councillors, each representing a *dako* or sub-tribe. Each *dako* also has a chairman responsible for his own people who settles disputes and carries out welfare activities.

A regular source of finance for the Corporation and *dako* treasuries are the dues collected from seamen when they return from their voyages. A similar type of organization has developed among the Kru of Freetown. The Corporations are still tribal in membership, but they are an urban phenomena, drawing people from all parts of the Kru coast into a new community which in some senses takes the place of the old lineage and age-set system.

Women also have shown adaptability in evolving a new way of life in the city. They can no longer grow much of the family food, for there is little cultivable land in the vicinity of the urban 'Krutowns', but some have been able to get an education and enter wage-employment, although the chance of educational advancement is much slimmer for women than for men. Many have taken up trading, with great success—selling fish, peppers, rice and other vegetables—and a wife who can turn household income into trading capital is greatly esteemed, and gains new authority and independence.

Until recently, the Kru have stood outside the Liberian social hierarchy. They seldom sent their children to be brought up in *élite* families, formerly the main avenue to individual economic, educational and social progress in Liberia. For this reason they have only recently been involved in the gradual incorporation of the indigenous Liberian peoples—particularly the peoples of the coastal area—into the Americo-Liberian *élite*. In the last few decades, however, and particularly since other West African countries attained independence from colonial rule, they have entered the Liberian civil service in increasing numbers and many have achieved prominence in government, in the universities and in the professions. □

Ian Berry/Magnum

Malinke
MALI, SENEGAL AND GUINEA

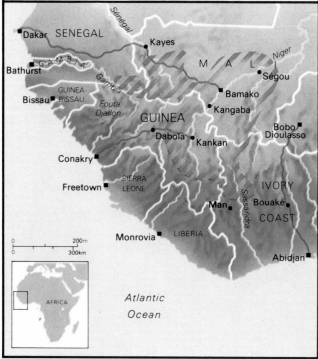

The Malinke, Bambara and other Manding peoples of West Africa are famous for their rich musical heritage. Their bards, or *dyeli*, preserve in song and recitation the history of their folk-heroes and the musical traditions of the ancient Mali empire. Individual bards specialize in the playing of different instruments, like the elaborate *kora*, or 21-string harp-lute of the Malinke, the more rugged *ngoni*, or 4-string lute of the Bambara once used to urge on warriors in battle, and the *bala* or Manding xylophone.

All these instruments, and others, were described by the first European to reach the Manding heartland at the end of the 18th century, the Scottish explorer Mungo Park. Park was as impressed by the rich musical culture of the Manding as he was by their hospitality. The continuation of that culture is reflected in the fact that no less than four West African nations have adopted traditional Manding themes as the basis of their national anthems.

The Malinke (or Mandinka) and Bambara are the two largest of a network of related peoples speaking dialects of the same Manding language. Today, the Manding-speaking peoples represent an important part of the population of nine African states. They extend from The Gambia in the west to Upper Volta in the east, and from the desert margins of Mali in the north to the humid forests of the Ivory Coast in the south.

The name 'Manding', of which Malinke is a corruption, is derived from the name of a small mountainous area astride the present-day borders of Mali and Guinea, from which most of the Manding-speaking peoples trace their historical expansion. This Manding heartland, once rich in wild game, lies at a strategic point along the fertile course of the Niger River and has deposits of iron and gold which provided an early source of wealth for the local population. It formed the centre of the vast medieval empire of Mali, which dominated the larger part of West Africa.

The most famous Mali Emperor was Mansa Musa, who after his pilgrimage to Mecca in 1324 distributed gold so lavishly in Cairo that he flooded the market so that the value was seriously affected. Long after his death he was commemorated by inclusion in several early European maps, his kingdom standing in the middle of an otherwise uncharted Africa.

The Emperor most frequently remembered among the Malinke and Bambara today, and whose praises are most widely sung by their bards, is Sundiata, the 'lion-king' who first established the Mali Empire in the early 13th century. As a result of Sundiata's conquests the Manding language, economic power and tightly-knit social system spread far in all directions.

Neither clan nor caste is really adequate to describe the Manding social system, which can no more be compared to the 'clans' of Scotland than to the 'castes' of India. There is the *dyamu* or patrilineage, whose members share a common name and common prohibitions (such as a taboo on eating their particular 'totemic' animal), while there is also the *nyamakala* or 'craft group', embracing patrilineages or branches of patrilineages, traditionally associated with a specific craft or profession. The *dyamu* has been important in integrating the Manding-speaking world, as individuals sharing the same patrilineal name traditionally accord each other hospitality

The mosque now dominates life in Djenne. Of the two main Manding peoples, the Malinke have been more profoundly affected by Islam than the Bambara. The religious laxity of the Bambara caused the orthodox Fula reformer al-Hajj Umar to launch a religious war against them in the 19th century.

wherever they may meet.

The Manding *dyamu* include the two noble patrilineages of Keita and Traore: Sundiata and subsequent emperors of Mali bore the name of Keita, and it is significant that the first two presidents of the Republic of Mali have been a Keita and a Traore, respectively. But other *dyamu* are associated with particular craft groups, such as the Dyabate and the Kuyate, who frequently belong to the important 'guild' of Manding bards. The two other main craft groups are the smiths working with iron, gold or silver, and the leatherworkers. Peasant-farmers have their own patrilineages, but are normally outside the craft group system or *nyamakala*.

Bards are a special craft group. From all over the thousand mile-wide Manding-speaking area, from points over a thousand miles apart, they maintain their ritual solidarity by gathering every seven years at the small town of Kangaba, in the Republic of Mali, for a ceremony which is both secret and ancient.

Kangaba, near the banks of the Upper Niger, is in the very centre of the Manding heartland. At first sight, it appears a typical farming community in an area where the northern savannah merges with the more wooded country further south. The buildings are either mud-walled compounds, square houses roofed with corrugated iron, or the more traditional round houses roofed with thatch. It is one of these small round houses, only a few feet in diameter, which is the focus of the bards' seven-yearly gathering, marking the central point of the whole Manding world. Known as the *kama-blon* or 'sacred vestibule', this unique house is ceremonially re-roofed by the assembled

(Above) The Dyula people, of part-Malinke, part-Bambara origin, are the main Manding traders. Their language is the lingua franca of merchants in many West African states where the Dyula sell goods like these richly coloured cloths.

(Right) A National Dairy Board using modern equipment has encouraged traditional herders to boost production by improving the quality of their cattle. Like other peoples of West Africa the Malinke did not milk their cattle until the practice was introduced by Fulani herdsmen.

(Left) The Malinke are distinguished by their aquiline noses and high cheekbones. Women wear gold earrings which they regard as a form of wealth to be melted down for sale in times of hardship.

bards, and the secret of its contents is guarded by them most jealously.

Although Islam is the principal formal religion throughout the Manding-speaking area of West Africa, it is often practised in a less rigid and orthodox way by the Bambara and Malinke than by some other neighbouring peoples. The Manding bard plays his own traditional part alongside the Moslem priest, for example, at naming-ceremonies for infants, and it is probable that the bard may have had a specifically priestly-role in the original pre-Islamic religion of the Manding. Ancestor veneration is still of great importance and it is the bard who continually reinforces the links between the present generation and those of the past.

The Bambara of the open savannah have proved generally more resistant to Islam than have the Malinke of the more wooded and forested areas. This has been in contrast

John Bulmer

to the stricter orthodoxy of the Fula as reflected in the 19th century holy war conducted by the Fula reformer al-Hajj Umar against the Bambara and other 'infidels'.

Resistance to Islam has been associated with the survival of some of the richest West African traditions of modelled art, as shown in the exquisite lines of the stylized antelope head-dress of the Bambara. The carved antelope, known as the *tyi-wara* or 'beast of cultivation', represents the mythical antelope which brought the secret of cultivation to the first farmers—perhaps reflecting a period when the Manding, originally hunters, began to embrace an agricultural economy. *Tyi-wara* head-dresses, one male and one female, are traditionally carried on the heads of two youths during rituals for the fertility of crops. Such ceremonies are now becoming rare, as the impact of the West completes the work which Islam began in undermining one of the richest African civilizations.

Some of the more ancient traditions of the Manding probably survive among the Dogon of Mali. Although the Dogon now speak a different language, there is a tradition that their ancestors in the male line were originally refugees from Manding, who fled in order to preserve their non-Islamic culture and religion. As among many other non-Manding peoples of West Africa, wood-carving is carried out by smiths, who are also often responsible for the ritual and magic surrounding the use of masks. These include a wide range of face masks, representing humanised animal types, such as the lion, hyena and crocodile, and associated with 'secret' societies. One among the Manding is the *ntomo*, whose function is to prepare young boys for the initiation into the adult community. Equally important, from the artistic viewpoint, are the stylized human fertility figures, carved by Bambara smiths.

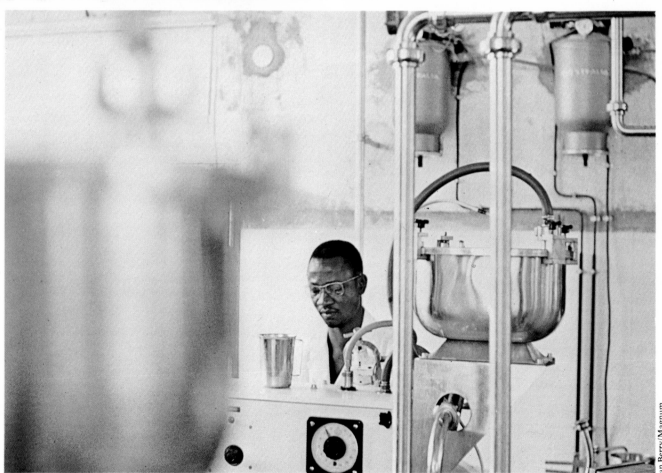

A.A.A.

A Malinke bard or dyeli uses a 21-string harp-lute kora to accompany his recitation and singing. The history of the ancient Mali empire is still related in this way; especially the popular legend of Sundiata, The Lion King, who founded Mali.

Decorative leatherwork is prepared with local skins by the professional leatherworkers, and the various traditional forms of dyed cloth are prepared by women from both locally woven and imported materials. These cloths include batiks and tie-dyes, using indigo, and also the distinctive brown and white 'mud-cloths' worn by Bambara men, on which intricate designs are prepared by a complex process involving the use of a special type of earth. Manding women from even the poorest rural communites will appear in elegant gowns and 'head-ties' when the occasion demands, and will display the delicate gold jewellery which is their personal insurance policy.

The Manding tradition of trading has been encouraged by modern developments rather than undermined by them. They export local crops like millet, rice, maize and sorghum, along with shea butter and cloth while importing milk and butter from the Fulani and salt and livestock from the north.

The Manding term *dyula* means trader, and a people now known as Dyula, of part-Malinke and part-Bambara origin, are important traders in many countries of West Africa, especially in Ivory Coast and Upper Volta. The Malinke speak a dialect of the Mande language. The traders speak their own dialect known as Dyula which has become the trade-language throughout the area in which they operate.

In the latter half of the 19th century, a Dyula-trader, Samori Toure, attempted to recreate the ancient Mali empire, which had declined over the centuries to a tiny chiefdom around Kangaba. For several decades he ruled a wide area of the savannah and forest-fringe, playing off Britain against France, but was eventually defeated and exiled by the French. Sekou Toure, President of Guinea, even though he is a Marxist, used his descent from Samori Toure to appeal to nationalist sentiment in his bitter fight against French colonialism.

The importance and extent of Manding language and culture have been obscured in recent times by the superimposition of many national frontiers, and by the even greater divide between Francophone and Anglophone Africa. These divisions, of colonial origin, have been added to the existing ethnic divisions of Manding-speaking Africa. Although the Malinke and Bambara, and other Manding-speaking groups, speak the same language and share so many common traditions, they still regard each other as distinct and separate peoples.

Strangely enough, it was in London that there was the first concerted attempt to focus attention on Manding culture as a whole. A conference and exhibition on Manding civilization were held in 1972 sponsored by President Senghor of Senegal, himself part Manding in ancestry. A most striking cultural contact between Africa and Europe occurred when a group of white-robed Manding bards played a hymn in praise of the lion-king Sundiata at 10 Downing Street, against a background of Gainsborough portraits. □

Masai
KENYA, TANZANIA

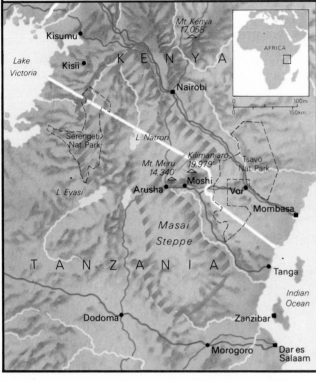

In the beginning Ngai, husband of the moon and Creator of all things, living on snow-capped Kilimanjaro, created the Masai. He then created all the cattle of the world for them to live by. So recounts Masai legend. Ever since, the Masai have loved their cattle and have justified cattle raids, which terrorized their neighbours, as reclamation of their God-given property.

The Masai, a group of clans who migrated from the Upper Nile in the 17th and 18th centuries, developed into a military élite with complete dominance over the grasslands of the Great Rift Valley. Today 100,000 of them live in equal numbers in both Kenya and Tanzania. They are not a homogeneous group, but belong to separate clans. Those who have traditionally cultivated crops, like the Arusha, are 'agricultural Masai'; others have always permitted the consumption of game and fowl, such as the Samburu and the Baraguyu clans; and there are those who live solely off the products of domestic animals, the 'pastoral Masai', or Masai proper.

Quick-drying cattle manure is used for building houses. In the villages, small, sun-baked rectangular huts are arranged in a circle and surrounded by a thorn fence to protect the stock from predators. The animals are taken off to graze every morning by the boys and they return at dusk to the security of the village. There are usually several families, each with their own herd, in every village. But the animals are herded as a single unit by the sons of the village elders.

The Masai keep cattle, sheep and goats, but cattle are valued more than the small stock which are grazed close to the village by the youngest boys. Bullocks are kept for slaughter on ceremonial occasions, and it is the adult milch cows which are the basis of the Masai economy. Most villages are semi-permanent, moving every three or four years when the accumulation of mud in the cattle kraal makes it unusable. In the dry seasons, the herds may be driven to distant watering-places where the men will erect a temporary camp.

Masai warriors, the moran, often hold bundles of soft aromatic leaves under their armpits as a deodorant. In the past moran went into battle bearing a 50lb buffalo-hide shield and an 8ft spear.

Brian Boyd/Colorific!

Mirella Ricciardi/Virginia Fass

Europeans did not succeed in penetrating Masailand until the 1880s, although they had been at Mombasa and Zanzibar on the Coast for some time. The Masai were reputed to be extremely fierce and warlike—a reputation fostered by the Arab merchants who fought them over the routes into the interior where they traded for ivory. When Joseph Thomson reached Masailand in 1883, he found them decimated by a bitter war between the Laikipiak, a powerful group of agricultural Masai, and several sections of the pastoral Masai, who were unified for the first time by their greatest *Laibon*, or prophet, Mbatiany. The Laikipiak were eventually routed, never again to exist as a separate people.

These events were followed by a devastating epidemic of rinderpest in 1890, which killed off many cattle, and by a severe drought which killed off many more in 1891. The two disasters plunged the Masai into another serious war, this time between different sections of the pastoral Masai who are divided into 19 territorial sections. In each section the men administer the pasture which is held in common by all members of the section; domestic animals are owned by individuals. The civil war started when the *moran* of the Loita section raided other sections for cattle. By the end of the war, nearly all the sections had been caught up in the conflict on one side or the other.

Mbatiany died before the war broke out and two of his sons, Senteu and Ole Nana, competed for the succession to his position as chief *Laibon* of the Masai. They made use of the conflict to forward their personal claims. Senteu used his prophetic powers to advise the Loita while Ole Nana advised their opponents. The war ended in 1902 when the Loita were decisively defeated and sued for peace.

The British authorities in Nairobi immediately recognized Ole Nana as Paramount Chief. They believed

Masai women adorn themselves with large necklaces, headbands, metal armlets and bracelets. Like their men, they spend hours decorating their bodies.

(Right) Smiths live apart from other Masai who think them inferior because they slaughter the cattle they earn by their work. To the Masai the only worthy occupation is herding and the persistent killing of cattle for food is considered gluttonous.

At first the sky and earth were one, according to Masai legend. After their separation, Ngai the Creator went to live in the sky above Mount Kilimanjaro and sent cattle to the Masai to sustain them.

Mirella Ricciardi/Virginia Fass

incorrectly that he had authority over the Masai. But when he died the Masai made no attempt to appoint a successor – authority was in fact exercised through the age-grade system.

Every adult man belongs to an age-set. When he is circumcised at about 16 years of age he joins the age-grade of *ilmurran* (usually known as *moran* and often translated as 'warriors'). He remains a *moran* for between 7 and 14 years and then all the existing *moran* are simultaneously promoted to the status of elders when for the first time they have the right to take snuff, chew tobacco and settle. At this point they receive their own particular age-set name which they keep as they move up, as a set, through the various grades of elderhood.

The name of the latest age-set to reach the status of elders is *Ilterekeyani*. These men are now the most junior elders, and their influence is not very much felt. The set above them occupies the 'senior elder' grade and they are now beginning to take most of the important decisions in the territorial sections, although the next set, the 'retired elders', remain very influential. There are usually a few representatives of the age-set above the retired elders who are consulted on matters of religious and ceremonial detail but their role in decision making is small.

The Masai trace their history by reference to the time when particular age-sets were serving as *moran*. Thus 'the time of the *Ilterekeyani*' corresponds to the years between 1956, when the first members were circumcized, and 1971. By then they had completed all the ceremonies and were promoted as elders. Estimating 15 years for each age-set, historians can date events as far back as the 1790s.

The age-sets are based on sections and are egalitarian in structure. Every man can have his say at councils and decisions are reached democratically. Councils have traditionally been the primary forum for legal and political decisions. They settle disputes, administer the pastures, organize rituals and, today, discuss propositions for cattle-dips, ranching schemes and other development projects. Every age-set nominates from among its own members an official known as *olaiguenani*—'the one who discusses'—who is *primus inter pares* or first among equals.

Olaiguenani must be a man respected for his wisdom and his diplomacy. Men's councils meet under the shade of trees and any wise, kind man is said to 'give out shade' because peope are drawn to him for help and advice. *Olaiguenani* chairs age-set councils, but he cannot make even the smallest decision without calling a meeting and referring the issue back to his age-mates for discussion. If the matter is an important one affecting other grades or other sections, a council will be convened of representatives from all the groups affected.

The *moran* acted in the past as the Masai army, responsible for the defence of the country. They were never conquerors, merely marauders who besides capturing or 'reclaiming' their cattle sought to prove their manhood. Often the clans fought among themselves in arranged tournaments as there was no one left to fight on the grasslands where they had become the undisputed masters.

Visitors to Kenya and Tanzania often express surprise at the continuing survival of the institution of moranhood, when there are no more wars to fight and cattle-raiding has been virtually suppressed. In fact, fighting may never have been the primary function of the *moran*. In practical terms they form a mobile core of young men who can be called upon to help in any arduous work such as moving herds in search of new pasture during a drought. Indeed, in many parts of Masailand the *moran* are totally responsible for the herds when they are a long way from the

R. D. Waller

permanent villages during the dry seasons. Travelling widely during their period of service, they can be relied upon to know of all the available pastures as well as the latest news from different territorial sections.

When a man is first initiated, he is ignorant of much that an adult Masai must know—about politics, religion and herd management—and moranhood gives him a thorough education in these subjects. He also makes wide contacts, not only with *moran* but with others outside his own family, contacts which he will draw upon in later life when he is looking for a wife or is in need of help.

Moranhood forces the young men away from the security of their homes. They live in rough camps called *manyattas* and return to society as adult men, having acquired the skills of social life and public debate which are needed for the administration of their communities. They also bring with them a sense of superiority towards those

who have not been through the same experience, namely, women, children and outsiders. Traditionally the pastoral Masai are an extremely proud and self-assured people. They pity the cultivators like the Arusha who have no cattle and are forced to grow crops and so humiliate themselves. The smiths they despise. Their work is thought unworthy of a Masai.

Western education has been accepted gradually. By the 1950s and 1960s, many boys went to primary school. In the more traditional areas a significant number left school as soon as they were circumcized, choosing to become full-time *moran*. But today, many more are returning to secondary school, shortly after circumcision.

The function of the prophets, *Laibons*, was primarily to bless the ceremonies of the *moran* and to advise on propitious times for raiding and for war. In times of conflict, their influence became much greater than in times of peace.

Mirella Ricciardi/Virginia Fass

Moran painstakingly plait each other's hair, which they inter-weave with strands of ochred string to form long plaits. They live and work together for 15 years sharing everything—an experience which develops great loyalty between age-set members.

Today *Laibons* deal mainly with individual clients who bring them such problems as infertility or persistent misfortune. In the old days, important prophecies took place in a state of trance. No such prophecy has taken place for many years now and the *Laibons* admit that their general powers to foretell the future are on the wane. But they still claim to be able to divine the causes of personal calamities. Divination relies on a complicated method of counting pebbles thrown from a calabash.

Women are married at about the age that men are entering moranhood. They too are circumcized, shortly after the onset of physical maturity. The operation is regarded as parallel to male circumcision; for both it marks the social transition into adulthood, and women may not marry until they have been through the ceremony. There are various marriage restrictions. A man has to marry a woman from one of the five clans outside his own. He may not marry the daughter of a man belonging to his father's age-set, nor may he marry two sisters or a woman belonging to his mother's immediate family. Before he marries, however, he may choose his girlfriends freely, provided that they do not belong to his own or his mother's immediate family.

When a woman marries, she leaves her father's home and goes to live with her husband. She will eventually build a house for herself with the assistance of the other women in the village (a task which may take up to a month). In the meantime she will stay with her mother-in-law, or in the house of one of her husband's wives. There is no limit to the number of wives a man may take but, in practice, he is restricted by the size of his milch herd as he must be able to provide enough milk for each wife and her children.

On the first morning in her new home, the bride is given milking-rights over several of her husband's cows. Nine is a magic or 'perfect' number for the Masai as it symbolizes the nine orifices of the body. So nine of these cows are marked in colour patterns which are regarded as 'perfect' and therefore holy. Her husband must not alienate milking-rights previously allocated to another wife and it is usual for a man to keep some stock in hand. As the sons of each wife grow up, she allocates specific animals from 'her' herd to them. When they reach manhood and start to set up herds and families, they are entitled to these animals and their progeny.

On the wife's death, all unallocated animals go to her youngest son; the unallocated animals of a man go, on his death, to his oldest son. The youngest son of a woman is automatically responsible for looking after his mother in her old age; correspondingly, the eldest son is responsible for his father. But this is a formal rule which is modified, in practise, according to individual preferences. If any child were to abandon an aged parent, he or she would be cursed.

The amount of formal bridewealth asked by the father and brothers of a bride varies according to her family traditions. But it usually consists of four 'perfect' animals: two cattle, for example, and two small stock. This is very modest compared with some of the agricultural neighbours of the Masai, such as the Kikuyu, who may ask for 40 head of cattle. Furthermore, the bridewealth is rarely paid until the woman's oldest child is ready to be circumcised, though the ceremony cannot take place if this debt is outstanding. But the obligations of a husband to his wife's kin are considerably more far-reaching. They may call upon him for help of any kind and he cannot refuse unless it is quite beyond his means. Childless women will usually try to adopt a son or daughter and the adoption will be considered final if the child is circumcised in her house after the payment of her bridewealth.

Relationships in Masai society are established or consolidated through gifts. Brothers, co-wives, in-laws and friends give presents which lend their names to the relationships. Thus, it is customary for a man to give his full brother an adult cow. The Masai word for cow is *en-kiteng* and, after the gift has been made the brothers will cease to use each other's proper names but will, instead, address each other reciprocally as *Pa-kiteng*.

The staple diet of the Masai is cow's milk. This may be supplemented with milk from the small stock although sheep's milk is rarely drunk. In the dry seasons, Masai used to mix their milk with cow's blood to eke out the food

Cattle are central to Masai life and are killed only on special occasions.

(Far right) A Masai girl.

A 'Laibon' casts pebbles from a gourd to divine the future. He seeks answers to questions ranging from family matters to the success of cattle raids, and will be paid up to 20 cattle for the prophecy.

supply. But this is rarely done today: people prefer to buy grain or even to grow maize themselves. Meat is eaten at nearly all ceremonies, in case of illness (when the patient may need fat or meat to build up strength) and sometimes to celebrate the arrival of visitors. Beer is an important element of celebration. In the old days, the Masai made a type of mead, with honey collected by the Dorobo hunters who live in pockets all over Masailand. But now they must usually make do with beer made from sugar or from a mixture of sugar and honey.

Masai use almost everything produced by their animals. Cow-hides are made into thongs and bed-coverings or sold to traders. The softer hides of sheep and goats are used for ceremonial cloaks and skirts. Horns are made into containers, while fat is stored in the form of lard. Everything else they need they buy from outside. Dorobo hunters provided them, in the past, with rhino horns for snuff containers and tusks for armlets. The much-despised caste of Masai smiths forged their metal weapons and other implements. But now the Masai go to shops for cloth, grain, tea, sugar, soap, tobacco and other provisions.

The Masai believe in one god, *Ngai*. '*Ngai*' is the word for the sky and air and, to the Masai, god is a very abstract concept. *Ngai* is ultimately responsible for everything that happens and constitutes a moral force which automatically punishes certain gross sins, such as the needless, deliberate killing of a helpless creature. People pray to *Ngai* for health and fertility at any time of day, but sunrise is particularly favoured. During droughts, women sing prayers for rain; during storms they pray that lightning may not strike. Women also sing prayers at most ceremonial occasions.

But the majority of Masai ceremonies are primarily concerned with the passage of the individual or the group through the formal stages of the life-cycle, rather than with abstract religious beliefs. The only important step in the life-cycle which is virtually unmarked by ceremony is death itself. Masai do not believe in an after-life, and the death of all but the oldest members of society is regarded as a deep affront, to be ignored as far as possible out of respect for the feelings of the bereaved. If the deceased had a nickname, then a new word must be found for the idea it expressed.

Both Kenya and Tanzania are trying to draw the Masai further into their national economies whilst bringing them the advantages of schools and hospitals. There are ambitious co-operative ranching schemes and herd management training programmes, along with innoculation schemes and cattle-dips to counter tick-borne diseases. Much of the Masai land is very arid and the stock has to be moved long distances during the dry seasons. There is now a growing realization of the efficiency of the traditional Masai techniques of herd management. The traditional system is flexible because land is not fenced or owned by individuals, some of the ranches are now trying to incorporate this flexibility into their own controlled situation where diseases are more easily eradicated.

Such recognition of the value of traditional practices is a success in the integration of the Masai into the modern economy. But social problems still exist. As one Masai politician said, they do not want to be treated as the vagabonds of East Africa. Prejudice against the Masai by people who once feared them is a cause of great offence.

Tension is often present when the *moran* move outside their own areas. They are sometimes looked on as a backward and unco-operative people who are relics of a pre-colonial past and who must change their ways in the post-Independence era of nation states. Their own future will indicate whether the dilemma between traditional and modern Africa is resolved satisfactorily. □

Merina
MADAGASCAR

The history of the Merina is known in detail only from the end of the 18th century. Before then the Merina were divided into many small and very unstable kingdoms. These were replaced by a unified state when Andrianampoinimerina, defeated his rivals and established himself in Tananarive. His name means 'the Prince of the heart of the land of the Merina'—a place he can still be said to hold today. After his military success Andrianampoinimerina built his capital on a hill in Tananarive. Not only did he unify the country but he began to conquer his neighbours, a process which his descendants carried on so successfully that in the end they ruled practically the whole island.

This success was in part due to contact with Europeans and especially to the guns which the Merina kings obtained from them. This contact was of two kinds. There was contact with Britain and France, both eager to influence the Merina but with an eye to possible colonization, and there was contact with missionaries, especially with British congregationalist missionaries who were active from the beginning of the 19th century. A period of anti-Christian reaction followed and when Christianity became dominant again, the queen was converted, which was seen by the Merina as a symbol of their nationhood. Today the Merina are probably one of the most devout Christian people in the world, having adapted Christianity to their own customs.

Soon, however, the 'European friends' of the Merina kings began to show they wanted more than simply to convert them to Christianity and to teach them new skills. The British and the French slowly gained influence until finally the French invaded the island and exiled the Merina monarchs. This was the end of the Merina Empire and although Madagascar is independent today, the Merina are not any more in exclusive control. Their political fortune has fluctuated in a turbulent period when they have contested for power with other less privileged islanders.

Merina villages are often situated on the hilltops and one of the Malagasy words for 'hill' also means 'village'. They are often surrounded by massive fortifications and moats—at night the villagers used to roll an enormous stone over the entrance to close it off.

The houses are two-storied tower-like buildings, usually with bright red walls made from the red earth which is found all over Madagascar. All the houses open out towards the west, which makes the village streets look very strange, as it seems as if the houses on one side of the road have no windows or doors.

Inside the house too, everything is orientated in a particular direction. The kitchen is always to the south, the water is always to the east of the fire, and the bed of the master of the house is in the northeast corner—the holy corner of the ancestors. The most important people sleep nearest the northeast, with the less important more to the south and west. Merina sleep with their heads pointing towards the northeast out of respect for the ancestors.

Rice is the staple food of the Merina, and this fact is reflected in many aspects of their culture. The phrase 'to eat a meal' means to eat rice. For the Merina rice is the only real food—everything else is flavouring. Rice is the basis of their life and thus the basis of their social organization. Every Merina village has its irrigated rice fields and a group of these villages centred around nearby rice fields forms the basic unit of traditional Merina society. The inhabitants of these villages are all members of one group,

The location of Madagascar in the Indian Ocean off Mozambique would lead us to expect peoples who by race, language and culture are related to the African continent. But the only definite ties which have been established are with people living several thousands of miles to the east, around Indonesia. All Malagasy speak one language which, although it is divided into many dialects, clearly belongs to the same great Malayo-Polynesian family as the Indonesian, Malay, and Maori languages. In culture, too, the Malagasy show clearly their South-East Asian relationship.

The Indonesian racial element is strongest among the Merina, many of whom have straight black hair and light coppery skin. Their customs, religions and beliefs are all reminiscent of South-East Asia. Today the Merina live mainly in the mountainous central plateau area as farmers or craftsmen. Many also live in towns, especially in Tananarive which is not only the Merina capital but also the capital of all Madagascar. They are reputed for their many skills in wood, iron and textiles and are especially successful in commerce and the professions. Most of the teachers, doctors and lawyers of Madagascar are Merina by origin. Nevertheless many Merina still live as peasants in a way that has changed little for centuries.

Apart from some royal tribes, all Merina use garlic as a relish. They call it male onion, for 'garlic' in French and 'male' in Merina sound similar. The onion is now known as 'female onion'.

(*Above*) *In Tananarive, the capital of Madagascar, many Merina are successful in business and the professions. From this hill King Andrianampoini-merina created a unified state during the 18th century —the basis of present-day Merina prosperity.*

(*Right*) *A Merina tomb may cost ten times as much as a house. For to have a tomb is a sign that a person belongs to a particular group, has rank and has legitimate access to rice fields.*

and their unity comes largely from the fact that as a group they are the rightful owners of the rice lands on which they and their ancestors depend. To ensure that their lands do not go to outsiders they insist that all their daughters marry other members of their group so that no non-group member is ever an heir to the rice fields of the group. Such a marriage is often described as closing up a breech in a wall or as an 'inheritance not going away marriage'.

At marriage the groom makes a payment to the bride's family and must give his bride new clothes. This is balanced almost exactly by the dowry of bedding and other household objects which the family of the girl must supply for the groom. As the girl goes to live in the groom's

Alexander Low/John Hillelson Agency

Women work in the rice fields which surround Merina villages. Rice is not merely their staple food, it is the only real food as far as the Merina are concerned—anything else is just flavouring.

house, to keep the balance the marriage ceremony is almost entirely concerned with the reverse process. The bride's father makes the groom a 'son' who then recognizes his family's authority. This is done first by jokingly humiliating the groom by forcing him to beg for his bride.

When the groom's family comes to the bride's house they must knock three times before the family of the bride is willing to notice them. Then the family of the groom must ask for the bride in a beautiful speech. If the speech is not well enough prepared, the family of the bride will fine the groom. Nothing may be said which could be construed as improper, such as mentioning the name of the bride and the groom in the same sentence. That is not the only pitfall. If the groom's family has been too circumlocutary, the bride's family will pretend not to have understood who was meant and will produce a little girl of three whom they will only substitute for the right girl on payment of another fine. This is all something of a game, much enjoyed by all, but it is underpinned by fundamental social principles.

Merina marriage can only be understood in the light of their interest in keeping the rice fields within the groups. This is also true of the other major principle of organization of their social life, the family tomb. A Merina tomb normally costs ten times as much as a house, and is made of stones while the houses are of earth. Some of these stones are massive slabs of up to 15 feet square or even more. The tombs are partly overground with an underground chamber which is capable of holding a large number of corpses. The external part is today often covered by cement and decorated by balustrades or arcades owing something to traditional folk art and much to various European styles often of the last century.

Everywhere these tombs dominate the countryside. Many villages which have long since lost all their inhabitants maintain a ghostly existence by the presence of the tombs which survive the houses and where the present-day descendants of the villagers, living elsewhere, will ultimately be buried. In this lies the importance of the tombs: they are the signs of the permanent association of the Merina groups and their rice fields.

To have a place in a tomb is the sign that one belongs to a particular group, and therefore to have a particular rank. It is the sign that one has a legitimate right of access to rice fields, and it means that one's ancestors were associated with the glorious history of kings and princes; in other words it is the only true warranty of being a Merina. Not to have a tomb is to be nobody, probably the descendant of slaves, although even these are now building tombs; it is to have no family since the most likely explanation is that one has been expelled from entry into the tomb by relatives outraged by an act of gross immorality. In this way the tomb is the pivot of an individual and his society as well as the pivot of the individual and his homeland.

The Merina are often described as having a form of ancestor worship but this is today a very misleading statement. For, as we have seen, they are all Christians and apart from minor beliefs in nature sprites and ghosts, which they do not take very seriously, they are quite orthodox. However, the importance of tombs and the importance of linking the living to the previous generations buried in the tombs has meant that several famous ceremonies have developed. Being placed in a tomb is of paramount social importance but the time of death may well be unsuitable for a great ceremony, for two reasons. First, such a ceremony is expensive and death may come unexpectedly. Secondly, it takes a long time to gather together the whole family of the deceased.

To resolve the problem, the Merina carry out a second burial some years after the death when they exhume the corpse to rebury it properly in its ancestral tomb. Today

The two-storied red earth houses built by the Merina always face the west. Merina sleep with their heads pointing northeast, the holy corner of the ancestors.

(Far left) A Merina wagon train.

this is also necessary, as with the mobility of Merina society people often die far away from their ancestral homes. They must be buried temporarily where they die and later on, when the body is reduced to a skeleton and the preparations completed, they are returned to their ancestral homeland, and their ancestral tomb. In the season when these ceremonies take place, long processions of relatives, preceded by a flag, return the corpses of their kinsmen to their tomb for the second funeral. This is a cheerful occasion for it is a time of reunion of the family in a practical and a spiritual sense.

These second funerals are the largest feasts and ceremonies. Large numbers of people gather for the opening of the tomb. For the people most closely concerned the funerals are intensely personal affairs and as the corpses are exhumed the close relatives are frightened and shocked. There follows a period for piety towards the dead. A eulogy is spoken while the corpse lies wrapped in a mat on the laps of close female relatives. New multicoloured silk shrouds are then offered to the corpse by each of many descendants so that the corpse may be completely rewrapped in twenty of these costly offerings.

Then comes the most surprising element. The relatives dance with the corpse on their shoulders and treat it with sacriligious disrespect. In fact the behaviour seems to be a way of transforming and breaking the ties of the living with the individual dead. It depersonalizes them and merges them with the tomb, the group and its ancestral land.

The Merina attachment to their tombs, to the locality in which the tombs stand and ultimately to their history is encapsulated in these ceremonies. It has enabled the Merina to maintain their identity and cohesion through the dramatic changes which the society has undergone and which it is continuing to undergo. □

Maurice Bloch

Moors
MAURITANIA

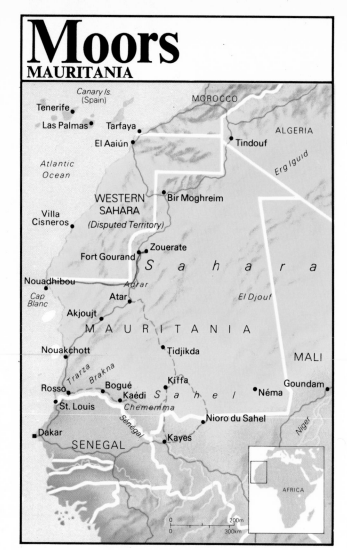

The word 'Moor' (in French 'Maure') comes from the Latin and has been applied over the centuries to Moslem peoples from Spain to West Africa. Since the French conquered the Sahara in the late 19th and early 20th centuries, however, the term has been used to describe the inhabitants of a vast stretch of the western desert, known in the Arab world as Shinquit.

Today this enormous geographical area lies within the Islamic Republic of Mauritania, which covers an area almost twice the size of France and contains a population variously estimated at between 500,000 and 1,500,000. The Moors comprise about three-quarters of the population of the republic, and fall into two broad ethnic groups known by their Arabic names: the *bidanis*, or 'Whites' of Berber origins, and the *sudanis* or 'Blacks', whose origins are mainly Sarakolé, Bambara, Wolof, Toucoulor and Fulani.

In the past the *sudanis* were generally subservient to the *bidanis*, but the divisions between the two groups are based not on colour but on class. There are numerous very dark-skinned *bidanis*—the result of intermarriage with *sudanis*—and a man, black in colour but with a noble genealogy, may be accepted as a *bidani*. In the 19th century, some *bidanis* held social positions on a level with *sudanis* because their genealogy was not noble.

The Moors occupy a harsh and difficult land. In the northern and central parts of Mauritania, Saharan conditions prevail, with vast areas of shifting sand dunes, barren rocky plateaux, and little vegetation. Rainfall increases in the Sahel, or 'shore', the name given by the Moors to the fringes of the desert in the south of their country, and reaches over 20 inches along the River Senegal. This region is characterized by more stable dunes, with scrub trees and summer grasses. Over half of the Moors live in the southwest Sahel in the plains of Trarza and Brakna.

Tradition has it that the first ancestors of the Moors came into Mauritania with the Almoravid chieftain Abu Bakr ibn Umar. Other Moors claim to be descendants of invaders from Morocco or Touat in Algeria during the 12th and 13th centuries, while a third influx, of people descended from Hassan of the Beni Maqil tribe, occurred from the 15th century onwards. The Hassaniyya language takes its name from the last group, who became known as Hassani. Their predecessors, however, appear to have spoken a Berber dialect, Zenaga, which still survives in a few places in Trarza. As these migrants moved south into the more hospitable regions of Shinquit, they encountered Negro peoples living along the banks of the Senegal River, and incorporated these *sudanis* into Moorish society as tributaries of noble families.

Traditionally the direction of Moorish society was shared by two groups of *bidani*, the Hassani and Zawiya tribes—comprising about one-fifth of the population— who were served by a number of tributary classes, including slaves, freed slaves, musicians and poets. Legend has it that the origins of the division of Moorish nobles

Moors of the Hassani group have traditionally been warriors and many still carry arms. In the past, the Hassani protected the more numerous but peaceful Zawiya in return for tribute payments.

Peter Carmichael

Jon Gardey/Jacscam

A family of Moors rests for tea, the usual beverage of desert peoples throughout North Africa. Many nomadic herding routes have been regularized since the French strengthened the wells with cement.

Moorish women demand better treatment and conditions in the independent Republic. After Arabic, French remains the second language of Mauritania, a legacy of the colonial era which ended only in 1960.

into Hassani and Zawiya was an event known as the War of Bubba between the established Berber inhabitants of the country and the newly arrived Hassani. At its conclusion, probably sometime in the late 17th century, the Hassani were victorious and the defeated peoples, who became known as Zawiya (people of the religious centres) agreed to abandon warfare, live according to the Koran and provide the Hassani with certain defined services. Later, some Hassani units renounced their militant past and became Zawiya.

Temporal power within Moorish society lay with certain dominant Hassani tribes. They achieved authority through their ability to protect allies and attack rivals, but their strength depended on the loyalty and fighting ability of their dependants. In each region of the country, the Hassani were commanded by an emir elected by a council of the tribal elders. He possessed little individual power and merely carried out the wishes of the council. The Hassani levied numerous taxes, and even extracted protection-money from passing caravans.

The Zawiya tribes were the spiritual guardians of the society, but they also controlled the country's economic resources. There was a strong tradition of literacy among the Zawiya and they were generally better educated than the Hassani—learned Zawiya acted as mediators in disputes and as spiritual counsellors to the Hassani. But the vast majority were neither mediators nor scholars. They controlled most of the livestock, the exploitation of salt, the organization of caravans and the gathering and

Peter Carmichael

145

selling of gum arabic obtained from acacia trees. Only Zawiya tribes could dig and maintain wells.

The Zawiya outnumbered the Hassani, but as most tribes were divided into small herding groups because pasturage was scattered, they were highly vulnerable to attack and needed the protection of the larger and more mobile Hassani. Their sheikhs, however, had very considerable power within the tribes and freedom to act on their own initiative. The Zawiya had their own system of taxation, mainly involving religious offerings.

Most noble Hassani and Zawiya families were served by a number of tributary families, whose food, clothing and general welfare were the responsibility of the head of the noble family. Class identity was subordinate to the bonds of family, clan and tribe, and slaves or smiths, for example, living within noble camps, took their status from their *bidani* nobles, not from their tributary strata.

European, particularly French, commercial interests came into contact with Moorish society from the late 18th century onwards, but it was not until the early 20th century that the French extended their control over the whole country. Mauritania became first a 'Territoire Civil', later a colony, and was administered from St Louis in Senegal until independence in 1960. The French 'pacification' brought a greater degree of security to the non-Hassani Moors, by putting an end to raiding. Tributary peoples were freed from their masters and, deprived of most of their traditional sources of revenue, the Hassani were forced to take up livestock-rearing and commerce. Nomadic migrations were regularized when the wells were cemented, while the introduction of motor transport brought a decline in the caravan trade and camel breeding.

Western education was introduced through a number of schools which taught both Arabic and French but this affected few Moors apart from emancipated *sudani* and

The drought which struck Mauritania in 1972 turned the entire country into a disaster area. Refugee camps sprang up around all the major towns, putting extreme pressure on the limited urban resources.

the former tributary classes, and did not replace traditional Zawiya scholarship. Although the economic position of the Hassani tribes was weakened, French subsidies greatly strengthened the political authority of their emirs, increasing the scope of their patronage and keeping the succession within particular families. Colonial rule had a further important impact on Moorish society—lands in the south of the country, inhabited by peoples who were not traditionally part of the Moorish society, were incorporated into the colony.

Mauritania was the last French dependency in West Africa to gain independence. The new state was extremely poor and its economic viability questionable. With no capital and only two towns of over 5,000 people, nomadic pastoralism was the main source of livelihood. The livestock herds of the Moorish tribes were the country's major economic resource and provided not only food for the population but also a surplus for export. In the Sahelian zone the Moors migrate with their herds of cattle, mainly African Zebu, between the Trarza and Brakna plains in the wet season and the pastures along the northern bank of the Senegal River for the dry season.

Animals are sold at the major livestock centres of Kaedi, Kiffa and Nema to middlemen who drive them into Senegal where they are fattened for the markets of Dakar. North of Trarza the pasture is unsuitable for cattle and in the Adrar the northern nomadic Moors cross vast areas with their herds of sheep, goats and camels; they also cultivate gardens in the scattered oases. The Negro population, concentrated in villages mainly along the Senegal River, cultivate millet and sorghum where the river flood has receded. The ground is not tilled; a forked stick is used to make the holes in which the seed is planted. Production does not meet local demand.

Since independence, the discovery and exploitation of the country's large mineral deposits has introduced a small but extremely profitable modern sector into the Mauritanian economy. The new mines are concentrated in the northwestern part of the country; iron ore, now the country's major export, at F'Derik, and copper at Akjoujt.

The iron ore is moved by rail to the port of Nouadhibou for export and the copper by road to Nouakchott, the country's new capital. A modern fishing industry is also being developed at Nouadhibou to exploit the rich fishing grounds off the Mauritanian coast.

The new industries are an extension of the modern industrial world and exist in sharp contrast to the traditional sector of the economy. They are highly capital-intensive and offer few employment opportunities for Mauritanians, but they provide the Government with important new sources of revenue with which it is improving livestock production and expanding the area of irrigated agriculture.

These economic developments have been accompanied by a gradual change in Moorish social structure. Although only about 10 per cent of the population are urban dwellers, this change is particularly apparent not only in Nouakchott and Nouadhibou but also in other smaller towns. The beginnings of supra-tribal organization—such as trade unions, women's and student organizations—represent a challenge to traditional tribal loyalties and established patterns of political authority. A new class of Moorish entrepreneurs is emerging, including Moors from the lower social strata, and a growing number of students return to Mauritania after studying abroad, seeking more radical solutions to the country's economic and social problems.

Yet these changes in Moorish social organization are overshadowed by the deep division between Arabic-speaking Moors and the non-Moorish Negro minority which affects every aspect of Mauritanian life. A considerable number of non-Mauritanian Negroes arrived after independence, attracted by the economic opportunities available in the new state. Today they hold a disproportionate number of positions in government and are indispensable in running the economy. They are anxious to establish closer economic links between Mauritania and Senegal and Mali and are deeply suspicious of close ties with North Africa and the Arab world. The Moorish majority feels threatened by this socially mobile Black minority and seems to have found a new unity and sense of Moorish identity by subordinating traditional divisions between Hassani and Zawiya, and *bidani* and non-*bidani*.

In 1972 a terrible drought hit Mauritania and the government declared the whole country a disaster area. The Senegal River failed to flood, and flood recession cropping was impossible for the first time in 50 years. The drought's impact on livestock production was even more catastrophic. About 80 per cent of the herd, some 1,600,000 head, were driven into neighbouring countries and it is not known how many died or were slaughtered prematurely. Death rates among young children and the very old have been much higher than normal and long-term physical and mental damage has probably been suffered by children on extremely low nutritional levels.

Serious social and economic problems have arisen, for nomads from drought areas flocked to the towns in search of emergency food supplies. The population of Rosso, for example, on the banks of the Senegal, trebled as a result of the influx of refugees. Some pastoralists may never return to their former way of life. The full impact of the disaster on the economic and social organization of the Moors is still unknown, but the consequences of this terrible event will be felt for many years. □

Three Moorish girls play on gourd harps of a design known in Ancient Egypt. In traditional Moorish society, the dominant Hassani and Zawiya tribes retained sudani (Black) musicians to chant their praises and provide entertainment.

Ndebele
RHODESIA

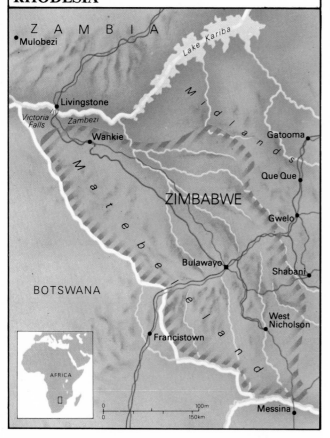

Ndebele could not withstand the wave of invaders who were lured northwards by the prospect of gold and diamonds. Dreams of goldmines were never realized but the mineral and agricultural wealth of the area was adequate recompense. Expansion continued across the Zambezi and rich deposits of copper brought added wealth to the settlers. Forced evictions and treaties, often of dubious morality and minimum legality, left the African people without rights in the land of their birth.

The White settlers elaborated their rule with an imported political system. Eventually they consolidated their control over a vast area of Central Africa by forging Southern and Northern Rhodesia and Nyasaland into the Central African Federation. It lasted barely 4,000 days—destroyed by increasingly organized African nationalism in 1963. After Northern Rhodesia and Nyasaland became the independent African republics of Zambia and Malawi the White settlers realized that the colonial government in London no longer supported their minority rule. By U.D.I. —Unilateral Declaration of Independence—they sought to retain their power and wealth which could only be defended by preventing African rule spreading south across the Zambezi into white-ruled Rhodesia.

Within Rhodesia, African resistance to colonialism found expression in political parties whose names changed as each in turn was banned. Zimbabwe, from the name of the ancient Shona seat of government, came to symbolize a desire for their own identity and a new political system. When many nationalist leaders were detained without trial a new challenge faced the independence movement. Its answer was that uncompromising attitudes and re-

Ndebele acknowledge two 'mothers'. The individual, natural mother is the 'little' one, but when she is away working, ill or otherwise unable to manage, there is a 'big' mother who will take over.

The Ndebele of Zimbabwe are very clearly aware that the days of their great kings who reigned supreme over the country are gone; yet they have never fully accepted the domination of their nation by White settlers and their descendants. Although only 14 per cent of the population, the one million Ndebele have played a part in all the liberation struggles against foreign domination.

After eighty years of colonialism this warrior people is extensively integrated into the urban economy developed by the White settlers. As labourers, miners and factory workers they live in the crowded townships outside the major cities of Bulawayo, Shabani and Wankie. While many of the women work as servants for the Whites the men refuse to take work as garden or kitchen boys—their warrior tradition is still strong and their submission to colonialism is far from complete.

The Ndebele, or Matabele, as they were known, call themselves amaNdebele. Their history began when, at the beginning of the 19th century, they fled from the oppressive power of the Zulu king. Mzilikazi led a breakaway section, who came to be the Ndebele, northwards away from the Zulu territory. They settled in the thickly wooded *bundu* and grey uplands of western Zimbabwe except for a few who made their home in the northern tip of the Transvaal. SiNdebele, their language, has the same sort of relationship to Zulu as American has to English. Mzilikazi's heir, Lobengula, lost the Ndebele kingdom to representatives of Queen Victoria led by Cecil Rhodes after whom the country was called 'Rhodesia'.

The advent of the settlers was met with stiff resistance beginning with the Matebele Rebellion in 1891. But spears and shields were no match for European guns and the

pression could only be met with violence. Guerrilla warfare started in 1967 to win back by arms what had been taken by force and trickery. Some Ndebele joined small guerrilla groups to fight beyond the borders of Matebeleland. This guerrilla war forced the settlers to negotiate once again with the leaders of the African National Council in 1975.

Traditionally the Ndebele are cattle rearing and millet growing people, though maize has now largely taken the place of millet. They are both pastoralists and cultivators. This versatility has enabled them to withstand the capriciousness of Nature in the different areas they have inhabited. The cattle are reared for their milk and for pulling ploughs. Cereals are the Ndebele's staple diet; made into a thick porridge, *isitshwala*, eaten either with soured milk, drained of whey, or with vegetables selected from a variety of wild spring greens that thrive in the fallow fields and around cattle kraals. Meat is eaten extensively. While most meat is now provided by cattle herds, in the past it was obtained through hunting. Then cattle were never slaughtered unless they were sick, barren or no longer of use.

The Ndebele hunt usually in small family groups, armed with *knobkerrie* clubs and specially trained mongrel dogs. The quarry is driven towards the hunters who strike the animal's heart or the centre of the head. If conditions permit, larger hunts are organized in search of big game like kudu.

There is a special procedure for sharing out the spoils at the end of the hunt; the choicest cuts from any kill—the choicest being the fattest by Ndebele standards—are left to the man whose *knobkerrie* or *assagai* provides the blow that finally brings the animal down. The only other priority is that if a man first spots a beast hiding in the thickets, he will receive the first cut it if is killed. The man who supervises the share-out is always the senior member of the hunt, either in age, or more commonly according to his close relationship with the royal family, or local headman.

The Ndebele have a special liking for all kinds of uncooked meats, either after they have been flavoured with salty extracts and herbs and thoroughly dried in the sun, or when the animal has been freshly slaughtered. Tripe, locusts, birds and hens' eggs are all eaten raw. Such delicacies as caterpillar, turtle and all manner of insects are roasted. The flesh of dogs, cats, monkeys and varieties of fish are taboo and no explanation is given beyond '*kunjengo, kuganga abadala bathi akuqalwa*' . . . 'it is just like incest; the ancients have decreed that it shall not be, if you break the rule you will die'.

The search for food is a major preoccupation of the Ndebele and the *assagai* has been as important in hunting as in war. Standing armies were used extensively in bad harvest years for raiding neighbouring tribes for cattle and crops. Slaves were also taken to tend the fields and fetch water from distant rivers in cases of extreme drought. Any villages raided and found with inadequate supplies were punished by the assassination of a few of their leading males. This ensured that weak neighbouring groups kept adequate supplies of food in case of an unexpected Ndebele raid.

In the past boys were taught war games, before being eventually initiated into warrior groups. Educational instruction was carried out for the young through work and play, and boys learned to handle the *knobkerrie* and the *assagai*. Girls underwent instruction through work and play, in child care, cooking, the selection of non-poisonous foodstuffs from the bush and the care of the fields. At the initiation ceremony all initiates, male and female, had their ear-lobes slit, a mark which identified them as belonging to the Ndebele nation.

Education is lifelong; any Ndebele always expects an older one to teach him something from time to time. But the education of the young is particularly intensive, and is carried out jointly by both sexes. Breast-feeding is shared out equally amongst all child suckling mothers in case a mother's milk supply runs dry.

Ndebele house decoration relieves the barrenness of the industrial landscape. Many Ndebele live in these overcrowded townships frequently 10 or 15 miles from the factories or shops where they work.

Alan Hutchison Library

(Above) Traditionally, cattle herding was a task for young Ndebele boys before they became warriors. Today cattle are killed for meat, something unthinkable in the past when meat was obtained by hunting.

All children are assured of a stable upbringing. Illegitimacy and orphanhood, in the Western sense, are unknown. Each child has its natural or 'little' mother as well as a 'big' mother who acts as a substitute should the natural mother no longer be able to care for her child. No distinction is made between biological relationships and social ones. An ordinary Ndebele child thus has several potential parents, and such mishaps as death, divorce and rejection do not result in neglect of the child.

Social life is based on the extended family, with wide ranging relationships determining the family's obligations. A man can still marry as many wives as he can support, but women may only have one husband. Female infidelity is socially unacceptable and often results in the heavy fining of both the wife's father and her lover. If she persists she could be, and very often is, divorced and deprived of her children. A man's infidelity commands no more than a severe rebuke from the wife's male relations, who often politely suggest that they are not averse to providing a further wife if he can justify his need and ability to support her.

The system of government in Matebeleland since the annexation of Rhodesia by the British has adapted the former governmental institutions. The focus of power is now the Native Commissioner and the chiefs and headmen are his appointees. Their main task is to keep him informed of activities that might upset the settler regime. Chieftainships are maintained on the lines established by the Kumalo Dynasty in the 19th century.

In traditional Ndebele society authority resides with the king and his court consisting of family hangers-on and provincial representatives. Each province has a paramount chief—*induna*—selected by the provincial representatives and elders who express the *abantu batini*—the people's opinion. Very often the son of a previous chief succeeds to his deceased, or deposed, parent. Women are never chiefs but do sit at court; their intelligence and social position influence a man's qualification for high office.

The paramount chief has under him a series of headmanships or sub-chieftains ('*mlisa*). The headmen in turn control the various military leaders of respective clans. The current system makes the chief Native Commissioner the king figure; his appointee chiefs become imitation provincial leaders.

The system was based on a well ordered style of military command. The king was always the political and military leader, but never religious leader. Religion was left to the expert control of the king's medicine men and women. The chief medicine man, on the advice of his peers, appointed the nation's religious leader—always a woman of advanced age with a successful record in medicine. She became the chief prophetess (*igoso*) and the people's representative to the spirit of the departed, who are supposed to intercede on behalf of the living to *Nkulnkulu*, the God of the Ndebele. The Supreme Being is sometimes called *Nkosi yama-'Kosi* (King of Kings) a title now taken by such White leaders as the premier, the chief Native Commissioner and the President.

The authority of chiefs has virtually disappeared although they still inflict physical punishment. This is deeply resented by the people who respect them no more and therefore maintain that the basis of a chief's rule, consent, no longer exists. The chiefs' position has been further eroded by educated Ndebele who deliberately returned from the towns to the villages to oppose the chiefs' complicity with the government. The rural Ndebele rejected their chiefs after the 1958–63 campaign which was directed against the Land Husbandry Act and the forced evictions from land taken for White farmers. Since then the chiefs have been provided by the government with armed bodyguards—something the traditional warrior chiefs never needed. Another change since the days of the old warrior chiefs has occurred in the towns. Here the Ndebele work, mix and intermarry with what their forbears would have deemed lesser beings (*amahole*).

Over 20 per cent of the Ndebele—probably half the active workforce—live in the overcrowded townships which surround the urban centres, but they still retain close links with their homes in the rural areas. Many only live in the towns for six months of the year when there is no work to be done in the fields. At the weekend, town workers pour back to the countryside where they all have fields and cattle cared for by a trusted wife or relative.

To travel home at weekends, workers band together into travel associations to pay the running costs of a vehicle which a driver borrows from his employer. Urban funeral and credit associations also cater for the needs of their subscribers. They supplement the assistance provided by the traditional extended family system. This system still survives despite urbanization, although economic power and missionary education now give the young greater independence.

These educated younger Ndebele are now more important than the elders. They are prominent in the African National Congress which is locked in negotiations with the settler regime. In spite of their support for guerrilla fighters, most of the Ndebele would welcome a peaceful transition to the state of Zimbabwe. □

Nyoro
UGANDA

There are today some 200,000 Nyoro, or Banyoro, living in northwestern Uganda. Their country, known as Bunyoro, lies in the fertile uplands to the southeast of Lake Albert. Until recently it was the seat of a powerful monarchy which claimed to have ruled for at least five centuries.

The Nyoro *Mukama*, like other divine kings, was important not only as the supreme secular ruler, but also ritually. He carried out special ceremonies, some of them associated with cattle, at regular intervals 'for the good of the country'. As the head of the kingdom and the source of all authority within it, his personal well-being was mystically identified with the country as a whole. Any injury to the king would affect the entire nation, it was believed.

The *Mukama* was not allowed to become seriously ill, or enfeebled by old age; if either of these things happened he was supposed to poison himself or to be put to death by his wives. It is said human sacrifice took place in connection with accession and other royal ceremonies in order 'to strengthen the king'. His uniqueness was further stressed by the use of special titles and greetings, reserved for him alone, and there was even a special court vocabulary. Senior officials had to kneel down respectfully if they wished to hand something to the king, or to receive anything from his hands.

It was consistent with the emphasis on the *Mukama*'s pre-eminence in a hierarchical social system that almost all social relationships in Bunyoro were characterized by what has been called 'the premise of inequality'. In almost any relationship one person was considered as being clearly superior to the other. Naturally this was especially true of relationships between subjects and chiefs of any rank, between the king and everybody else, and between nobles and commoners. But it was also largely true of everyday relationships of kinship and neighbourhood among the ordinary people.

Even today, older Banyoro speak a little nostalgically of fathers 'ruling' their sons, husbands their wives, fathers-in-law their sons-in-law and so on. Special deference between these and other categories of relatives is still expected. Interpersonal relationships in Bunyoro were probably hardly less egalitarian than in other traditional kingdoms. But as in some neighbouring states, the idiom of supremacy and subordination is a striking feature of the culture.

Despite this, Banyoro often contrast the easy and relaxed atmosphere that prevails—or should prevail—at the level of the local community with the very much more formal quality of their relationships with the superimposed state and its officials. Their traditional concern with the maintenance of good local relations is well exemplified in the characteristic Nyoro institution of neighbourhood courts or moots. Disputes arising out of cases of theft, assault, adultery or trespass by stock, may be taken to the official courts. But older Banyoro much prefer if possible to deal with such matters within the community where they belong. This is done, quite informally, by a tribunal, made up of a few of the senior local householders, who hear the parties and their witnesses before deciding on the issue.

Whatever the decision, a standard penalty is imposed on the guilty party. Early in the morning on an agreed day, he is required to bring to the house of the person he has wronged a substantial quantity of meat and banana beer. A feast is at once prepared—the meat, usually goat,

George Rodger/Magnum

Special trumpeters are part of the Nyoro kings' retinue: they perform at biennial festivals held to celebrate and renew the kingship. The trumpets are made of gourd and covered with hide and cowrie shells.

George Rodger/Magnum

Sir Tito Winyi Gafabusa, said to be the 49th Nyoro Mukama, returns with his regalia keepers and retainers from a palace building. The Nyoro kingdom was abolished by President Obote's government in 1967.

is a luxury—and both parties to the dispute, together with the members of the tribunal and neighbours, partake. Singing and dancing soon begin, and the party continues until all the food and beer is finished. After this the two disputants are supposed to be reconciled, and the quarrel between them should never be referred to again. Evidently the aim of such proceedings is not so much to punish a wrongdoer but to effect a reconciliation and restore good neighbourly relations. Far from being rejected by the community, as he would be if he were taken before the official courts, the culprit is explicitly reintegrated into it.

Of course such reconciliatory procedures do not always work. With the development of a money economy and the growth of opportunities for cash-cropping and wage labour, men are no longer dependent on the good will and cooperation of a group of kinsmen and neighbours. Lawbreakers can, if they wish, defy the judgements of such neighbourhood courts with impunity, and many do so. This is just one sign of the breakdown of traditional structures under a new economic system.

As with their Baganda neighbours to the east, the great majority of Nyoro are small farmers, although an increasing number are officials, professionals or in trade. In the countryside they live in scattered settlements rather than in compact villages, and their homesteads, surrounded by fields and food-gardens, are usually sheltered by a banana grove. But, unlike Baganda, Banyoro do not use their bananas for food; they prefer to grow beer-making varieties from which the national drink *mwenge*, is brewed. The staple food crop is eleusine (finger millet), but sweet

potatoes, cassava and various kinds of peas and beans are also grown. Cotton and tobacco are cultivated as cashcrops.

In pre-colonial times the Banyoro owned large herds of cattle, just as the Bahima of nearby Ankole still do today. But by the end of the last century most of their herds had been destroyed by rinderpest epidemics and by the ravages of war. Today the tse-tse fly, which carries the dreaded cattle disease trypanosomiasis, prevents cattle-keeping throughout most of the country. But Banyoro are still very cattle-conscious: their language contains many idioms relating to cattle, and the loss of their former herds is still widely mourned, even by people whose ancestors are unlikely ever to have had any. Today, while most farmers do own small flocks of goats or sheep, as well as a few chickens, meat and eggs are rarely eaten and the diet of most Banyoro is short of protein.

As elsewhere in the interlacustrine region west and south of Lake Victoria a difference of status is recognized between the formerly cattle-owning Bahima—called Bahuma in Bunyoro—and the agriculturalist Bairu majority. But the distinction seems never to have been as important as it is, for example, in Ankole. With the loss of the Banyoro's former herds it has become practically irrelevant—except as implying a rather dubious claim to special hereditary prestige.

In Bunyoro the group which has claimed the highest social status, and the privileges that go with it, were until very recently the members of the ruling Babito clan. Their forbears are believed to have come to Bunyoro from the Nilotic regions to the north (the present Acholi and Lango districts) some three centuries ago. They are said to have peacefully taken over the country from an earlier dynasty. This was the shadowy and at least partly mythical Bachwezi, a race of light-skinned hero-gods with remarkable skills, who after performing many miraculous feats conveniently vanished from the earth just before the Babito arrived. Stories of Nyoro origins, and of the wonderful doings of their early kings, are vividly recounted in Bunyoro's exceptionally rich and complex mythology, which composes a major body of oral literature.

Bunyoro's last king was Sir Tito Winyi Gafabusa who claimed to be the 49th king, and the 26th of the Bito dynasty. He died in retirement in 1971, aged over 80, having outlived his kingdom by four years. As a small boy, he had seen his father's kingdom subjugated by the British, in alliance with Bunyoro's neighbours and traditional enemies the Baganda, after a long and bitter military campaign. This ended in 1899 with the capture of the Nyoro king Kabarega, who had fought for a number of years, against hopeless odds, to retain his country's independence. Exiled by the British to the Seychelles in the Indian Ocean, he was only allowed to return to Uganda as an old man, more than 20 years later.

With the conquest of Bunyoro, its two largest and most important and fertile counties which were the traditional heartland of the old kingdom were handed over to Buganda, which profited handsomely from the downfall of its old rival. After 1900, the truncated Bunyoro kingdom was administered for over 60 years as part of the Uganda Protectorate; its two succeeding kings (both of them sons of the redoubtable Kabarega) exercising a limited authority under colonial rule. Sir Tito reigned for the longer part of that period, after succeeding his older brother in 1924. In 1967 with the abolition of all four of Uganda's traditional monarchies by Premier Obote's first post-Independence government, the Bunyoro kingdom ceased to exist.

The design of some Nyoro drums shows Ganda influence. The Baganda supported the British against Bunyoro and after the conquest in 1899 were rewarded by being given the two best Nyoro counties.

George Rodger/Magnum

Even during the colonial period of 'Indirect Rule', and especially from the 1930s onwards, when some of the king's supposedly traditional powers were restored to him, Bunyoro's native ruler managed to exercise a good deal of influence. This was particularly so in such sensitive areas as the appointment, promotion and dismissal of his regional chiefs. In his civil service, loyalty to his own person counted for as much as, or even more than, conformity to modern bureaucratic values. In the later years of Sir Tito's reign this state of affairs began to give rise to some resentment among the growing intelligentsia, especially among the younger and better educated chiefs. A new constitution enacted in 1955 effectively reduced his status to that of constitutional monarch.

Today most Banyoro are at least nominally Christians, while a few are Moslems. But many still retain some of their traditional beliefs. Bunyoro's traditional religion is associated with the ancient Chwezi hero-gods. As well as being thought of as the ancient rulers of the kingdom, some of the 19 Chwezi spirits are associated with such elemental forces as thunder and lightning, rain, earthquakes and the sun and moon. Like the ancient Greek gods, they are thought of as variously related to one another. Banyoro say that when the Chwezi spirits disappeared from the world they left behind them a cult of spirit mediumship of which they are themselves the objects.

Though the Chwezi are no longer physically present, their spirits may 'possess' those properly initiated into the cult which is widespread throughout much of Uganda and beyond. When the spirit is in the head of its medium, a goat or fowl may be sacrificed to it. The spirit is asked to bless its devotees, and to grant them health and, especially, fertility. The birth rate in Bunyoro is low, and the efforts of European missionaries to suppress the cult have been attributed by many Banyoro to the White man's supposed desire that the Nyoro people should die out, so that their country could be taken over by the Europeans.

Mediumship ritual is concerned with other spiritual forces too, especially the ghosts of dead kin, which may harm the living particularly if they died with a grudge against anyone. Their mediumship cult has enabled Banyoro to cope with forces conceived to be dangerous and beyond human control. So it is not surprising that in modern times a variety of non-traditional elements have been incorporated. These have included various illnesses, motor cars and aeroplanes, even such abstractions as Islam, and the mysterious foreign forces of 'Europeanness' and 'Swahiliness'.

To determine the cause of misfortune—barrenness, illness, the early death of children—Banyoro have recourse to divination. There are many techniques, the most popular being the casting by the diviner of nine cowry shells on a mat. The resulting patterns are interpreted as either auspicious or inauspicious. As well as diagnosing the action of a Chwezi spirit or a ghost, the diviner may attribute the trouble to sorcery by a jealous or offended neighbour. For a fee he will provide a magical antidote.

Bunyoro is not unique in having undergone extensive and massive change during the past century, but its experience of Western contact has perhaps been more radically disruptive than that of most African states. Banyoro say, with resignation rather than bitterness, that the Europeans have 'spoiled' their country. It is a little ironic, at least from the viewpoint of Nyoro monarchists, that growing economic prosperity, the increasing democratization of the kingdom, and the restoration in 1965 of the 'lost counties', should have been followed so soon by the final dismantling of the ancient kingdom. □

Pygmies
CENTRAL AFRICA

To the Pygmies, the great tropical rain forest of Central Africa is a benevolent, friendly, comfortable and healthy place: it is a conscious being to be trusted, respected and loved. So intimate and protective is the relationship that the Pygmies call the forest 'mother' or 'father'. As they say, *ndura nee bokbu*, the forest is everything.

Pygmy hunters and gatherers are still spread widely from the west coast of Africa to the mountainous borders of Uganda, Rwanda and Burundi. Out of the total pygmy population of between one and two hundred thousand, two major groups have undergone less assimilation than the others—the Binga of the forests to the west of the Ubangi River, and the Mbuti, several hundred miles to the east, in the Ituri Forest. Recent studies of blood types throughout the equatorial region indicate that the Mbuti are probably closest to the original pygmy type, and culturally this also seems to be the case.

In their relationship with the neighbouring villagers the Mbuti have established a dual world, where that of the forest is set in classic opposition to that of the village. For the anthropologist the fascinating thing about this relationship is that it averts rather than fosters hostility; indeed the relationship is generally characterized by a great deal of amity. For the historian, however, it means that the Mbuti have, in their forest world, been able to keep much closer to their traditional hunting and gathering form of life than those pygmies who have been drawn more closely into the village orbit and become increasingly dependent upon the villagers in all respects, including food, to the point of almost total cultural change or degeneration.

This relationship has been grotesquely, but understandably, distorted through superficial observation by travellers and administrators. To outward appearances, in some villages more than others, the Ituri Mbuti seem to be virtually slaves to the villagers. They can always be seen in subservient if not menial roles, working for the villagers with little evident return. Closer observation, however, reveals that even in these villages there are certain important ritual occasions on which the Mbuti are honoured and respected, as in the first fruit offerings from the village fields. In the various life-cycle crises of the villagers, too, the Mbuti play a vital ritual role—most of all in the *nkumbi* circumcision initiation which is now shared by most of the surrounding village tribes, even those that formerly were non-circumcisers.

The respect is mutual, though both peoples tend to deride the chosen life style of the other as being not quite human. Outside observers have found it difficult to assess the situation accurately because they have generally thought only in terms of economic exchange, in which terms the Mbuti certainly are the losers. They provide the villagers with all the forest products so essential for survival: protein from game and nuts, other forest foods such as mushrooms and honey, saplings for house frames and phrynium leaves for roofing. In return the Mbuti get cast-off clothing, a few cigarettes, scraps of food, and metal arrow and spear heads. They also provide a labour force for the village, particularly at harvest time, although the villagers have no political means of coercing the Mbuti into any of this activity.

The Mbuti perform these tasks willingly, because in return for their economic contribution to village life they get exactly what they need—to be left alone in their forest world. If they did not provide for the villagers in this way, the villagers would have to invade the forest for essential products, as they have done almost everywhere else. This would quickly destroy the viability of the Ituri forest as a haven for the 35,000 Mbuti hunters and gatherers now living there. By accepting the role of subservient suppliers, the Mbuti keep the villagers out of the forest, in enclaves distributed around the periphery of the major hunting area.

The Mbuti unwittingly fulfil another vital political function: just by being in the centre they form a common point of reference for all the highly different tribes of cultivators that surround them. This is formalized in the ceremony of the *nkumbi* ring. This is the initiation of the village boys which some Mbuti also undergo. Held every three years, for boys between the ages of eight and twelve, it lasts for over two months. Without the ceremony a village boy cannot achieve adult status or join the ancestors when he dies. It makes the Mbuti initiates blood-brothers although they are still looked down upon. Nonetheless, Mbuti participation in the *nkumbi* is a prerequisite, although this is entirely a village and non-pygmy festival in origin.

Even in the *nkumbi*, the Mbuti seem to play a subservient role, without any ritual authority, but their presence is ritually essential. For in this way alone are the villages able to come directly to terms with what they conceive of as the powerful and hostile spiritual forces of the forest. The forest is the neighbours' chief enemy, closing in and choking gardens and homesteads alike, and forcing regular migration; a fearful place, full of wild animals and evil spirits. They believe that by undergoing the initiation the Mbuti are themselves placed under non-forest supernatural sanctions, which from the village viewpoint are as effective as the political coercion they would like to apply, but cannot. However, it is exactly by going through the *nkumbi*, and testing the power of the village's supernatural world, by deliberately flaunting it, that the Mbuti know that they are indeed not constrained in any way, political or ritual.

In the forest it is often as if the village world did not exist. This varies from one part of the forest to another, and in some sectors, particularly to the east and south, the Mbuti are, like other pygmy groups, becoming increasingly dependent. This process has been accelerated since national independence by the influx of other peoples who are not part of the traditional relationship and who invade the forest deliberately to exploit its resources, rather than relying on the Mbuti to bring them what they need. However, in the central region, until the present at least, the forest life of the Mbuti is much as it always must have been.

There they live in small bands of anything from seven to thirty households. Each band within its own defined territory is constantly changing in size and composition throughout the year according to the availability of game and vegetable resources. Those to the west hunt more with bow and arrow. For both there is one time of year when all families within each hunting territory come together for communal hunting, and a time at which they split into tiny fragments, sometimes of only two or three families. A territory may extend for several days fast march from the village into the centre of the forest.

The 'family' is clearly defined as an economic rather than a biological unit, and the whole band is in effect the grand-family in which everyone addresses everyone else in kinship terms normally appropriate only to a nuclear family. Behaviour is expected to follow these lines, regardless of actual kinship. The band can thus change composition frequently without ever losing its tight-knit integrity. The constant changes are a prime mechanism by which disputes are averted, since as soon as a dispute begins to brew, one or other of the parties simply leaves and joins another band, justifying such a move on the grounds of the hunting being better elsewhere. These grounds, even if incidental, are frequently real, and the process of fission and fusion within each territory is also a vital part of the Mbuti role in the overall forest ecology.

The Mbuti have no leaders, no political centralization, no legal system, no social classes, no ritual specialists and no rigid rules of descent. Authority is clearly divided between the four age levels: children, youths, adults and elders. Each level is given essential responsibilities that grant it some measure of social control, making total co-operation indispensable for survival. For children and elders the responsibilities are primarily ritual and religious, since they are closest to death and therefore, as the Mbuti see it, closest to the ultimate source of all power and authority. Adult responsibility is primarily economic as they are the hunters and gatherers; for the youths responsibility is political. It is they who sanction social behaviour and who have it in their power to bring about social change.

Mbuti life is remarkably unfettered by formal social organization and structure; for them flexibility is the key to survival. But on occasions of death or when their survival is threatened they have a ritual, the *molimo*, which reinforces their sense of dependence upon the forest and their independence of the villagers. During this time they prefer to move camp as far away from the village as possible, ritually closing the trail behind them, and living only off forest products.

A relatively small part of their day is spent in the communal food quest, the remainder being spent in individual activities in camp. These include making bark cloth, repairing nets, making new bows and arrows, and weaving baskets. But it would be rare for the rest of the day to pass without some other form of communal activity such as the telling of legends, dancing or singing. The Mbuti have songs for particular occasions, such as honey-gathering, elephant-hunting or death, but all are addressed ultimately to the forest. Again these activities, while providing a wealth of entertainment and relaxation, make a major contribution to the integrity of Mbuti forest life, to their self-perception as forest people, and to the maintenance of their informal rules of economic and political behaviour, including their obligations to the villagers, for as long as they wish to keep them at a distance.

Their contribution to village economic and religious life, and to the overall inter-tribal political alliance, often seems minimal. Villagers are always complaining about shortage of supplies. But being a living part of the forest the Mbuti have learned that excess is as dangerous to survival as deficiency. For the villagers, as for themselves, they provide just enough of both goods and services, no more and no less. If the Mbuti seem happier, and indeed their life is characterized by an exuberant joy, it is because while the villagers are all relatively recent immigrants to the forest, to the Mbuti the forest has always been their father and mother.

It is not an empty romanticism that leads the Mbuti to call themselves *bamiki ba'ndura*, children of the forest. It is their world and they know it; it will remain theirs for as long as they can continue to exclude the villagers. The recent post-independence fighting between mercenary and Congo government forces throughout the forest threatened to destroy the relationship by driving the villagers into the forest for refuge. There was a danger that the refugees might learn that the forest is not such a hostile place after all, and could be exploited without the mediation of the Mbuti. But the Mbuti cunningly continued to play the game of being servants; they continued to feed and support the villagers economically, and thus continued to keep them ignorant of how to survive on their own.

In 1970, as soon as peace was restored, the villagers were only too happy to flee back to the periphery, rebuild their dusty villages, and restore the duality—the opposition—by which both they and the Mbuti are able to keep their own way of life. □

P. Muller/Hoa Qui

(*Right*) *Dancing, drumming and singing enliven Pygmy life. They sing about such special occasions as honey gathering, elephant hunts and death, but all their songs are addressed ultimately to the forest, which they call their 'mother and father'.*

(*Below right*) *The small physique of Pygmies, who are on average four and a half feet tall, has long fascinated foreigners: in 1851 some were sent to the Great Exhibition in London. The accumulation of fat on their buttocks suggests they are Bushmanoid in origin.*

(*Above*) *The forest provides Pygmies with most of their needs. The frames of their houses are made of saplings and the roofs of leaves. Nuts, mushrooms and honey are also gathered in the forest.*

It was once believed that the Pygmies were virtually slaves of neighbouring villagers. But in fact they cultivated this relationship of servitude to keep the villagers away from their forest home.

(*Below*) *Armed with spears and bows and arrows Pygmy hunters pursue their quarry into the depths of the forest, their natural habitat. The Pygmies hunt antelope, monkeys and even elephants.*

Colin Turnbull

Victor Englebert/Susan Griggs Agency

Colin Turnbull

John Moss/Colorific!

Colin Turnbull

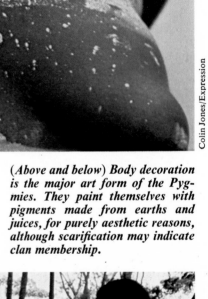

Colin Jones/Expression

(Below left) The presence of Pygmies is considered essential at the initiation ceremonies of neighbouring villagers. In this way the villagers come to terms with what they see as the powerful and hostile spiritual forces of the forest.

(Above and below) Body decoration is the major art form of the Pygmies. They paint themselves with pigments made from earths and juices, for purely aesthetic reasons, although scarification may indicate clan membership.

Colin Jones

Shilluk
SUDAN

In the 16th century, from the 'land of Duwat' in the south, came the legendary hero Nyikang and his warrior son Dak to found a dynasty on the west bank of the Nile. Tradition says that Nyikang was accompanied by Dengdit and the Dinka, Gilo and the Anuak, and Odimo and the Luo; the tribes he conquered were united into one people, the Shilluk.

Despite a long history of contact with Arabs from the north and other Sudanese peoples, Shilluk beliefs have survived. The spirit of Nyikang still provides the focus through which the Shilluk interpret and understand their existence. They trace the roots of their social order back to Nyikang and the central institution of their society, the dynasty which Nyikang founded, still exists.

The Shilluk have a rich tradition of stories, myths, and hymns: Nyikang is at the centre of these expressions of their elaborate cosmological ideas. They recognize three main divisions of their universe—earth, sky, and river— the only elements they know in the savannah where there are no mountains, ravines or forests. These three regions are significant in both their religion and mythology, and their economic life which revolves around cattle herding. The Shilluk also keep sheep and goats, and cultivate millet, maize, sesame, beans, pumpkins and tobacco. They recognize that their existence depends on the sky sending rain and the river rising to sustain the grass and crops.

Nyikang is said to be able to change natural and celestial phenomena. Two of the most important events in Shilluk mythology concern these powers—the crossing of the river and the fight with the Sun. The migration of Nyikang and his followers was halted by the Bahr el Ghazal, a river covered with floating vegetation. According to one legend, an albino follower asked Nyikang to clear a path for his people by spearing him in the river. Nyikang did this and the albino's blood cleared a way for the Shilluk to reach their present home. The Shilluk still cross and recross the crocodile infested Nile, eliciting the help of Nyikang. They call out his praise name 'crosser of the river' to gain protection in their journey.

While the Shilluk were waiting to cross the Bahr el Gazal, it is said that Nyikang lost a cow. It was reported to be in the herd of the Sun, and Dak set off with his followers to reclaim it. He fought with Garo, the son of the Sun, and cut off Garo's hand or finger to get a silver ring or bracelet. During the battle, Nyikang drove the Sun back into the sky, and revived his army by sprinkling them with water, or by touching them with the silver bracelet.

Another version is that Nyikang made the Sun shine at night so that the fight could continue. The silver from the ring or bracelet is said to have been used for the silver emblems—a bracelet and spear—still given to Shilluk kings at their installation. In the Shilluk savannah, the sun is hottest at the end of the dry season, just before it rains: the rains are said to overcome the heat as Nyikang overcame the Sun. He is believed to bring the rain, and thus still revives his people by sprinkling them with water.

The earth, the sky and the river are encompassed in the figure of Nyikang, and he is assimilated into them. Since Nyikang unites the elements of their natural world, it is through him that the Shilluk understand the nature and coherence of these elements in their universe. Nyikang's exploits are recorded in his many praise-names and titles. He has the names 'heaven' or 'the above', he is called 'son of the Nile' and 'son of the river'; and in hymns he is called 'our earth' or 'master of the earth'.

The birth of Nyikang is linked in alternative accounts to heaven or to a special creation of God. In one story, he is the son of Okwa, but Okwa traces descent through several forefathers to a great white or grey cow, which was created by God in the river. Nyikang's mother was either a crocodile, or partly crocodile. She represents in Shilluk thought the totality of river beings and phenomena and offerings are still made to her on the river banks where crocodiles emerge.

The Shilluk believe that it was Nyikang who first separated them from others of the same stock, and who differentiated them by associating different lineages with different territories, and sometimes with different totems. He is said to have made people for his kingdom out of insects, fish and animals. The ordinary Shilluk are thought

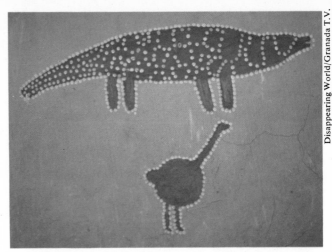

(Above) Crocodile and ostrich paintings decorate the Akurwa shrine where effigies of Nyikang and Dak, the nation's legendary founders, are kept. Nyikang's mother is said to have been part crocodile.

(Left) The cattle which the Shilluk king acquires as gifts or fines are kept in the royal village. These treasury cattle are given away by the king to people in need or used for special feasts.

In language and physical appearance, as well as in their social and political ideas, the Shilluk illustrate their descent from the early Pre-Nilotic peoples many thousands of years ago.

to derive their humanity from him.

Divided into about 100 descent groups, the Shilluk trace descent through the male line. These groups are dispersed throughout the kingdom, living in different settlements. In each settlement one descent group is dominant, and provides the chief of the settlement. In the past, these settlements were politically opposed. However, since the beginning of the dynasty, the Shilluk have all recognised a common head, the *reth* or king, who always comes from the *kwareth* or royal clan. Throughout Shilluk history, the kingship has acted as a focus of political loyalty and national identity, uniting competing localities into a totality.

It is unlikely that the later Shilluk kings were more than theocratically omnipotent. Their importance was limited to a religious function which revolved around making sacrifices, particularly for rain and victory in war, and carrying out ritual obligations to Nyikang. Their major judicial role seems to have been the settlement of disputes, as peacemaker rather than as judge. A further reduction in their powers came about with foreign rule in the Sudan. At the end of the 19th century Anglo-Egyptian rule introduced another and more powerful authority in the land—central government.

Since Sudanese independence in 1956 the government has formalised the *reth*'s position by appointing him magistrate second class. That is the extent of his legal power today, but he remains the focus of loyalty for those Shilluk who lead a predominantly traditional life. In recent years, the kingship has circulated amongst three families. The 33rd king was installed in 1975.

Nyikang is thought to have come to Shillukland from the south west, near Tonga, and travelled along the west bank of the Nile until he reached Muomo in the north. Muomo and Tonga respectively became the most northerly and southerly settlements of the kingdom and the country is now divided into two provinces, Ger in the north and Luak in the south. Sometimes these territorial and political divisions are opposed to each other. The really important divisions of Shillukland are, however, Gol Dhiang in the north and Gol Nyikang in the south—the religious divi-

Ostrich feather effigies of Nyikang and Dak are carried to the coronation at Fashoda on a ten-day journey from Akurwa through the villages. Coronation ceremonies reassert the unity of the nation.

Ayang Anei Kur was crowned 33rd reth, or king, in 1975. The reth's powers have declined since the arrival of central government: Khartoum recognizes him only as magistrate second class.

sions corresponding to the political divisions of the kingdom. The boundary between them is the inlet of a river called the Arepejur, which means 'the gathering of the peoples' just to the south of the royal capital, Fashoda.

The Arepejur divides two settlements, the political chiefdoms of Golbany and Kwom, the chief of each representing his religious division. It is these leaders, acting as the spokesman for Gol Dhiang and Gol Nyikang, who must reach agreement on the choice of a new king. This choice is then confirmed by an electoral college which consists of the chiefs of Muomo and Tonga, nine chiefs representing the original settlements of Shillukland and three chiefs of dominant branches of the royal clan. The backing of all parts of the kingdom is necessary before a prince can be made king.

Even when agreement has been reached, there remains ceremonial opposition between the two religious divisions until the king is installed. Then the divisions unite to form the single kingdom that Nyikang created. The ceremonies begin with the journey of two effigies, representing Nyikang and Dak, from the shrine at Akurwa in the extreme north to Fashoda. As the effigies pass through each district the people gather to pay their respects to Nyikang, for the Shilluk believe that the effigy contains the spirit of Nyikang.

At Arepejur, the effigy of Nyikang and his followers from Gol Dhiang meet the king-elect and his supporters from Gol Nyikang in mock battle. The two protagonists represent the different parts of the Shilluk kingdom. Nyikang is victorious and captures the king-elect. Symbolically, the office is more powerful than the man. In Fashoda, the effigy is placed on the royal stool before being removed for the king-elect to sit in its place. The spirit of Nyikang is then thought to enter him, and he trembles with possession. He is then king of the Shilluk. The diversity of the Shilluk is overcome, and the nation is symbolically united.

All sections of the population are represented in the investiture. Different settlements and clans are responsible for performing various parts of the ceremony and providing certain ritual objects such as ostrich feathers, antelope skins, sacred spears and royal drums. The kingship represents the whole country, and the king can only be made by rites in which the whole country takes part. In the final phase of the ceremony, the king receives homage and exhortations from the chiefs.

Only the son of a former king can become king of the Shilluk. There is, however, no customary order of succession, and so theoretically any son of a previous king is eligible if he can press his claim. In the past, disagreement over the choice of king led to fighting between Gol Nyikang and Gol Dhiang; individuals were only able to retain the kingship if they could defend themselves against rival claimants. The Shilluk say that kings should be put to death if they grow senile or become sick, and that any prince may at any time challenge the king to mortal combat.

The Shilluk believe that their king should be in a state of ritual purity and physical perfection. If he is not, then he should be killed to avoid some grave disaster; he must be killed to save the kingship and with it the Shilluk people. The king may be strangled, or walled up in a hut and left to die, if he fails to satisfy his wives or shows other signs of physical deterioration. There are traditional but contradictory accounts of regicide. It seems most likely that those kings who died violently were the victims of internal rebellions and discontent.

The power of any individual king clearly rested on his identification with Nyikang, for the Shilluk believe that an individual does not reign but rather Nyikang does: 'Nyikang is the *reth* but the *reth* is not Nyikang'. The Shilluk also say 'that if Nyikang should die, the whole Shilluk race would perish.'

Somali
SOMALIA, ETHIOPIA, KENYA

The Somali Democratic Republic, or Somalia, is almost unique among the states of modern Africa. Instead of a patchwork of ethnic and tribal groups inside an arbitrary colonial frontier, it contains only one people: the Somali. Altogether, there are estimated to be about seven million Somali, of whom two million live outside the Republic. These occupy large areas of Kenya, Ethiopia and the (French) Territory of Afars and Issas. There are also Somali communities in most of the major cities of East Africa and Arabia, and small groups scattered throughout the world's seaports and capitals. All these people share a similar culture and language, the same religion—Islam—and a sense of common identity.

The Somali have always been known for their ferocity as warriors and stubborn independence and individualism —characteristics developed in a beautiful yet hard and pitiless environment. This is the northern part of the 'Horn of Africa', where Africa juts out to meet the Arabian peninsula. The Somali, like most of the peoples of this region, are racially of the intermediate type which was once called Hamitic; dark-skinned, but more similar in cast of face to Arabs and Europeans than to Negroes. They probably originated as a separate people near the Gulf of Aden coast, in the northern part of their present territory.

In this harsh and arid region, there are no permanent rivers, rainfall is sparse and the country consists of dry savannah plains and semi-desert, with a mountain escarpment in the north, facing the coast. Though crops are grown in the highlands of the northwest, over most of the area the only feasible means of livelihood is by pasturing animals. The people are nomads, constantly moving with their stock in search of water and grazing. It is a harsh

life at the best of times, and should the rains fail, the result is famine: in 1974, 7,000 people died from the drought which gripped Sahelian Africa.

A Somali poem describes the interior in the dry season:
> Bush thick and impenetrable, scorched trees,
>   the hot air rising from them,
> Hot wind and heat, which will lick you like
>   a flame . . .
> The swelling of feet pricked by thorns, a
>   thorny thicket, plants prickly and spiny.
> Charred plants, hot stumps of burnt trees,
>   the hot air rising from them . . .

To the nomad, water and rain mean everything that is sweet in life; the composer of a love song will compare his mistress's beauty to fresh grass that springs up where rain has fallen, or to a tree growing beside a spring, that will remain green and fertile even in the drought.

During the 9th and 10th centuries AD, the Somali accepted the Moslem faith. It was perhaps the most significant step in their history: Islam was subsequently the basis of their culture, and the mark of their identity as a people. In this and many other ways the influence of the Arab world, so near to them across the sea, has been crucial. Today, the Somali Republic is the only non-Arab country in the Arab league.

In the early period, Arab traders founded a chain of ports along the coast of the Horn; their population and distinctive culture have survived to be incorporated into the Somali nation. One such port, Mogadishu, is now the Somali capital. This debt to Arabian civilization is enshrined in the tradition that the ancestors of the Somali clans came from Arabia and were kinsmen of the Prophet Mohammed himself.

The expansion of the Somali people southwards began about the same time as their conversion. By the 16th and 17th centuries, they had conquered the region where the Juba and Shebelle Rivers run down from the Ethiopian highlands. Those Somali who moved here found a very different habitat and circumstances from the north. The land along the rivers, and the plain between them, is fertile and well suited to farming; indeed it was already farmed by groups of Bantu speakers who came from the south.

Conquering or entering into alliance with these people, many Somali groups settled in their turn, to till the earth or have it tilled for them by slaves or clients. The Southern Somali are generally more peaceable, open and easy going than those of the north. This is because they live in an easier environment where they have developed peaceful institutions so as to dwell permanently together in villages and towns. Here they have assimilated the Bantu. Their habits and traditions differ in many ways, and some of the southern dialects are almost unintelligible to a northerner. Northern nomads have traditionally tended to see the southern farmers as soft and slow-witted, not proper Somali; southerners in their turn see the northerners as uncouth and lawless.

While the river area was being settled, other Somali groups bypassed it and pushed yet further south, as far as the Tana river in what has since become northern Kenya. Here conditions are similar to those in northern Somalia, and they have kept their pastoral nomadic way of life.

Somali social organization is based on this way of life. The usual living group among the nomads consists of a

Annunziata/Explorer

Somali nomads are particularly proud of their camels which are lovingly portrayed in their poetry. These camels, which are herded separately from family flocks of sheep and goats, are being watered in the Northern Frontier District of Kenya where some of the two million expatriate Somali live.

Somali Koranic schools have taught Arabic for over 1,000 years. But widespread literacy was not achieved until a modified Roman alphabet was adopted as the official script for the Somali language in 1972. The government claims that a campaign started in 1974 has raised the literacy rate from 5 to 70 per cent, a remarkable achievement.

Kosy Rouleau/John Hillelson Agency

Tony Carr/Colorific!

163

Alan Hutchison

man, or two or three related men, with their wives and children and perhaps a widowed mother or other dependants. Each married woman has her house, a collapsible structure of mats over a framework of branches, which can be dismantled and packed on to a camel when it is time to move camp. The encampment is surrounded by a fence of piled thorn branches to keep enemies and predators out, and the sheep and goats in, at night.

These animals are the principal part of the nomad's stock; looking after them is the job of the women and young children. But the pride of the nomad is his camels: objects of prestige and beauty as well as providers of milk and meat. Since they can go for long periods without water, they are herded separately from the family flocks which have to stay within reach of a pool or well. The camels of several kinsmen are herded together by boys who spend their lives from the age of seven, until their early twenties and old enough to marry, looking after the animals.

For people constantly on the move, there are no such things as 'neighbours'. The only ties are therefore to one's kin. Until recently these ties were very strong and absolutely essential: without kinsmen to support him, a man was helpless. 'Kinsmen should be as the thorn fence protecting the encampment', one poem says. Descendants of the same man form a group, and such groups were the basis of traditional Somali society. Groups of kin competed and fought for scarce water and pasture. Decisions were taken by consultation between the adult men; there was no central 'government' among the Somali until modern times.

Somali women, unlike most Moslem women, have never gone veiled or been segregated from the world. Nevertheless, they live according to a code of strict decorum. Traditionally, female virginity is safeguarded by infibulation, the surgical joining of the lips of the vulva. The operation is carried out at eight to eleven years old; it is

In 1974 the Somali government sponsored 'Operation Clean-Up' to sweep the streets of its capital, Mogadishu. This is typical of the mass mobilization campaigns based on self-reliance which attempt to make the most of Somalia's limited resources.

not only very painful but ensures that a girl's wedding night is no joyous experience. This is one national tradition which most modern educated Somali reject and would like to see changed, but it is still prevalent, and its strongest supporters tend to be older women.

Somali life is reflected in their great tradition of poetry. Until recently, the Somali language was not written down, so poems circulated by word of mouth, and those judged the best were carefully transmitted from one generation to the next. Classical verse is a highly complex and demanding art. Poems are comments on the poet's own experience; often on political themes, argument and propaganda. One of the most famous of their poets was the religious warrior leader, Mohammed 'Abdille Hassan (nicknamed the 'mad Mullah' by the British) who at the beginning of this century led a 20 year-long guerrilla campaign against British, Italian and Ethiopian colonists.

In modern popular song, which uses a simpler version of the old verse techniques, love is the favourite theme. Many of the lyrics have a romantic intensity which can be best appreciated against the background of the sexual restraint of traditional Somali culture.

Somali society is changing rapidly. After the disastrous Sahelian drought of 1974, nomads are being settled as farmers and fishermen. Now under a government committed to 'scientific socialism', the Somali of the Republic have to learn how to transform their old pride and independence into a new national spirit, abandoning—so their leaders hope—the loyalties to clan and lineage, which formerly divided them, for the brotherhood of all Somali. ☐

Sotho
LESOTHO and SOUTH AFRICA

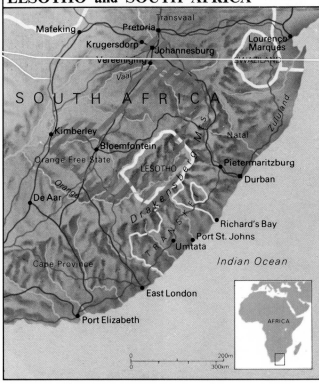

Sotho men can be distinguished by the way they wear their blankets, imported from South Africa. The cloak characteristically envelops the left shoulder, while the right arm remains free.

The kingdom of Lesotho lies astride the watershed of southern Africa, perched among the dramatic peaks of the Drakensberg Range from which flow three great rivers, the Vaal, the Tugela and the Orange. This range, which rises to over 10,000 feet, divides the lush and fertile valleys of the lowveld, along the Indian Ocean coast, from the arid plains of the highveld. It also divides the traditional settlement areas of the two major branches of Bantu-speaking peoples in Southern Africa—the Nguni and the Sotho. To the south and east are the Nguni, who include the Zulu and Xhosa; to the west are the Sotho (sometimes known as Basotho).

The name Sotho (pronounced Sutu) is loosely applied to those peoples of the interior plateau who share a broadly similar language and culture. The Sotho are distinguished from the Nguni peoples by their preference for living in concentrated settlements, for marrying close kin and by their use of animal totems for their clans. They are divided into three groups. The Tswana live in Botswana and western Transvaal; the Northern Sotho, in northern and eastern Transvaal; and the Southern Sotho, in Lesotho, formerly Basutoland, and the Orange Free State.

Early in the 19th century these Sotho clans were dispersed all over the highveld in small autonomous chiefdoms. Only the Pedi, the largest tribe of the Northern Sotho group, had emerged as a major political force in the 18th century, through their control of trade between the interior and the Portuguese settlement at Delagoa Bay. In the 1820s, however, Shaka Zulu's military revolution in Natal unleashed two decades of turmoil in southern Africa: the terrible years known to the Sotho as the *Difaqane*, a time of constant warfare, wandering and hunger, which completely altered the old settlement patterns and led to the emergence of new political entities.

One of the new states was that of Moshoeshoe who established himself with the remnants of scattered Sotho clans in the Caledon Valley, in the western shadow of the Drakensberg. These were the people whose descendants describe themselves as the Sotho of Moshoeshoe, whose country became the British protectorate of Basutoland and, in 1966, the self-governing kingdom of Lesotho. Since it is the only Sotho state which today retains its integrity in the form of political independence, Lesotho can be considered as being representative of the Sotho tradition, although strictly it is representative only of that branch known as the Southern Sotho.

Moshoeshoe was a minor chief of a section of the Kwena (Crocodile) clan which now forms a hereditary aristocracy in Lesotho. Through an astute combination of military tactics and diplomacy he was able to maintain his defensive stronghold at Thaba Bosiu, the Mountain of Darkness, and to consolidate his political position against a series of powerful adversaries. He emerged at the end of the period of turmoil in control of the area between the Caledon and the Orange rivers.

His followers were diverse but their descendants invoke a common identity as the Sotho of Moshoeshoe. They celebrate the exploits of the past in a vigorous tradition of praise-songs (*dithoko*) and a rich body of literature. Although the nation comprises many Sotho clans—the largest are the Kwena, Fokeng, Taung, Sia and Tlokwa—they all share one language and culture and a unique historical consciousness. Consequently they do not experience the acute ethnic rivalries which mark the politics of some other African countries.

Moshoeshoe and his people also had to contend with the Afrikaners who had trekked from the Cape Colony in search of new farming land and settled in the region north of·the Orange river. Recurring conflicts over territory broke out into open warfare in 1858 and again in

Lesley Garner

165

Norman Meyers/AAA

Daily Telegraph Colour Library

(Above) Sotho villagers live at heights of up to 8,000 feet in the Drakensberg Mountains. Higher still, herdboys occupy temporary grazing posts where they tend sheep and cut grass for fodder.

Dredging for diamonds in northern Lesotho has provided a few jobs, but has done nothing to stem the tide of migrant labourers going to work in South Africa. The profitable exploitation of diamonds is still uncertain but the De Beers company of South Africa recently invested in a new attempt.

1865. The Sotho were forced to cede much of their land; and Moshoeshoe sought British protection which was reluctantly granted in 1868.

The population of Lesotho expanded rapidly throughout the following hundred years, to reach the figure of one million in 1966. The Sotho gradually settled all the mountain areas, and the Kwena clan extended its political domination through the 'placing' system by which senior chiefs granted rights of territorial jurisdiction to their junior kinsmen. The chiefs held the prerogative of allocating arable land to their subjects; they controlled the distribution of cattle, the most important economic resource; and they pursued a strategy of arranging marriages between close kin. As commoners point out, 'the chiefs like to marry each other', for the strategy had both economic and political advantages.

Marriage requires the transfer of bridewealth cattle, known as *bohadi*, from a man's kin to his wife's kin to ensure the legal validity of the union and to give the man paternity rights over the children. The Sotho say, 'the child belongs to the cattle'. Delay in payment of *bohadi*—the customary requirement is quoted at 20 head of cattle but is now often paid in cash—can give rise to uncertainty over whether a man has 'sufficiently' married his wife to claim paternity of her children. Marrying a cousin helped to prevent the dispersal of family wealth in stock.

Chiefs were usually polygynous—one important chief, Jonathan Molapo of Leribe, was reputed to have 96 wives. Often half-brothers were competing for succession to office, and expected to draw on the political support of their respective mothers' kin. Marrying a close kins-woman was a means of creating a powerful factional alliance.

In the 1870s, despite the early years of privation, the country was the granary of southern Africa. The discovery of diamonds at Kimberley attracted thousands of fortune-seekers from all over the world and ensured a ready market for surplus grain from Basutoland. The Sotho themselves joined the flow of migrants seeking work, so that the export of grain and labour rapidly induced the trans-formation to a cash economy.

One hundred years later the position is reversed. Today Lesotho imports grain and is listed by the United Nations as one of the poorest nations in the world. This has happened through a rapid increase in population combined with a steady deterioration of the land, as a result of erosion, over-grazing and poor cultivation techniques. The Lowlands were described in 1834, when the first missionaries explored the country, as fertile and teeming with game.

Now the once rich area is deeply scarred with *dongas*, or erosion gulleys, in which the torrents of the rainy season carry away vast quantities of good soil every year. There is an acute shortage of arable land and most families cannot earn a living from the desultory cultivation of hard and exhausted soils. Sotho staple crops are maize and sorghum, supplemented by wheat, pumpkins, peas and beans. Many families also grow green vegetables and root crops with some success in small enclosed gardens near the homesteads.

The only way to increase crop yields under the existing system of land tenure is the use of intensive techniques. These include improved seed, fertilizer and proper plough-ing by oxen or hired tractor, all of which require con-siderable investment. Lesotho has few minerals and little industry so that there are very few employment oppor-tunities inside the country. The result is that most house-holds depend for their livelihood on the export of their menfolk to the towns and farms and to the gold and the coal mines of the Transvaal and Orange Free State.

Migrant labourers spend most of their adult lives moving alternately between their rural homes in Lesotho and the industrial centres of South Africa. Their cash earnings provide the means for their families to buy food and clothes, and to invest in agriculture and the *bohadi* ex-changes which legitimate marriage. This is the measure of Lesotho's dependence, surrounded as it is by its powerful neighbour, South Africa. The consumer goods of indus-trial society may be found in the midst of hunger, and the international malaise of inflation reaches the remotest mountain villages.

The migrant labour system has drastic consequences for village social and economic life. It causes a shortage of male labour for the critical task of ploughing in October and November. Men cannot take their families with them to town, so husbands and wives live apart for repetitive periods of indefinite length which leads inevitably to

Some Sotho girls still undergo initiation. During the second and public stage of the ritual they often per-form elaborate parodies of male behaviour such as imitating the swagger of courting youths.

Colin Murray

Wim Swaan/Camera Press

domestic tensions and a high illegitimacy rate. Women must often rear their children single-handed, and they have to plan the domestic budget with unpredictable resources and, perhaps, differing priorities from their absent husbands. Most manage remarkably well.

In the later stages of her life a woman increasingly assumes the responsibilities incumbent upon her position as the focal point of a 'house'. A house is the basic domestic unit, consisting of a woman and her children; it has clearly defined property rights as against other houses of a polygynous man. Entitled to general deference on account of their age and status, widows have also held important political offices in Lesotho if only in the capacity of regent after a husband's death. The 'senior mother' of the present king, Moshoeshoe II, was Regent for 20 years.

Both boys and girls are initiated at any time from puberty to their early 20's, although only a minority go through the ritual today. Boys are circumcised and live in harsh seclusion in mountain areas well away from habitation; girls are secluded near the village. During the second, public, stage of their initiation, the girls perform elaborate songs and dramas which involve an element of parody of male behaviour. In their respective 'schools' both boys and girls are shown mysteries and learn secret songs called *dikoma*. There is a strong taboo against revealing any of these mysteries to the uninitiated, madness is said to afflict anyone who does so.

The Sotho believe that after death senior kin continue to exercise moral authority over the living. People celebrate their obligations to the *badimo*, or shades of the ancestors, through the occasional sacrifice of a cow or sheep for a feast, in propitiation of ancestral wrath or in anticipation of good fortune for the family. The profession of medicine is dominated by men who learn it

Horses are symbols of prestige in Lesotho, where they are used principally for transport. The Basuto pony is particularly prized for its adaptation to the mountainous terrain.

either through dream-revelation from the family shades or through apprenticeship to another doctor.

A variety of divining techniques are used to diagnose sorcery and other agencies of misfortune, and a profusion of herbal remedies to deal with all manner of disorders ranging from trivial complaints to a woman's failure to conceive. Barrenness is regarded as a tragic condition while conversely, motherhood enables a woman to fulfil her natural part in the social order. In the past, doctors also had the duty of invoking rain in periods of drought.

The Sotho today retain a lively respect for their chiefs, and an equally lively awareness of their rights as citizens. 'A chief without people is no chief' well expresses the reciprocities of office: yet, with the bureaucratic structures of the central government superimposed upon the hierarchy of chiefs, the Sotho find their traditional loyalties distorted.

In successive political crises since independence, the ruling party under Chief Jonathan has maintained control by manipulation of constitutional power. This has left many Sotho disillusioned with self-government. Politically independent, Lesotho is economically dependent on a country with an alien philosophy of rule—the idea of White supremacy enshrined in South Africa's apartheid system.

The outlook for the future is uncertain. Lesotho achieves a precarious livelihood only through the export of her manpower. This stark fact cannot but undermine the prospect of fulfilling national aspirations whose foundations were so proudly laid 150 years ago. □

Swahili

KENYA, TANZANIA

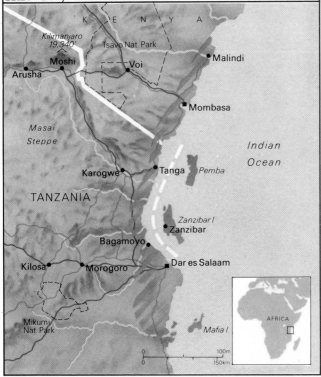

Colourful kitenge cloth is replacing the traditional black material worn by the Swahili women of the Comoro Islands. The new fabric is made at the Chinese-built Friendship Textile Mill in Dar es Salaam.

Alan Hutchison

Swahili is the name given not only to East Africa's most widespread language, but also to some of the people who live along the coast of Kenya and Tanzania: the word Swahili comes from the Arabic *sahel* and means coast dwellers. They form a collection of populations who share a common culture and language but the boundaries between the Swahili and their neighbours are never defined very clearly. It is always open to argument who are 'true' Swahili and who are 'marginal' people, claiming higher status in the complex society of the region.

The East African coast is ecologically and historically unique. It consists of a highly fertile but very narrow strip of land, with many small offshore islands, between the Indian Ocean and the arid plains that stretch back to the uplands of the interior. This coastal strip is quite distinct from its hinterland—an intermediate region with ties both to the interior and to lands across the ocean, belonging fully to neither. The Swahili have lived here for centuries, with links both to the people of the interior and to those from elsewhere on the Indian Ocean coast, especially the Arabs.

The Swahili do not stand alone as a distinct ethnic or tribal entity but form an element in a wider, mixed coastal society. Little is known of the shadowy groups who were among their earliest ancestors—the Diba, Debuli and others from Persia and India whose ancient ruined settlements lie largely unexcavated in Zanzibar, Pemba and elsewhere along the coast. The identity of the indigenous peoples who previously occupied the coast, and who intermingled with the immigrants to form the Swahili, is also unknown. But from the 8th century onward, there were varying degrees of intermixture with Arabs, who slowly began to settle along the coast setting up small trading colonies.

The Swahili had emerged as a distinct people with their own way of life by the 12th century at the latest. Their stone-built towns along the coast were the capitals of small city-states. Dynasties of Swahili kings, with their own small armies, left behind them stone palaces and mosques, written chronicles and minted coins. These towns still exist, mostly as overgrown ruins on raised coral promontories and off-shore islets.

Pate and Kilwa were perhaps the most important towns along the coast during the 15th century; Kilwa was an entrepot for the gold trade of Monomotapa. On the islands off the mainland were the states and towns of Zanzibar and Pemba, and far to the east those of the Comoro Islands. These petty states were in continual competition, and their decline after the 15th century was due largely to the arrival of Portuguese colonists, who were ousted in turn by the Omani Arabs in the 18th century. The Arab Sultanate had its seat of government in Zanzibar, and during the 19th century it effectively controlled the whole East African mainland as far as the Great Lakes. Zanzibar declined eventually with the abolition of the slave trade and the advent of British and German colonial rule.

Language and religion are the main cohesive features of the Swahili culture. There are many dialects of KiSwahili, but all are mutually intelligible except in minor details of vocabulary. Unlike other Bantu languages it has long been a written language, using Arabic script, and there is a tradition of elaborate poetry and written verse chronicles. Their Moslem faith has linked the Swahili to the wider Islamic world and also distinguished them from the peoples of the hinterland. The mosque is the centre of any settlement, however small; the larger Swahili towns often have several dozen mosques, each the centre of a small neighbourhood.

The Swahili are essentially town-dwellers. With their 'stone' (coral) town-houses and mosques surrounded by

John Middleton

(Below) A Swahili craftsman painstakingly carves a door post in Lamu on the Kenyan coast. Ornately decorated doors are an indication of Arab cultural influence along the shores of East Africa.

(Above) Swahili are essentially urban dwellers. Outside the towns, in the wooded areas of the coast, Swahili farmers live in coral houses which are thatched with palm leaves.

Sheila Unwin

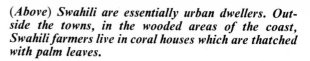

Alan Hutchison

Swahili housewives buy most of their fruits like oranges, cherries and paw paws from roadside traders. The black bui bui robe of this woman is an adaptation of traditional Arab dress.

Swahili women wade out into the Indian Ocean to catch fish by hand. They encircle the fish, moving closer and closer together, until they can scoop them up into their baskets.

Peter Fraenkel

lesser mud-and-palm thatch houses, the compounds and streets of Swahili towns and villages are very different from those of their non-Swahili neighbours. Today the larger, two-storey, stone houses are often abandoned or derelict, but at the height of Swahili culture they were central to the Swahili way of life—they had special quarters where women could be secluded, and slaves formerly occupied the ground floors. Plumbing and stone bathrooms, stone carving, elaborate plasterwork, and finely carved doors were indications of high status, as were elaborate chairs, beds, chests, and other furniture. Traditional Swahili products included gold and silver jewellery, woven silk and cotton fabrics, leather goods and fine iron-work: wealthier families imported Chinese and Indian porcelains.

All this demanded great wealth: slaves and ivory provided it. The Swahili, together with the Arabs of Zanzibar, went into the interior of Africa to carry off slaves and collect ivory. These were exported to the countries of the Indian Ocean along with cowrie shells, gum, gold, timber and agricultural produce.

The Swahili have always produced for their own consumption millet and some rice, as well as coconut products and fruits in abundance. The importance of fishing is evident in an elaborate marine culture and technology that permeates everyday life, while high status has always been given to landowning and farming. Retail trade however, has been looked down on as suitable only for Arabs and Indians, an attitude that has cost the Swahili dear in recent years.

Although still wealthy, the Swahili coast and its peoples have lost their former substance and glory. Today the Swahili see themselves as emerging from the decline they suffered under colonial rule, although they cannot seek to re-establish their former power. But their language and culture, established for so many centuries, are widespread in independent Kenya and Tanzania, and ensure them high cultural prestige and a unique identity. □

Tswana

BOTSWANA, SOUTH AFRICA

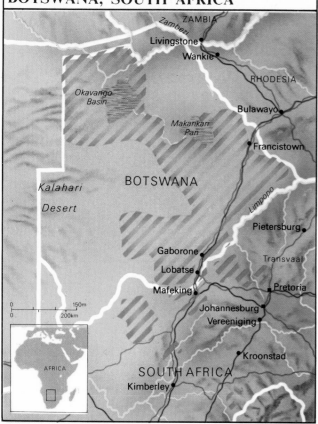

On the edges of the Kalahari desert the Tswana are occasionally victims of drought. This mother has just been given powdered milk for her malnourished child at a government centre in Serowe.

Little is known for certain of the genesis and early history of the Tswana of Southern Africa, but it is widely accepted that they split from the Bantu-speakers of the East African lake region centuries ago. Indeed, two of the explanations for their name's origin emphasize this: *-tswa*, in Setswana, means 'go out' or 'come from', and *-tswaana* means 'separate from one another'. Dating their southward migration is a matter of guesswork, but the move is reliably estimated to have been completed at the latest by 1600 AD.

The Tswana, who constitute the western group of the Sotho peoples, are a linguistically and culturally homogenous population of some two million. Before European colonization of the interior, in the mid-19th century, Tswana territory was considerably larger than it is today. But the area of the chiefdoms was progressively reduced by White expansion. Today the Tswana live mainly in eastern and north-western Botswana and in Bophuthatswana, their 'ethnic homeland' in South Africa, which comprises some 20 widely scattered blocks of land. Bophuthatswana was granted 'total and complete independence' by South Africa in December 1977, but the separate blocks do not constitute an economically viable independent state – nor one that is internationally recognized.

On the borders of the Kalahari desert, rain and well-being are synonymous in the Tswana world-view; the term *pula* describes both. In the west of the territory, annual rainfall varies between 10 and 20 inches; in the east, between 15 and 25 inches. It is, however, both unreliable and subject to high rates of evaporation and drainage. But economic life depends on the rain and, whether or not they continue to cultivate and herd, Tswana are inveterately interested in the subject. In traditional cos-

mology, two types of rain are distinguished: *pula ya medupe* is 'white' and, being gentle and soaking, irrigates agricultural and pastoral land; *pula ya dikadima* is accompanied by thunder and lightning and falls in violent bursts, frightening people and animals and damaging crops.

The relationship between their ecology and their social and political arrangements makes the Tswana noteworthy among the Southern Bantu. They have never constituted a single political community with a king or a single government, but comprise approximately 80 separate, named chiefdoms, located mostly in South Africa, with populations varying from a few thousand to over a hundred thousand people.

In general, the territory of a chiefdom is dominated by its densely populated capital, in which most citizens live. They hold pastoral and agricultural land in the surrounding hinterland, where satellite villages are usually situated and often organized into districts under recognized headmen. According to customary law, everyone must live in a village. A large number move to their rural holdings in the agricultural season from November to June, but they usually return after the harvest.

Each individual in the Tswana chiefdom belongs to a household unit made up of a monogamous or polygamous family and sometimes other dependants. A number of neighbouring households form a family group. Their heads, who are usually related through their fathers' line, are ranked according to relative birth status, the first

E. R. Watts/Robert Harding Associates

Dr. Comoroff

The Tswana have built up large cattle herds which they sell at regular markets. Livestock provide some 80 per cent of all income earned in both the cash and traditional economies.

among them holding the position of family group 'elder'. A number of elders and their descendants, in turn, will collectively constitute a ward, the most significant unit in Tswana society.

The core of a ward is usually composed of a few related family-groups descended from a common founder, and the senior group provides the ward headman. While virtually all wards contain unrelated families originally placed there by the chief, these eventually become referred to as 'distant relatives'; for the idiom of kinship is used to express internal ward relationships.

The ward occupies its own residential site in the village, which is usually circular, with homesteads along the perimeter and a communal cattle-byre and meeting enclosure in the centre. For the average Tswana, the ward is the focus of social and economic life. The headman is responsible for the maintenance of law, order and amicable relations within the unit: aided by a council and advisers, he manages its affairs and is empowered to try minor disputes. The ward headmen also provide a link between their members and the government of the chiefdom. They sit on the *lekgotla* (chiefly council) and, as such, are closely involved in its administration.

Although each individual belongs to a household, family-group and ward, it is not only this which links him to others. Everyone is affiliated to a series of four groups and categories which cut across local divisions. First, while lacking corporate lineages, the Tswana recognize

mutual rights and obligations with many kinsmen and in-laws, some of whom live in different wards. Preferring if possible to marry cousins of all types, they do not distinguish sharply between their paternal and maternal kin groups, for the two overlap.

The transmission of property and position is patrilineal, and relations with close male kin are often competitive; maternal relatives, on the other hand, do not compete and are a focus of reciprocal obligation. This explains a major advantage of cousin marriage—it either transforms rivalry into, or perpetuates, ties of friendship and support. Kinship and affinity link each person to a wide ranging network, both within and across local groups.

Tswana communities are heterogeneous: during its history every chiefdom has incorporated immigrant groups from other chiefdoms, sometimes as separate wards under their own leaders. Each political community has its own totem, and a further affiliation is determined by the stratification of society: the ruling descent group forms the nobility; commoners rank next, and immigrants or their descendants from other Tswana chiefdoms after them; lastly, non-Tswana serfs were formerly attached to the households of prominent men.

The final category is the male or female age-regiment which every youth traditionally joined. These age-regiments were formed every four to seven years, following an initiation ritual. This no longer occurs, but today most Tswana enter voluntary associations: membership of churches, soccer clubs, co-operatives and other interest groupings now cross traditional residential, class, age, ethnic and kinship affiliations.

The principles of social organization are expressed primarily in the village context, for it is here that all

Peter Fraenkel

More than 35,000 Tswana miners work in South Africa, where companies encourage the use of migrant labour which is cheaper and less likely to cause political repercussions.

Christianity in the 19th century transformed, among many other things, social practices such as polygamous marriage. But, unlike other Southern Bantu converts, who often lived in segregated mission stations, Tswana Christians were integrated into the community, the structure of which changed little as a result.

Similarly, the incorporation of the Tswana into the Southern African economy, and the impoverishment of the rural areas, has compelled many adults to migrate as labourers to the cities and White farms. As a result, households have been severely disrupted as economic and social units. Nevertheless, this has been largely accommodated by the fact that they are embedded in larger local groupings, into which their members may be absorbed. Thus, while labour migration has had many negative effects on Tswana life, it has not led to structural breakdown.

Recent changes in national political environments, however, have begun to bring about structural transformations. The Tswana live in two states with dramatically different ideologies: in Botswana, the emergent regime has explicitly eliminated the power of chiefs who, in colonial times, suffered less interference than those in other British territories.

With independence in 1966 local government passed to District Councils and, while they retained some judicial and administrative functions, chiefs became junior civil servants. Apart from participating in an advisory House of Chiefs, they were specifically barred from national or local politics. Indeed, 'tribalism' and 'traditionalism' have negative connotations in modern Botswana; her current leaders are men who have become successful in the new politico-economic conditions.

In contrast, the South African regime has ostensibly encouraged the incorporation of traditional institutions into modern government. The ideological and moral premises underlying this rural aspect of the Republic's *apartheid* system have been bitterly debated, but its implications are clear. The creation of 'ethnic homelands' placed a measure of local control in the hands of traditional leaders. The architects of the policy, however, treated the chiefship as a purely administrative role, rather than the fulcrum of a dynamic political order. As a result, the political dimension of the office has—unwittingly or otherwise—been eliminated.

Despite their contrasting approaches, Botswana and South Africa have both transformed the indigenous system, leaving office-holders as bureaucrats with little effective political control. In the past it was precisely this control which underpinned the social order; so there can be no question that the processes of structural transformation set in motion by government policies will continue and be thoroughgoing.

When Botswana's small population of 600,000 won independence in 1966, their vast country possessed little hope of substantial economic development. Most people were herders or farmers, or went to South Africa to find work. But discoveries of mineral desposits, made soon after independence, have changed Botswana's economic fortunes.

Diamonds, copper, nickel, coal, manganese and asbestos are now all part of Botswana's mining wealth. Nevertheless the mines only employ some 5,000 people whereas 60,000 Botswana citizens still work in South Africa and Rhodesia. This figure underlines the country's dependence upon her wealthy and hostile White neighbours. □

social groupings are centred. During the agricultural season, when people move to their holdings, they live in relatively isolated domestic units. In fact, it would serve their material interests to remain scattered throughout the year—given the problems of dry land crop production and stock management in these conditions.

This is appreciated by the Tswana themselves, many of whom would prefer to settle permanently outside the village. But the tribal chiefs and headmen resist this: it is to their advantage that tribesmen should be concentrated, since political control is most effectively exercised when they are. The chief's success in enforcing laws of domicile, however, depends upon the extent of his power. Until recently, this in turn was determined largely by complex internal political processes.

The chiefship underpins their political universe, and the Tswana share a profound reverence for it. But they distinguish sharply between office and holder. Although entitled to honorific respect, the chief is seen as a fallible human, who may rule efficiently or ineptly and be powerful or weak. As this implies, he is involved in continuing debate in which his performance is publicly evaluated. In this way the chief can lose public support and executive control—in extreme circumstances, he may even be deposed. Continuing competition is a central theme in Tswana politics: indeed, they see it as the foundation of their democracy.

The Tswana social structure has endured in the face of dramatic external change. For example, the spread of

Tuareg

SAHARA

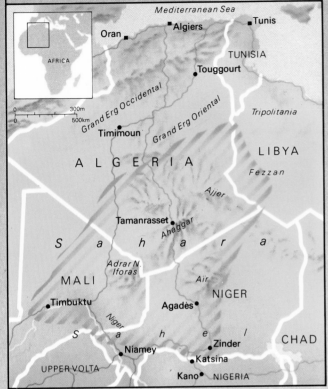

The Tuareg—the illustrious 'warriors of the blue veil'—inhabit a vast area of the Sahara and the Sahel in northwest Africa: in terms of modern state boundaries, the southern part of Algeria, south-western Libya, much of Niger and also northern Mali. No one knows when the first Tuaregs entered this immense desert region, but they appear to have travelled southwards in a series of migrations as early as the 7th century AD. The Air massif in Niger was once inhabited by a Negro population, but by the beginning of the 11th century had already been invaded by fair-skinned Berber pastoralists.

Arab tribes arriving in North Africa during the 11th century invaded Tripolitania and Fezzan, and this resulted in a further migration of Tuareg tribes. By the end of the 14th century Tuareg groups had established themselves as far south as the Nigerian border. As they advanced, the Tuareg came into contact with the Songhay and the Hausa, who were forced to acknowledge their suzerainty.

The first French military expedition entered Tuareg country in 1899 and met with fierce resistance, particularly in the Tanut region. But European power was not to be denied, and after their eventual defeat many Tuareg fled to Chad, although the majority returned later. After the French advance into the Air massif, some Tuareg settled as far away as Darfur in Sudan; their descendants still live near El Fasher. In 1917, following agitation by the Sanusiya religious order in the Fezzan, there was a general uprising against the French, and many Tuareg were killed or displaced during its suppression. Perhaps as many as 30,000 Tuareg from the Air fled into Nigeria at this time, settling in villages around Kano and Katsina.

The Tuareg are divided amongst seven major groups—the Kel Ahaggar, Kel Ajjer, Kel Adrar, Kel Air, Kel Geres, Aullemmeden Kel Dennek and Aullemmeden Kel Ataram. The two northernmost groups, the Kel Ajjer and Kel Ahaggar, are found almost exclusively within the mountainous massifs of Ajjer and Ahaggar in southern Algeria. The Kel Adrar inhabit the Adrar n Foras mountains in northern Mali, and the Kel Air, the Air massif in Niger and the plains to the west and south. In the plains around Tessawa live the Kel Geres; the Aullemmeden Kel Dennek or eastern Aullemmeden inhabit the plains around Tawa, and the Aullemmeden Kel Ataram or western Aullemmeden live in the plains around Meneka and along the Niger River.

The Kel Ajjer and Kel Ahaggar are frequently referred to as the Northern Tuareg, while the groups who live in the Sahel on the fringes of the true desert are known as the Southern Tuareg. Although estimates of the total number of Tuareg vary considerably, there are perhaps half a million. The vast majority are concentrated in the Sahel, which is thus the centre of gravity of the Tuareg world. The Northern Tuareg who live in the Sahara itself constitute only about 3 per cent of the population, while the Aullemmeden alone represent between one-half and two-thirds of all Tuareg.

Tuareg country ranges from savannah in the south, with 10–20 inches of rain per year, to barren desert in the north, dominated by the mountains of Ahaggar, Tassili-n-ajjer, Adrar n Foras and Air. The whole region is very hot in summer, when the day temperature is normally higher than that of the human body, and the temperature of sand and rocks can rise to 140°F. Violent winds are also common and add considerably to the discomfort of the climate. Travelling is extremely hard under such conditions and most people spend the day in the shade of rocks and trees, sleeping and drinking water—as much as 16 pints a day for adults. Winter temperatures in the northern part of the Tuareg country average about 50°F; frost is very common during winter nights, and snow is not unknown on the higher slopes of the Ahaggar.

In the south, winters are much milder—frost is rare and snow unknown. There is a fixed rainy season in summer, although the amount of rain can vary dramatically from year to year and drought is no stranger. After the rains, pastures of annual plants spring up and a mixture of grasses and thorny shrubs and trees grow over the plains. In the country of the Northern Tuareg there is no special wet season; four years out of ten are almost completely dry and when rain does fall it is normally in short violent thunderstorms. Here there is little or no vegetation, even in the mountains.

Tuareg society is extremely hierarchical. The main division is between the noble class (Ihaggaren or Amaher) and the vassal class (Imrad), which may originally be a result of pastoral camel breeders conquering nomadic goat breeders. In the past, each of the noble tribes with its respective vassals formed a political unit, under a chief whose authority was symbolized by a drum. The drum chief held supreme political and judicial authority in the drum group, and it was he who had to regulate all relations between nobles and vassals within that unit.

Among the Kel Ahaggar, for example, the division of Tuareg society into nobles and vassals corresponded well to their economic interdependence. While the nobles engaged almost solely in warfare, raiding and the control

Picard/AAA

Foto Hetzel/Leimbach

than one per cent of the total Tuareg population. Meanwhile, some Ineslemen tribes have achieved considerable political importance. Under the protection of the colonial authorities they acquired large herds, and among the Aullemmeden Kel Dennek they now exert a controlling influence.

In contrast to the true Tuareg are the negroid classes who have formed an integral part of Tuareg society for centuries, and are known collectively as Iklan. Many were originally slaves, taken during raids and warfare in the south or bought from Sudanese slave markets. The institution of slavery was allowed to continue among the northern groups by the French military administration, but the independent governments of the region have since taken firm action to abolish it. Today some Iklan live as servants in the pastoral camps of the Tuareg, some are cultivators, while others are blacksmiths who make weapons and silver ornaments for the Tuareg women.

Both the true Tuareg and the Negro classes speak the Tuareg language, which is known as *tamahak* in the northern groups and *tamachek* in the south. It forms a part of the Berber language group and has four main branches or dialects, which are on the whole mutually intelligible. The alphabet, known as *tifinar*, is known to all Tuareg groups and is related to the ancient Libyan script—the Tuareg language is the only Berber dialect with a written form. In addition, the Tuareg have contact with many people speaking different languages – Arabs, Hausa, Songhai and Fulani – and most Tuareg men know one or two languages as well as their mother tongue.

(Left) The veil worn by Tuareg men is their most distinctive feature. Yet it is not used primarily for protection from the desert sands; men often leave their faces uncovered when travelling.

of the caravan routes, the vassal tribes were occupied in goat herding and had their own caravans trading in cereals and dates. The vassals owned few camels themselves, but were rich in goats, whose products were essential for the nobles; and the nobles left many camels in the care of the vassals, who used them for their own caravan trading and raiding.

The major Tuareg federations were each composed of several drum groups and the drum chief of one of the drum groups took the title of *Amenukal*, or chief of the whole federation. The *Amenukal* was the war leader of the entire federation and also the arbiter and the supreme judge in disagreements between the different drum groups, but he could not meddle in their internal affairs and was rarely influential enough to stop their frequent quarrels.

In most Tuareg groups there are also whole tribes of Ineslemen or Marabuts—the religious class established after the introduction of Islam—led by their own chiefs. In the past their political position varied greatly from one group to another. Certain Ineslemen tribes in Air had the same status as true vassals, while others, like the Iforas of the Kel Ajjer, had much the same status as noble Tuareg although they had no vassals. Their traditional role was that of teachers, counsellors and judges in all matters concerning Islamic law and traditions.

The relationship between Ihaggaren, Imrad and Ineslemen was deeply affected by European intervention. The noble class was decimated during the revolt against the French in 1917, and today represents probably no more

Life is extremely harsh in the Sahara itself—in summer the sand temperatures may reach 140°F, and violent winds are also common. Apart from brief thunderstorms, most years see no rain at all.

In direct contrast to Arab custom, all Tuareg men wear a veil while their women are unveiled. The main function of veiling seems to be social, for many Tuareg men will leave their face uncovered in family camps or on journeys, but they will always cover mouth, nose and forehead in the presence of foreigners and of their parents-in-law. Tuareg women wear a headcloth which is similar in shape and form to the veil worn by the men, and in the presence of foreigners or fathers-in-law they will draw the head-cloth over their mouths. Both young men and young women adopt the veil or headcloth at initiation or marriage, which indicates that their social functions are identical.

The traditional veil or headcloth was made from a piece of Sudanese indigo cotton, made from narrow strips or bands, sewn together, and this type of cotton is highly esteemed for many other garments. Today, however, such cotton is expensive and saved mainly for festive occasions while daily dress is made of European cotton, which is indigo and white. There can be little doubt that this imported cloth has even replaced the traditional skin and leather garments in daily dress, which for men comprises the veil, a poncho-style shirt, and baggy trousers. In addition to their headcloth, the women wear a poncho-style cotton shirt and a shawl to cover the shoulders and head. Both men and women wear sandals.

There are a great many activities forbidden to a Tuareg, and there are many situations in which he must act in a special way if he is to be regarded as a man worthy of respect and prestige. Tuareg attitudes to etiquette are not easily described in words, for gait, gestures and postures

Smiths are numerous among the Southern Tuareg, making weapons for the men and silver jewellery for the women. They speak a language of their own and are believed to have magical powers.

Peter Carmichael

Peter Carmichael

all express qualities of elegance, arrogance, refinement and strength. Vanity in regard to dress and ornaments is further characteristic of all true Tuareg and many men wear Islamic amulets which they believe make them great and important. Prestige is a constant concern of the Tuareg, who are much more sophisticated than the other peoples living within their country.

Before the arrival of the Europeans most Tuareg were nomadic stockbreeders, with large herds of camels, cattle, sheep and goats. With the exception of the nobility, all Tuareg engaged in caravan trading which enabled them to exchange their surplus livestock products for dates and millet produced by cultivators at the oases and in the southern Sahel and Sudan. Moreover, throughout the 19th century great caravans crossed the Sahara bringing gold, ivory, ostrich feathers and slaves from West Africa to the Mediterranean, while south-bound caravans carried salt and Arab and European goods.

Raiding expeditions were common, with the Kel Ahaggar the most prominent warriors. The two dominant chiefdoms, the Kel Rela and Taytok, frequently raided the Aullemmeden Tuareg and the Arabs living north of Timbuktu, for these southern pastoralists were rich in livestock and in slaves. Some of the southern Tuareg and Arab tribes even paid fixed dues to chiefs of the Kel Ahaggar as protection against their raiding activities.

The Tuareg economy was profoundly changed by the arrival of the French. Raiding was suppressed by the colonial authorities, which profoundly affected the relationship between nobles and vassals and led to the breakdown of the traditional political systems of the Tuareg. Trans-Saharan caravan trade declined after the European occupation of West Africa, as a result of competition from faster and cheaper sea-routes and the construction of railways linking the interior with the coastal ports.

Only the trade in Saharan salt remained active, but independence brought a further blow to caravan trading—the caravans were forced to pay customs duties at the new frontiers, which further reduced the meagre price advantages which had made the journey worthwhile. But mobility and trade are built into their culture, and some Tuareg now use their camels to transport goods on cross-country routes where there are as yet no roads. For example, they move potash from eastern Niger to northern Nigerian markets, and groundnuts from producing areas in northern Nigeria to buying stations along the railway.

Many Tuareg remain nomadic, moving their herds between dry and rainy season pastures according to the quality and distribution of rainfall. The colonial powers, however, imposed a series of conventions regulating and limiting nomadic movements to specific territories for each federation, and post-independence frontiers have further restricted their movement. Wells have been improved and their edges cemented in order to improve livestock production, and disease prevention and eradication campaigns carried out. As a result the total number of livestock increased dramatically, resulting in serious overgrazing of pastures.

Other Tuareg have abandoned their nomadic life to settle permanently in one place. Some, but by no means all, have abandoned their tents for permanent dwellings—store houses with flat roofs, or huts made of mats or grass bound with ropes. The colonial authorities encouraged this process particularly among the southern Tuareg, and the independent Algerian government has embarked on a programme of forced sedentarization, grouping the Tuareg in agricultural co-operatives.

Jon Gardey/Robert Harding Associates

(*Below*) *Tuareg families gather at a relief centre in Niger during the long drought in the Sahel. The rains finally came in 1974, but Tuareg society has been changed permanently by the disaster.*

(*Above*) *Thousands of Tuareg have moved south into Niger and Nigeria since the drought began. Many are abandoning their tents for permanent housing and have turned to agriculture as a way of life.*

Sarah Errington/Alan Hutchison Library

Victor Englebert/Susan Griggs Agency

A few Tuareg struggle on with their traditional work as desert caravaneers—these are transporting salt, once a valuable commodity. But customs tariffs and paved roads signal the end of an era.

In the southern Sahel many Tuareg, particularly from the Negro classes, are now settled cultivators living in villages surrounded by millet fields; indeed agriculture expanded so rapidly in Niger that the government was forced to limit cultivation to certain areas in order to protect the pasturelands of the nomadic tribes. As agricultural work is seasonal, many of the young men also take jobs as porters or dockers in Nigeria, Ghana or Ivory Coast for part of the year.

The severe drought which struck the entire Sahel in 1972—the worst for 50 years—brought disaster to the Tuareg and put severe stress on their social structures and relationships. The nomads, although bred to disaster, have been particularly badly hit and have suffered more than the farmers. In Niger's two Tuareg-populated departments of Agadez and Tahoua, 80 per cent and 50 per cent of the population were designated drought victims. Most farmers lost only current income, but herders lost their capital stock. Government intervention since the beginning of the present century has reduced the nomads' power to protect themselves against the uncertainty of the natural environment and prevented them from recovering their losses.

Realizing by early autumn 1972 that the rains had failed disastrously after a run of bad years, the nomads and their families were forced to trek south in search of pasture for their herds. This massive southward migration intensified as water supplies began to fail, and generated conflicts over rights and obligations among the people and governments of the region. Many animals perished of thirst and hunger or simply from fatigue during the long journey; others were slaughtered prematurely or sold at buyer's prices. Thousands of Tuareg nomads, having lost everything, drifted to the bigger villages and towns, where they set up cowhide shelters and lean-to shanties on the outskirts of the settlements; for example, some 13,000 Tuareg nomads from Mali gathered at the vast Camp Lazaret on the outskirts of Niamey in Niger until they were forcibly transported back to Mali early in 1975.

In spite of emergency food aid and relief efforts, there was a high death rate among the Tuareg. Fatalities would have been higher still but for the tendency of the stricken groups to congregate in accessible places.

The rains in 1974 and 1976 were good, but even if they usher in a cycle of better rains in the Sahel this will not wash away the serious economic and social effects of the drought. Life for the Tuareg can never be quite the same again. Many young men, have drifted from the camps to the coastal cities from Dakar to Lagos and are widely employed as guards, while gangs of Tuareg children begging in the streets are a common sight in Lagos today. Others have been settled on experimental stations to grow crops and raise stock on small ranches. However, the majority of the Tuareg refugees have since returned to pastoralism, although on average each family has only a fraction of their former herd. Unfortunately, the official development programmes now being implemented in the Sahel merely repeat the inappropriate measures adopted before the drought – dams and pumps, cattle schemes, intensive agriculture, the provision of credit, and resettlement projects – 'modernization' policies which in no small measure contributed to the recent crisis and, moreover, weakened the Tuaregs' capacity to withstand it. Yet the Tuareg have the skills and aptitude needed to exploit huge areas of western and northern Africa and this land, though a harsh environment, is essential to the development of the states within the region.

Watutsi
RUANDA, BURUNDI

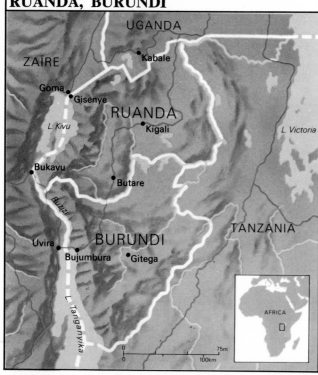

The mountainous region between Zaire and Tanzania has witnessed the partial overthrow of one of Africa's oldest ruling elites. In Ruanda the Watutsi had lost power to their subjects the Hutu before the Belgian government left in 1962. In Burundi the aristocratic Watutsi have managed to retain control, but only after ruthlessly suppressing a Hutu revolt in 1972. This further consolidated the Tutsi power, for all literate Hutu – some 100,000 – were exterminated.

Thousands of Watutsi had earlier died in pre-independence uprisings in Ruanda. Some 160,000 fled to the safety of neighbouring Burundi, but the bulk of over 600,000 remained. In Ruanda social differences were reinforced by physical ones. For the Hutu, who comprise 86 per cent of the population, average 5 feet 6 inches in height and are sturdy and thick set, with features and hair resembling those of the West African Negroes.

The Tutsi (plural: Watutsi) are taller, of average height of about 5 feet 10 inches. Slimmer in figure and, lighter in colour than the Hutu, they were traditionally pastoralists, rather than cultivators. In spite of forming less than 13 per cent of the population, they established a complete political and social domination over the Hutu majority, adopted the Hutu language and forgot their own.

The Tutsi system of domination worked through four channels of authority. For each district, there was a land chief responsible to the *Mwami* or king. It was his duty to

These aristocratic wives of Watutsi chiefs belong to one of Africa's greatest kingdoms. Their tremendous self-confidence and tall slender frames set them apart from their Hutu subjects.

Actualit

collect taxes of grain and other crops from the Hutu cultivators and to see that they provided labour for certain duties. He also settled any disputes about land or cultivation, and would appear at first to correspond with the European colonial idea of a district commissioner. But there was an important difference, because parallel with the land chief was an official equal in rank, the cattle chief.

The cattle chief collected dues in cattle, milk and dairy products and settled disputes about grazing rights and the ownership of cattle. The people of Ruanda did not consider land as the property of one man for all purposes; one man might have the right to a crop from the land, but someone else might have the right to graze cattle on it after the crop had been gathered. And one man might look after a cow and have the right to the milk and to male calves, but someone else, who had leased the cow to him, had the right to female calves and could revoke the lease and call the cow back to his possession.

In addition to the land chief and the cattle chief, there was an army chief. Everyone, whether Watutsi or Hutu, belonged to a regiment; only chosen young men of the Watutsi were actual fighting soldiers, but if the regiment was mobilized or called up for duty a certain number of Hutu would go too, as labourers, servants and porters. In peace, when the regiment was not mobilized, the members recognized an allegiance to the army chief and paid a tribute to him and his subordinates. A proportion of this was passed upwards till eventually some of it reached the *Mwami*.

The fourth channel of authority and tribute was supposed to be voluntary. Any Hutu or Tutsi could put himself under the protection of a rich or influential man. This system did not usually have anything to do with land; it was personal. The vassal, if he was accepted, would periodically bring his lord presents; if the vassal was Hutu and the lord Tutsi, as was very often the case, the vassal would sometimes act as a servant or carry messages. He was a feudal retainer who could be called on when required.

In return, the lord might let the vassal have the tenancy —the milking and the right to male calves—of several cows. If the vassal was a Tutsi, he would not be expected to work as a servant and his Tutsi lord would probably let him have enough cattle to sub-let to one or two Hutu. In every case there would be agreed services to be paid by the vassal, agreed benefits to be granted by the lord, but also a general understanding that the lord would protect the vassal in every aspect of life and the vassal would give complete allegiance. Most of the Watutsi had vassals beneath them but were also vassals to someone above them. While the whole system was in theory voluntary, in practice a man who had no lord to protect him would be exposed to all kinds of dangers. It might well be that a man had not really much choice; it would be hard to break away from a rich and influential lord.

The strength of the Tutsi domination lay in the fact that the head of each household would usually have to pay gifts, tribute or service to the *Mwami* through the four distinct channels—land chief, cattle chief, army chief and personal lord. The total was not oppressive compared with many systems, but any dissatisfaction was very difficult to conceal. If it did not reach the ears of one chief it would reach those of another. Any combination between the chiefs would also be difficult to arrange and unlikely to be kept secret.

Sarah Errington/Alan Hutchison Library

(*Above*) *A medical orderly tries to comfort an innocent victim of the Watutsi system of domination. After an abortive Hutu revolt in 1972 the Watutsi retaliated by killing some 100,000 Hutu in Burundi.*

Marion Kaplan

(*Left*) *Villagers cultivate fields on the hillsides between the city of Bujumbura and the historic Watutsi capital at Gitega. The Watutsi were traditionally pastoralists who considered themselves above agriculture which was done by the subject Hutu.*

(Left)   Flowing headdresses are an essential part of Watutsi dance. The mane of hair accentuates the rhythmic movement of Watutsi dancing.

Often Watutsi herdsmen do not own cattle but hold tenancy from their lords. An influential and rich lord grants a vassal milking rights and any male calves in return for his services.

Strong as this system was, the Watutsi had a still stronger psychological hold on the Hutu. They had imposed on them a conviction that the Watutsi were quite different from themselves, not simply by training but by inherent hereditary qualities. There was an evident physical difference, in height, features and skin colour. On both sides the degree of physical difference came to be exaggerated. Similarly, there were differences of temperament and character, due partly to training and partly to the widespread human tendency to act as one is expected to act, but these too were exaggerated.

The fixed picture which each had of the other was very clear. The Hutu were regarded by the Watutsi as hardworking, not very clever, not very subtle, quick-tempered, lacking in polite manners, obedient, physically strong, greedy about food, and lacking in self-control. The Watutsi, on the other hand, were thought to have qualities almost directly opposite; they were intelligent, refined, courageous, accustomed to give orders and see them obeyed, cruel, abstemious and self-controlled. Both Watutsi and Hutu believed that very little change could be made; the differences were inborn. But training and upbringing among the Watutsi could hardly have been better calculated to emphasize differences.

In the first place, diet was different. Watutsi would begin the day with a pot of curdled milk and would repeat this at midday. In the evening, while talking to friends and

vassals, they would drink mead, a strong drink made from honey, or a kind of beer made from bananas—but never the beer made from millet which is the staple drink of Africa. This the Watutsi regarded as fit only for Hutu.

Only after dark, and in the presence of his family, all Hutu being excluded, would he eat the one solid meal of the day. This would most often be beans or bananas with hot salted butter, and milk would be drunk. On a journey, when he could not ensure privacy, he would take no solid food and some Watutsi claimed that they never touched anything more solid than curdled milk and butter. The Hutu, by contrast, ate two solid meals a day of porridge made from beans, peas, millet or maize with sweet potatoes in large quantities.

Young Watutsi men were chosen to attend the *Mwami's* court, where they were trained in skills with the bow and arrow and the use of sword and spear, in war-like dancing and in the recital of poems about the bravery of warriors in the past. They were taught to make such poems too and to remain imperturbable when teased by their seniors. The virtues they were encouraged to admire were bravery, power to command, readiness to take responsibility, generosity to the poor, and self-mastery; they must always be polite and never show emotion. Thus they deliberately cultivated aristocratic virtues which distinguished them from the Hutu and riveted on the Hutu the psychological bonds which held them in subjection. □

Wolof
SENEGAL

The Wolof are the dominant group between the Senegal and Gambia Rivers on the coast of West Africa. They number about 1,500,000, comprising about 36 per cent of the population of Senegal and 12 per cent of the population of the Gambia. They were first described as a distinct entity by Portuguese explorers in the 15th century. At that time the centre of Wolof power was the inland state of Jolof, and many of the older writings refer to the people as Jolofs.

In appearance the Wolof are by no means homogeneous, yet they are clearly distinct from the slender light-skinned Mauritanians to the north, and from the fine featured reddish-skinned Fulbe; a very dark skin being characteristic of many Wolof. They also tend to be taller than the peoples of the tropical forest zone to the south, such as the Jola. The original inhabitants of the area seem to have been the Serer, and the Wolof may well be the result of a mixture between invading peoples and earlier inhabitants.

The valleys of the Gambia and Senegal Rivers have long been routes followed by Mandinka, Bambara and Serahuli migrants from the east. But with increasing European influence and trade, after the 16th century, the inhabitants of the coastal states grew in wealth and power and began to assert their independence from Jolof. During the period of the slave trade the region was constantly torn by internal slave-capturing wars, stimulated by alcohol and arms provided by the traders. Over a period of several centuries the Wolof increased their domination towards the south in the Serer regions of Sine and Saloum, and in recent years have continued a peaceful expansion, moving across the Gambia and into the Casamance region

Today a traditional chief is left with only his regalia, his title and his wives. Instead of receiving large amounts of taxes and gifts, he is now the holder of a minor government office.

in increasing numbers seeking better farming land.

Islamic influence was slight in the 15th century, though Wolof rulers had religious teachers as advisers at their courts, but during later centuries Islam gained ground, and the 18th and 19th centuries were marked by a struggle for power between traditional pagan rulers and Moslem leaders, who waged war partly against the new colonial power, the French, and partly to convert non-believers. The military force of the French and their local allies proved superior, but the peace provided conditions in which Islam could spread more widely and rapidly. Today Islam and its associated culture is practically universal. Animistic beliefs survive to only a minor degree, while Christian Wolof are found only in very small numbers in the cities.

Traditional Wolof political and social organization was typical of the societies of the Western Sudan region. The ruler was elected from among several eligible candidates, and the death of a ruler was often followed by a struggle between rival factions. In some regions eligibility was determined matrilineally, but with the increasing effect of Islamic views, succession to power now generally follows the male line.

After selection a ruler went through a period of ritual seclusion to acquire the mystical powers necessary to maintain the strength and prosperity of the state. After this a formal 'crowning' took place. Power was exercised through a series of court officials who controlled the judiciary, the military forces, tax collection and so on. Representatives of the various craft groups—musicians, goldsmiths, blacksmiths and leatherworkers—were present at the ruler's court. Representatives of the chief were placed at strategic points in the state to report to him.

John Bulmer

At Dakar's beach market a Wolof housewife goes shopping with her gourd and bowl. Traders sell a wide variety of produce which comes not only from inland farms but also from the sea.

The ruler drew his wealth from taxes and special levies, fines, work carried out on his own farms, raids on neighbouring territories, and presents from those who wished to gain his favour. Under colonial rule the power of traditional chiefs was greatly reduced, and they became in effect minor salaried government officials.

An elaborate system of social stratification still exists in rural areas, and in somewhat modified form in the towns, where an individual's origin is not always known. Society is divided into three main strata—the freeborn, those of slave origin, and the low-caste group of craftsmen such as smiths, leatherworkers, and musicians. The highest ranking freeborn were the royal lineages from which rulers were selected. Next came those who had electoral powers, held certain titles, or traditionally controlled regions within the state. Below these were freeborn who had little wealth or power, but were independent.

Slaves fell into one of two categories—those born in the household, who were treated like junior members of the family, and those captured in raids or purchased, who were subject to much harsher treatment. The social distinction between slaves and freeborn is still felt to be strong. It is very rare for a freeborn woman to marry a man of slave origin. Slaves no longer work for the family of their 'masters', though they do help on ceremonial occasions. Slaves were also ranked according to the status of their owners, and those attached to a chief often had greater wealth and power than many of the freeborn. Smiths, leatherworkers, musicians and other craftsmen formed endogamous groups—marriage only took place between members of the same category. This conformed to the Wolof principle that no one changed their status.

The typical Wolof village is inhabited by several hundred people. It consists of a series of fenced off compounds round a central village square shaded by large trees, such as silk-cotton trees and baobabs. In the centre is the men's meeting place, a roofed-over platform. Women tend to gather at the well, and come to the central meeting place only when there is a dance.

The compound is a group of houses enclosed by a fence. In most villages the houses are round, the walls being made either from millet or reed stalks, or from mud, and thatched with grass or rhun palm leaves. In recent years a rectangular or square form made from mud and roofed with corrugated sheets has become common. Rich Wolof have houses made from concrete blocks. The inhabitants of the compound consists of an extended family—a man, his wives and children, his brothers and their families, possibly an aged relative or two, and unmarried sisters.

The compound head's house is opposite the entrance, and the houses of his brothers off to each side. When a man has more than one wife, each wife normally has her own house which she shares with her children. Near the entrance to the compound are the houses occupied by young men and strangers who come as seasonal workers to grow groundnuts.

Polygyny is permitted by Moslem law, and chiefs and village heads often have several wives, although three quarters of the married men have only one wife. There is felt to be a great deal of tension and jealousy between co-wives and divorce is fairly frequent. In rural areas men marry in their early twenties, women in their late teens. In the cities, because of a greater amount of time spent in getting an education, difficulty in obtaining housing and the high cost of living, the age of marriage tends to be later both for men and women.

Marriage with a cross-cousin, either a mother's brother's daughter or a father's sister's daughter, is favoured, as it is felt that this will produce a more harmonious marriage relationship. If there is a dispute between husband and wife, kinsfolk try first to settle the matter. If they cannot achieve a solution, the case may be taken either to a more formal meeting of the village elders or to court.

The Wolof life cycle is marked by a series of rituals which indicate a change of status for the individual, and involve the community in recognition of the event. Between birth and the naming ceremony which takes place on the seventh day, numerous ritual acts are undertaken to protect the child from evil influences. The naming ceremony involves shaving the child's head, pronouncing the new name, and incorporating the child in the Moslem community. Alms, in the form of food and kola nuts, are shared among the participants. The mother also ends a period of seven days seclusion at this time.

Boy's circumcision ceremonies are held between the ages of about eight and twelve. In rural areas they are taken to an enclosure outside the village until they have healed. During this period they receive training in traditional songs and beliefs. At the end of their seclusion a festival is held in which they are welcomed back into the community in their new status. In urban areas the pattern has changed. In many instances the actual operation takes place at a hospital, the period of initiation is held during the summer school vacation, and the ritual separation of the initiates is less rigid.

In traditional marriage arrangements, after negotiations between the families of the bride and groom, the marriage is 'tied' at a Mosque ceremony generally held after the regular Friday afternoon prayer. Representatives of the two families attend, but not necessarily the bride and groom. Arrangements are made for the payment of

Ian Berry/Magnum

'marriage money' to the bride's family, this depends on the wealth and status of the families. When payments are completed, the bride is transferred in a ceremonial procession accompanied by her friends and age-mates, singing ribald songs. In the old days a demonstration of virginity was made the following morning by displaying a blood-stained cloth.

There is little formality in divorce proceedings. The husband can divorce his wife by making a formal pronouncement. A wife, if she has been mistreated or neglected, has to go through court proceedings. Usually she returns to her parents. If she fails to return in a reasonable time, the husband formally asks that she return or that the marriage payments be refunded. The two families start discussions to determine who is at fault.

Funerals follow normal Moslem custom. The body is washed, wrapped in white cloth, taken to the Mosque and laid outside while prayers are said, and then taken to the burial ground. Participants share a 'charity' of kola nuts, and after 40 days a further distribution of alms is made.

The Wolof are primarily farmers who grow sorghum and millet as their staple food, and groundnuts as their cash crop. Some also invest in herds of cattle which they may entrust to the care of Fula herdsmen. Many Wolof villages have an arrangement with the Fula by which the herds graze on such crop residues as groundnut haulms, and in return are tied up on the land near the village at night to manure the fields. Most rural families keep some sheep and goats, which are generally owned by women and herded by children. Horses and donkeys, which at one time were decreasing in numbers, have been increasing in recent years because of their usefulness in pulling light ploughs, weeding implements and carts.

The Wolof practise a wide range of crafts including the

The wife of a Moslem trader sweeps the front of her house in a slum district on the outskirts of Dakar, Senegal's capital. Both Dakar and St Louis, Senegal's main centres, are Wolof towns.

making of farm tools by blacksmiths; of pottery—often by women of the smith caste; the weaving of cloth from local cotton on a narrow loom, and a variety of styles of basketry. The manufacture of gold and silver ornaments tends to be concentrated in the larger towns and trade centres.

Recently the Senegalese farmer has had to face continual soil deterioration due to overclearing and overcultivation, increasing periods of drought. He also has to contend with competition from more productive areas of the world, and rising prices for imported commodities. The 1960s saw the growth of co-operative societies designed to help the farmer out of debt. These provide credit, supply agricultural implements, and help in marketing. The system however has had a lot of bureaucratic troubles, and often the result is merely that the farmer shifted his indebtedness to the co-operative society.

The principal towns in Senegal, Dakar and St Louis, were established on Wolof territory. Consequently Wolof culture now ranges from life in remote rural villages to modern urban life; from illiteracy to university education and Arabic scholarship; from traditional forms of village government to political parties and state bureaucracies; from old forms of entertainment and traditional music to the world of radio, record players and films. Wolof culture is and has always been, a changing one, but its prestige is such that the other ethnic groups, particularly in the towns, adopt Wolof dress and hair styles and use Wolof as a language of general communication. □

Yoruba
NIGERIA

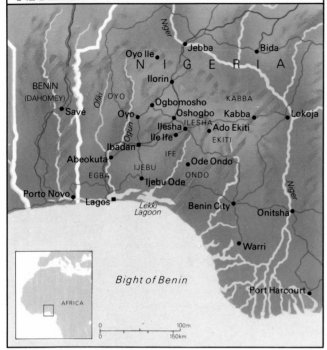

At international gatherings, the Yoruba are conspicuously resplendent in distinctive and colourful robes, demonstrating that they remain the proud heirs of their history and traditions. Today 12 million Yoruba live in the southwest of Nigeria and, across its borders, in neighbouring Benin (formerly Dahomey); in Nigeria they constitute one of the three dominant ethnic groups with their own language.

The Yoruba people, according to one variant of their creation myth, are descended from Oduduwa who came down from heaven by an iron chain, setting foot on the newly formed Earth at Ile Ife where he established a large city. His 16 sons then left to found their own kingdoms.

The Yoruba have their own pantheon of deities and their chieftaincy titles and rituals of kingship have a remarkable uniformity. Yet, save in the implications of the creation myth, there is no record that the Yoruba were ever united under a single ruler; in fact between the many kingdoms there are significant differences in political and social systems, though the cultural unity of the Yoruba is probably stronger now than ever before. In the past century differences in dialect have been eroded and the distinctive robes, formerly found only in Oyo, are now worn by all.

Their culture suggests that the Yoruba people have occupied their present homeland for thousands of years; there can have been little migration from outside though myths of individual towns and families suggest substantial internal migration as losing candidates in chieftaincy disputes travelled to seek their fortunes in new settlements. The present ruling dynasties probably date from the 12th century, though kingship, in some form, may have already existed.

From the Ile Ife the new rulers established the kingdoms of Oyo in the savannah and at Benin, the capital of the Edo people, in the forest. These two kingdoms grew in the following centuries to be mighty empires. Oyo controlled the trade route from the savannah northwards to the sea, while Benin had closer contact with the Spanish and Portuguese traders on the coast. At one time or another these empires established political control and cultural influence over most Yoruba areas. But between them lay a zone of small kingdoms, including those of the Egba in the west and the Ekiti in the east. These remained substantially independent for much of their history.

At the end of the 18th century the mighty Oyo empire was rent by civil war and collapsed completely in the 1830s with the intervention of Fulani armies pursuing their *jihad* or holy war. People from the fallen capital of Oyo Ile and the provincial towns fled southwards to swell existing towns along the forest margins. Iwo, Oshogbo, Ogbomosho, and Ile Ife—each of which now has a population exceeding 100,000—grew in size while the largest Yoruba city of all, Ibadan, was created by these refugees.

The granitic soils of most of Yoruba country are not very fertile but the rainfall which ranges from 80 inches a year at the coast to 40 inches in the north nurtures a luxuriant vegetation. Farmers practise a bush fallow rotation, cultivating a plot for three years and then allowing the bush to regenerate until, after five to 10 years, it may be cut and burned to restore fertility. With increasing population this fallow period is becoming seriously reduced.

The Yoruba grow a wide range of crops—many varieties of yam, coco-yam, cassava, bananas, plantain, maize and, in the savannah, guinea corn. Beans are an important source of protein and in earlier centuries supplemented the meagre supply of meat from wild animals. The oil

One of the most important Yoruba agricultural products is the red oil extracted from the flesh or the kernel of the palm-nut. It is used for cooking and in manufacturing processes like making soap.

Peter Lloyd

Corrugated-iron is replacing thatch as a roofing material in Yoruba towns, which closely reflect social and political structure. Family compounds are grouped in 'quarters' occupied by related families.

palm which grows wild everywhere provides the basis for their soup; a variety of green leaves, fruits and peppers provide relish in what is, by African standards, a rich and varied diet.

Although so predominantly an agricultural people, the Yoruba are urban dwellers. The capitals of the larger kingdoms probably contained 10–15,000 people in the past—today they are much bigger. The origin of town living is now lost, but it is perhaps to be associated with kingship and with an intensity of cultivation which allowed most men to live in town and walk daily to their farms. For the Yoruba 'a town without a king is no town'. These towns were enclosed by a high wall or earth rampart and ditch; in their centre, covering many acres, was the royal palace; in front of the palace was the central market; around it were grouped the compounds of other families. These were huge structures of linked rectangular court-yards housing 1,000 people or more.

The kingship is held by descendants of the town's founder, passing in rotation between several ruling houses but only to princes born 'on the throne' to a reigning ruler. Senior members of the royal family usually exercise little political power in the kingdom; in fact the complex ceremonies of installation of the new king symbolize not only his assumption of all the supernatural powers inherent in his predecessors but also his withdrawal from family commitments.

Political power resides in fact with the council of chiefs, men who are appointed for life, in most cases in northern Yoruba kingdoms by and from among the members of the constituent commoner families in the town. In the past the chiefs met daily in one of the outer courtyards of the palace, submitting their decisions to their king who then ordained them with the royal ban. The king remained hidden from public view, appearing only at certain annual

ceremonies and then heavily veiled by his beaded crown, which only descendants of the dynasty of Ile Ife may wear.

The chiefs chose their king from among eligible candidates put forward by the elders of the royal family. This apparent chiefly power over the throne was balanced by the king's greater supernatural powers, by his ability to divide his chiefs against each other and by his ability to increase the wealth of the throne, perhaps controlling a strong force of palace slaves.

Kings and chiefs were wealthy men, living in a luxury not shared by other members of their family and towns; they usually had scores of wives. Chiefly office was achieved by those who had already become rich through farming and trade; here it was hard work and astute financial management that counted. But a rich man had many sons and his property passed equally to the children of each wife, none received a sizeable inheritance. In fact the Yoruba often say that it is better to be born into a humble home—one learns to value work and this ensures success.

In the traditional government women held no political offices; very many are polygamously married and all are overtly submissive to their husbands. Yet it is a mistake to regard them as chattels. On marriage they retain full membership of their own families; they work independently of their husbands and have full control over their income; a Yoruba woman cannot inherit anything from her husband, but neither can he inherit from her. Divorce is easy, and at the instigation of the woman; the husband merely ignores his unloved wife so that she goes to another man or to her home. The Yoruba woman thus has most of the legal rights that Western women have been striving for in the past century.

Today the face of Yoruba country is changing. Cocoa, grown mainly by small peasant farmers, has brought

Bruno Barbey/Magnum

Alan Hutchison

Among the most important of the traditional Yoruba gods is Ogun, God of Iron, Hunting and War, in whose honour this festival is held at Ondo. Many Yoruba are Christians and over half are now Moslems.

Dominant in Western Nigeria, the Yoruba are the main population of the important towns of Lagos and Ibadan. They are thus closely involved in the rapid economic development taking place in Nigeria.

considerable wealth, supporting new categories of wealthy traders—the produce buyers, lorry owners and shop-keepers and a range of artisans such as builders, tailors and mechanics. The old compounds are replaced by one and two storey houses built of cement and with corrugated-iron roofs. Within the palace walls the kings have constructed sumptuous modern residences. New suburbs on the edge of the town attract those who wish to break with their families—or who can find no land within the town for a big house.

The new bureaucratic hierarchies have drawn educated Yoruba from both rich and poor families, thus maintaining the ideology that positions of power and wealth are open to all. Traditional deities have been displaced, and Christianity and Islam now have almost equal numbers of adherents.

And yet, with all these dramatic changes, many of the traditional features of Yoruba society have been reinforced. In the colonial period the kings were designated 'native authorities' and held responsible for the government of their towns; many literate rulers became benevolent autocrats, diminishing the power of their chiefs. Though the reputations of many rulers became tarnished through association with politicians, most are still highly revered in their town.

Most men live and farm on their family land, and the high market value of land particularly on the edge of towns helps to maintain the cohesion of the traditional family groups. Though their chiefs have lost much influence, most offices remain filled; local government ward boundaries often coincide with the compounds giving the family groups control over the election of councillors.

Thus while the face of the town changes, much of its traditional structure is retained. Chiefs still go about their daily business though their influence is rivalled by that of the well educated teachers and officials, and of the wealthy traders. Many more men are now engaged as traders and artisans; but the majority of the Yoruba still work on their farms employing techniques of cultivation which have changed very little.

An increasing number of Yoruba no longer live in the towns and villages of their birth. Probably one-fifth are migrants, living in the major cities of Nigeria and especially Lagos and Ibadan. These are the men who have left home to seek positions in the bureaucratic hierarchies or in wage employment, or to exploit more favourable opportunities in trading or craft industries. Most of these migrants maintain close ties with their home communities.

One might expect that it would be the poor who retain a close relationship; it is they who value more highly the security offered by their relatives and their continuing rights to land. In the urban areas it is they who are most dependent on relatives and townsmen for help in finding work and in coping with life's crises. However the more successful men, the wealthy and better educated, do not in fact sever their ties with their homes.

With their cars they can most easily make frequent visits home, can fulfil the common aspiration to build a house at home and have influence which can be useful in the promotion of civic projects. Each weekend there is an exodus of such men and women to attend weddings, funerals, chieftancy installations and the like in their home areas. Through such functions the ties between people from the same community are strengthened.

Within the cities migrants form 'Improvement Unions'

189

Marc & Evelyne Bernheim/Camp/Susan Griggs Agency

based upon their home communities. Usually it is the smaller towns and villages which have the strongest associations. The number of migrants is small enough not to make the association unwieldy; its members are more likely to be closely related by descent and marriage. The small community often engenders a stronger feeling of loyalty among its members as it competes for services with similar neighbouring communities and as it struggles against a feeling of inferiority to the large town to which it is politically subject. Thus small villages in a district have often produced more university graduates than the main town. This desire for achievement permeates the Improvement Union too, stimulating its activity in obtaining roads, schools and health services in the home area.

The larger Yoruba towns do not have such associations in which all migrants of the home community are members, irrespective of their status and urban success. But they have frequently had a para-political association, attracting to its branches the better educated and being concerned not with their individual problems but with broader

Akure lies to the east of Ife, the spiritual 'capital' of the Yoruba. The King, or Oba of Akure is dressed in his magnificent beaded ceremonial costume and surrounded by attendants.

civic issues, the election of members of parliament and the provision of major services.

A Yoruba who seeks prestige in his home town must maintain his contacts with it and be active in the urban associations. Such activity also gives a man esteem among his fellows from other communities. A man who does much for his home is praised, one who denies its claims is despised. Thus the Yoruba elite, whilst employed in national or state bureaucracies, or in business far transcending the local community, are still identified as Oyo, Egba, Ijebu, Ekiti and so on. These loyalties are manifest in countless situations. It is through these local bonds that a cohesion among all Yoruba is engendered, fostering their unity in the face of threats from without, stimulating their pride in their own history and traditions. ☐

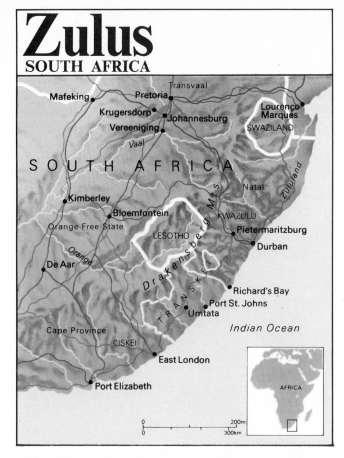

Zulus
SOUTH AFRICA

Chief Gatsha Butelezi, the Zulu Prime Minister demands an end to racial oppression and a greater share in the country's wealth for all non-White South Africans. He is a focal point for Black opposition condemning foreign investment and apartheid.

William Raynor/Camera Press

The Zulu kingdom was the creation of a great military genius—Shaka. In his short life from 1787 to 1828, Shaka welded many of the southeastern Nguni clans, living in the areas today called Natal and KwaZulu (Zululand), into an empire. They were the descendants of pastoralist people who had moved southward through Africa over many centuries. It is estimated that the Nguni reached South Africa between the 10th and 14th centuries.

The wars which established Shaka's political authority in Natal and Zululand precipitated waves of armed refugees fleeing through Southern and Central Africa. The period is known as the *Mfecane* (the Crushing). Today the people living in the old area of Shaka's supremacy, both those whose families were the victims of the *Mfecane* and those who were the subjects of the Zulu king, call themselves Zulu.

Shaka reigned for only 10 years but the kingdom he founded was to last more than 60 and was to present a challenge to neighbouring White colonists. Under Shaka's centralized military rule the kingdom was infused with a spirit of obedience and fear. Despite this, his genius as a statebuilder is undeniable and today he is upheld as the symbol of Zulu greatness.

Shaka was murdered in 1828 by his half-brother Dingane. According to tradition he died prophesying an era of oppression for his people as a result of the coming of the White men. At that time there were only a handful of traders living at Port Natal (today Durban) but within 10 years White power became a formidable threat to the Zulu kingdom.

In the 1830s Boer farmers in the Eastern Province of the Cape left their homes in protest against British frontier and racial policy. One of the parties of the Great Trek under Piet Retief crossed the Drakensberg into Natal and approached Dingane for a grant of land. But the trekkers' show of arms rattled the king and he had Retief and many of his followers murdered. The Boers retaliated a year later in 1838 and defeated a Zulu army at the Battle of Blood River. Dingane fled north and spent two years on the run, until in 1840 he was murdered in Swaziland.

Shortly after the Battle of Blood River Dingane's brother Mpande fled across the Tugela River with 17,000 followers seeking Boer aid to help establish him as king. After Dingane's death the Boer commandos proclaimed him King of the Zulus, but his land was restricted to that North of Tugela, while the southern land, today Natal, was divided into Boer farms. However it was impossible to maintain Natal as an all-White haven.

Many of the people who had fled during the *Mfecane* returned to their old homes in Natal. These Zulus experienced colonial rule long before those north of the Tugela. They were settled in reserves; chiefs were appointed by the British, who had annexed Natal in 1844, and they were subjected to Native Law, a code which restricted rights of movement and barred them from participation in the government of the colony.

In Zululand Mpande was able to preserve the essentials of Shaka's system. He was succeeded by his son Cetshwayo in 1872. The strength of the Zulu kingdom alarmed the neighbouring people of Natal and in 1872 a British conquering force marched into Zululand. One column of this force was defeated by the Zulus at the Battle of Isandlwana. This was one of the worst defeats a modern army ever suffered in a colonial war. Out of 1800 soldiers only 55 British and 300 of the Natal Native Corps survived the battle. However in subsequent operations the British defeated the Zulus and by the end of the year Cetshwayo was in exile and the country divided into 13 districts ruled by chieftains appointed by the governor of Natal.

This settlement was the prelude to a civil war which the

The creation of KwaZulu brought the Zulu people some relief from the harshness they had suffered since the White conquest of their land, but the imposition of taxes and the overcrowding of the reserves, which resulted from White appropriation of much of the most fertile land, forced the people to seek employment within the White economy. Men went to work in the mines of the Witwatersrand and the factories of Johannesburg and Durban.

Zulu workers in towns suffer separation from their families, poor living conditions, low wages, and gain little advantage from membership of trade unions. But in 1973 Zulus were among workers who expressed their discontent in a wave of strikes which swept South Africa. The strikes in Natal were highly successful and obtained wage increases and voiced the African workers' anger in an effective form of demonstration. They defied the law which made African strikes illegal.

The laws controlling influx into the cities have proved extremely difficult to enforce and as a result a large Zulu urban population has grown up in Durban, the Reef, and many of the smaller towns of the Transvaal and Natal.

Young married women stay in KwaZulu while men work in towns. On their return husbands may reject their traditional wives in preference for urbanized women whom they consider to be more sophisticated.

Gerald Cubitt

return of Cetshwayo only intensified until he was captured in battle by the British and died in captivity in 1884. He was succeeded by his son Dinizulu, whose reign saw the dissolution of the Zulu kingdom. It was annexed by the British, who imposed on the people a system of government similar to that of Natal. One attempt at armed resistance was made in 1906, but this did not involve all the Zulu people and was crushed. Earlier, in 1897, Britain had ceded government of Zululand to Natal and in 1910 it became part of the Union of South Africa.

In 1948 the Nationalist government came to power in South Africa with a policy of creating Bantustans—where each Black group could develop separately in accordance with the tenets of *apartheid*, an ideology which aimed at the preservation of White supremacy. The old nucleus of the Zulu kingdom in Zululand was designated as a Bantustan and named KwaZulu. The Zulu people were divided on the question of the acceptance of Bantustan status. Chief Gatsha Butelezi, one of the leading chiefs, considered the system had been evolved without the people's consent, as they were deprived of the vote.

In 1970, however, a meeting of chiefs decided to accept Bantustan status, as this would provide them with responsibility for some of their own affairs and give a platform from which to express their views. Chief Gatsha Butelezi was elected as the Chief Executive Officer and on a local level the people continued to be ruled by the chiefs and magistrates appointed by the central White government.

While some urban families retain rural links, others have evolved a more Westernized form of life. They often talk a distinctive urban argot and are deeply marked by conditions of life in the townships with their poverty, crime, violence and constant police harassment.

Urban Zulus were staunch supporters of the two mass Black political protest movements of this century, the ICU (Industrial and Commercial Workers Union) in the 1930s and the ANC (African National Congress) which staged large demonstrations in the 1950s and early 1960s. Both were concerned with elevating Zulus and all Black peoples of South Africa from their second class status. The Zulu president of the ANC, Chief Albert Luthuli was awarded the Nobel Peace Prize in 1960.

In recent years, world opinion has hardened against the policy of *apartheid*, and internal discontent is becoming increasingly apparent. For while mass Black political protest is no longer lawful—it was declared illegal in 1960 —opposition takes other forms. Already traditional leaders such as Gatsha Butelezi the Zulu Prime Minister are proving to be unreliable agents of social control as far

as the White authorities are concerned—they are openly critical of *apartheid*.

A cheering crowd of 16,000—many of them non-Zulus —in Johannesburg's Black township of Soweto heard Butelezi declare his demand for major change in the country. 'South Africa is one country' he maintained in March 1976. 'It has one destiny. Those who are trying to divide the land are attempting to stem the tide of history. Most Black people do not want to abandon their birthright. They intend to participate in the wealth of their land'.

This speech followed Butelezi's demands that foreign companies end their investment in South Africa. This does not provide any long term benefit for Black South Africans, it only strengthens the *apartheid* system as far as Butelezi is concerned. But for all the effectiveness of his speechmaking Butelezi cannot avoid the fact that he is a govern-

Zulus perform dances of their warrior ancestors at a 'village' set up for tourists. Despite increasing urbanization, many tribal traditions survive. Spontaneous dancing is still common among Zulu men.

On Shaka Day, Zulus in KwaZulu remember their glorious past. It was Shaka who in just 10 years before the Boer expansion welded the Zulu nation into the supreme military power in Southern Africa.

(Below) Police ruthlessly suppressed the wave of strikes which swept South Africa in 1973. African strikes are illegal, and show the increasing national and political consciousness of Black workers.

Peter Fraenkel

Traditional Zulu houses are still found in KwaZulu. The basic unit of rural Zulu society is the fenced kraal, with the houses of a man and his family in close proximity to the herds of cattle and goats.

ment employee who has to administer much of the legislation which he decries. However, it is not only the speeches of their Prime Minister that express Zulu resistance to White domination. Acting on the inspiration of old traditions Zulu thought and society have evolved in response to the new way of life.

Zulu traditional religion is concerned with belief in a supreme god, the creator. But most of its rituals centre on ancestor worship, as ancestors are believed to be directly responsible for the well-being of their living descendants. After more than a century of mission activity many Zulus are now Christians belonging either to orthodox mission churches—Anglican, Catholic, Methodist or Lutheran—or to one of the larger number of independent churches. Some of these have beliefs similar to those of mission Christianity but have Black clergy. Others include the 'Zionist' Spirit Churches which stress faith healing and trance-induced speaking with tongues.

Yet nearly all Zulu Christians preserve some of the older customs associated with belief in the power of the ancestors. In traditional religion, a year after a person has died a ceremony is held to incorporate him into the body of the ancestors. Today Christians hold a similar ceremony but erect a tombstone and pray. The name of the Zulu creator god is also preserved because it was used by early missionaries in their translations of the Bible.

As the Zulus were originally pastoralists, much of their ritual involved cattle. Birth, marriage and death were marked by the ritual slaughter of a beast. Today important moments in a person's life are still marked by ritual slaughter and cattle continue to play an important part in life. No girl is considered legally married until her husband has

paid *lobola*, a gift of cattle to a girl's parents. A common sight in townships today are large numbers of white goats and other animals on sale for slaughter. Zulus respond to the profound stress of urban life by sacrificing the white animals which are traditionally associated with purity and strength.

According to traditional Zulu thought there are two types of illness: natural diseases (*umkhulane*) like measles or the common cold, which 'just happen' and which anyone can cure, and diseases which only the Zulus understand (*ukufa kwabantu*) which result from bad human relationships and an imbalance in cosmological order. Only traditional diviners can cure *ukufa kwabantu*, preserving an old strain of thought and applying it in a changed world.

Traditional clan relationships also persist, as does polygamy, although this is not common among orthodox Christians. Clansmen may not intermarry; they eat milk food only at another clansman's house, and they seek assistance first from a clansman before turning to outsiders. Within the clans there are family groups whose members have religious and social obligations to one another. These people respect common ancestors and are forbidden to practise certain types of sorcery against each other. Despite the upheavals of conquest and urbanization traditional relationships provide a network of security.

KwaZulu today is a land marked by severe soil erosion, overcrowding, and poor agriculture. The same is true of many Zulu reserves in Natal. Government attempts to improve farming are ineffective because they cannot avoid the fact of insufficient and exhausted land. Similarly in the towns attempts to build new houses and provide some amenities are only palliative and cannot solve the major problems of poverty and state scrutiny. But in this bleak environment the Zulus have evolved a way of life that draws on old traditions and keeps potent the memories of past strengths. □

Index